Fine
Machine
Sewing

COMPLETELY REVISED AND UPDATED

Fine Machine Sewing

COMPLETELY REVISED AND UPDATED

Easy ways to
get the look of
hand finishing
and embellishing

Carol Laflin Ahles

The Taunton Press

For Ron, Daniel, and Emily

Publisher: Jim Childs
Acquisitions Editor: Jolynn Gower
Assistant Editor: Sarah Coe
Copy Editor: Suzanne Noel
Indexer: Lynda Stannard
Cover Designer: Ann Marie Manca
Interior Designer/Layout Artist: Carol Petro
Illustrator: Rosalie Vaccaro
Cover photographer: Jack Deutsch
Interior photographers: Jack Deutsch, Scott Phillips

The Taunton Press
Inspiration for hands-on living®

Printed in China
10 9 8 7 6 5

Fine Machine Sewing was originally published in hardcover
in 2001 by The Taunton Press, Inc.

The Taunton Press, Inc., 63 South Main Street, PO Box 5506,
Newtown, CT 06470-5506
e-mail: tp@taunton.com

Library of Congress Cataloging-in-Publication Data:
Ahles, Carol.
   Fine machine sewing : easy ways to get the look of hand finishing and embellishing /
Carol Laflin Ahles.— Completely rev. and updated.
     p. cm.
     ISBN-13: 978-1-56158-487-1 hardcover
     ISBN-10: 1-56158-487-8 hardcover
     ISBN-13: 978-1-56158-586-1 paperback
     ISBN-10: 1-56158-586-6 paperback
    1. Machine sewing. I. Title.

TT713 .A37 2001
646.2—dc21   00-051028

Acknowledgments

My sincere thanks to:

My husband, Ron; our children, Daniel and Emily; our new son-in-law, David; and our families, the Laflins and Ahleses, for their love and support;

My friends, especially Lydia Johnson, with whom I learned smocking, heirloom sewing, and much more; and Robbie Fanning for her inspiration and guidance;

Karen Kay Buckley, Carol Clements, April Dunn, Janice Ferguson, Terri Johnson, Patti Jo Larson, Kerry Reynold, and Suzanne Sawko who each generously contributed special expertise to this book;

The sewing educators who have taught me and those with whom I now teach for sharing their joy and excitement in sewing;

Those I have taught for their enthusiasm, which makes what I do such a pleasure;

Ann Henderson at *Creative Needle* magazine and Chris Timmons, David Coffin, and Karen Morris at *Threads* magazine for encouraging my contributions to their wonderful magazines;

Eileen Hanson for the initial development of *Fine Machine Sewing*, and Jolynn Gower, Sarah Coe, and Suzanne Noel at The Taunton Press for all their assistance with the revision;

Scott Phillips and Jack Deutsch for their beautiful photography, miraculously showing every detail we wanted.

I would also like to thank the following companies and their representatives for their support and willingness to answer my questions about their products:

Sewing-machine companies—

Gayle Hillert and Jane Garrison at Bernina; John Curtis and Jackie Andress at It's A Stitch Bernina dealership in Houston

Pam Mahshie at Baby Lock

June Mellinger at Brother

Chris Tryon at Elna

Sue Thornton-Gray at New Home

Kim Fillmore and Laura Haynie at Pfaff

Mary Griffin at Singer

Sue Hausmann, Nancy Jewell, and Cathy Wilson at Viking

Thread, needle, lace, notion, and stabilizer companies—

Ken Moore at American & Efird Inc. (Mettler thread)

Meta Hoge at Coats & Clark

Emma Graham at The Crowning Touch

Lisa Shepard at HTC

Pat Andreatta at Heirloom Stitches

Jill Repp and Katie Mirr at June Taylor

Jose Reyes at Schmetz Needle Corp.

Fred Drexler at Sulky of America

Pam Burke at Thread Pro

Lanny Smith at YLI

Contents

Introduction

About the Revision

The revision and expansion of *Fine Machine Sewing* incorporates many additional related techniques and reflects new machine models and products that have become available since it was first published.

There are minor changes throughout the text, but major new techniques covered in the revision include:

✗ Several methods to prepare and stitch perfect turned-edge appliqués and scalloped hems.

✗ New fagoting techniques, including fagoting narrow bias tubes on curves. (Only straight fagoting was covered in the original version.)

✗ A new chapter on replicating vintage lace and entredeux techniques, for creating heirloom garments and linens.

Other changes include:

✗ Revised charts for "Machine Settings for Decorative Techniques," including a few minor changes for previous machine models and stitch numbers and settings for many new machine models.

✗ Many new garments, projects, and stitched samples, which, along with those from the original book, have been shot in beautiful color with an emphasis on close-ups of the techniques. (The hands-on shots, old and new, remain in black and white because they show up exceptionally well that way.)

✗ Updated "Resources," including "Sources of Supply" and "Publications."

✗ An improved index to make it even easier to find a topic.

Fine Machine Sewing has gotten great positive response, and I know machine owners will be pleased with the new techniques, updated information, and color photography in this revision.

About the First Edition

This book is for all sewers who want high-quality machine stitching, finishing, and embellishing without headaches, whatever their level of expertise.

Whether I am teaching at a sewing seminar in Greensboro, North Carolina, or Kyabram, Victoria, Australia, I find that many of the frustrations experienced by machine sewers are universal. It is easy for me to empathize. I can remember years of:

✗ fighting puckered seams and tunneled decorative stitching, especially on lightweight fabrics (was my sewing machine a lemon or was "automatic self-adjusting tension" a hoax?);

✗ estimating seam-allowance and topstitching spacing (and living with less-than-perfect results) because I thought being precise would be too time-consuming;

✗ thinking that the only applications where I would consider built-in decorative stitches would be craft projects or children's playclothes;

✗ trying to copy by machine the classic look of hand techniques such as hemstitching, fagoting, decorative edgings, pintucks, and shadow work but finding both the process and the results unsatisfactory;

✗ struggling to machine-stitch blind hems and narrow hems that would be acceptable for something other than curtains.

Like most sewers, I blamed most of these difficulties on my sewing machine. Then, in 1981, my friend Lydia Johnson and I bought Buttons 'n' Bows, a three-year-old sewing-machine dealership/fabric store in Houston that specialized in smocking and heirloom sewing. I started teaching machine classes to sewers who, like us, not only sought perfection in their sewing but also were stitching on some of the most difficult and sheer fabrics. I researched, attended seminars, experimented, and refined, until little by little everything started to fit together. It was such a relief to learn that these common problems do not have to be inherent in machine sewing!

My classes grew. I started teaching nationally, then internationally, and wrote for *Creative Needle* and then *Threads* magazines. (Some of the material in this book first appeared in my articles for these magazines.) I have now taught over 8,000 students at seminars and have learned from them, too. In this book, I'll share this know-how with you.

Chapter 1 explains how to control the factors that affect all machine sewing in order to get the best results with everything you stitch. (Demystifying tension alone will allow more control over your sewing results than you probably thought possible!) This chapter also covers sewing with lightweight fabrics and stitching buttonholes—common areas of difficulty. Chapter 2 explains ways to achieve precise, accurate, professional-looking results with much less effort than you might have expected.

The balance of the book presents fine finishing and embellishing techniques for creating useful, classic details such as pintucks, hemstitching, and fagoting. These details, which are achievable on most sewing machines, can be seen on fine ready-to-wear garments and home linens. Appropriate areas for these techniques—such as collars, pockets, cuffs, and hems—can always be found on patterns as well as on purchased garments. (In this book, pattern information for photographed garments is given only for specialized patterns.) The refinements you will learn for blind hemming and narrow hemming will give you skills you can use in finishing almost any garment. To help with problem solving, each chapter ends with related questions and answers. For decorative techniques, stitch numbers and settings for many machines are provided on pp. 195-197.

The goal of this book is to get the most from the sewing machine you have, but "What to Look for in a Sewing Machine," on pp. 192-194, addresses the question of purchasing a machine for this type of work. It explains the features I look for most and their benefits (it will also help you understand features you may already have on your machine). "Caring for Your Sewing Machine," on pp. 198-199, covers maintenance as well as power surges, magnetic pincushions, and transporting your machine.

For years I have been asked to write a comprehensive book that includes the material from my magazine articles and classes. My hope is that *Fine Machine Sewing* will open useful and creative options for you and enable you to get greater joy than ever from all your machine sewing.

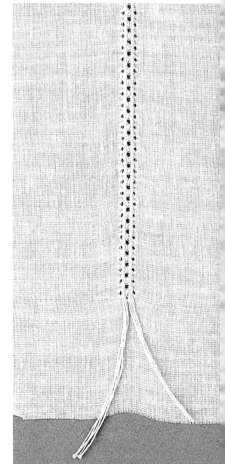

Getting the Best Results

Puckered seams and tunneled decorative stitching are not an inevitable aspect of machine sewing, even with fine, lightweight fabrics. When sewers encounter such typical difficulties, their first instinct is often to blame the sewing machine, specifically its tension mechanisms. But no machine, whether an older basic mechanical machine or a new top-of-the-line computerized model, can give its best performance if it is full of lint or is being used with cheap, uneven thread, a bad needle, the wrong presser foot, or the wrong settings. If you sew only on sturdy fabrics, such as denim, and you are not bothered by less-than-perfect results, it's possible to get by with less-than-ideal conditions. But when you want beautiful results on the more difficult lightweight fabrics, every factor is critical: machine condition, fabric preparation, thread, bobbins, needles, presser feet, settings, and tension. When these are correct, "tension headaches" will become a thing of the past.

The gentle curves of the collar are traced with decorative topstitching using the Parisian hemstitch. The folded tucks, also topstitched with the Parisian hemstitch, add textural interest to this beautiful batiste blouse.

Condition of the machine

Keeping your machine clean and oiled (if oiling is recommended for the make and model you have) is one of the most important things you can do to maintain high-quality stitching as well as to avoid expensive, time-consuming repairs. Lint, especially in the top and bobbin tension areas, is a prime cause of tension problems.

Before starting a sewing project, clean your machine following the instructions in your sewing-machine manual. If you do this regularly, it takes only a few minutes—a worthwhile investment to avoid possible problems. For more detailed information on machine care, including cleaning, storing, and transporting, see pp. 198-199.

When you have stitching problems, such as skipped stitches, follow the troubleshooting routine described in the sidebar at right.

Troubleshooting

If you have stitching problems, try the measures listed here. Also refer to the problem-solving section of your sewing-machine manual.

1. Turn off the machine, then turn it back on. This resets the machine. If the problem remains, perform the following corrective measures:

2. Unthread the machine.

3. Remove the bobbin.

4. Clean the machine. Oil, if required for that model.

5. Insert a new, good-quality needle of appropriate type and size.

6. Replace the bobbin carefully.

7. Rethread carefully.

Fabric preparation

Proper preparation of the fabric is essential. For the best results, some fabrics should be prewashed. Also, take grain direction into consideration when setting up your machine. Before starting your project, sew test samples to be sure that everything is in order.

PREWASHING

The safest practice is to prewash washable fabrics the same way the completed garment or project will be washed. This preshrinks the fabric, releases excess dye, and removes the sizing from the fabric surface. (And if the fabric does not wash well, you want to know before putting time and effort into stitching it!) Why do we remove sizing when we usually want the fabric to have body? Because the difficulty in penetrating such resins can lead to problems, such as skipped stitches and puckering. It is better to prewash, then spray-starch and press. Of course, prewashing is a judgment call. For example, I seldom prewash high-quality imported cotton batiste or organdy. I most often use these fabrics in light colors, and typically the garments I make with them are not fitted, so color bleeding and shrinkage are rarely a concern.

GRAIN DIRECTION

Grain direction often contributes to the problem of puckering. You can expect to have more difficulty when stitching woven fabrics in a lengthwise direction (parallel to the selvage), because lengthwise threads are stronger and have less give than crossgrain threads. You may have noticed that it is lengthwise decorative stitching and the side and center-back seams that pucker most often. The photo below shows an example of puckered lengthwise stitching and unpuckered crossgrain stitching sewn with exactly the same settings.

Should you change the grain direction when cutting the pattern pieces to avoid this problem? No, unless you are making something that will not be worn, such as a craft project. A garment may not fit or hang properly if the grain direction is changed. What you can do is use more care whenever you stitch lengthwise. For example, you may have to hold the fabric more taut as you stitch, and you may have to loosen upper tension, even if this was not necessary when stitching crossgrain (selvage to selvage).

STITCHING TEST SAMPLES

Always take a few minutes to stitch test samples of any decorative stitching (and of straight stitching as well if you are using a fabric you are not used to), before stitching the actual project. If you don't first perfect the stitching on a test sample, you may have to live with less-than-satisfactory results on the project or rip out your work and start again, both of which are time-consuming and frustrating. Stitch with conditions exactly the same as you'll use on the project, including the thread, needle, grain direction, number of fabric layers, stabilizer, and so on. Note any necessary adjustments (including tension) right on the fabric sample, and save it in a notebook for future reference (see the sidebar on p. 8).

Thread

If you are looking for top-quality results, start with good-quality thread. Choose thread that is appropriate to the stitching technique (generally seam stitching versus decorative stitching) and the fabric (for example, for fine fabric, choose fine thread). Don't waste your time and risk good results by using cheap thread with nubs, uneven thickness, or fuzziness.

In general, extra-fine cotton-wrapped polyester thread is appropriate for seaming most light- to medium-weight fabrics. Fine mercerized cotton can be used on fine, all-natural wovens if strength is not needed. For the additional strength needed for knits or heavier fabrics, use long-staple polyester. For decorative stitching on light- to medium-weight fabrics, use fine machine-embroidery thread, usually cotton (size 50/2 or 60/2) or rayon (size 40).

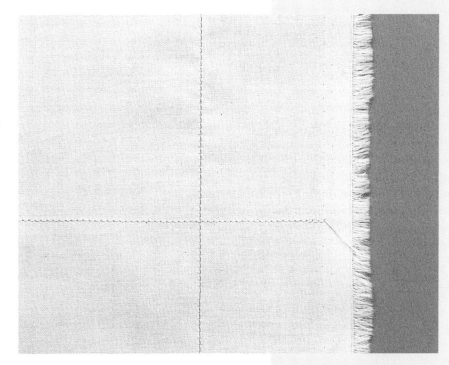

Lengthwise stitching (the vertical stitching on this sample) is naturally more likely to pucker than crossgrain stitching (the horizontal stitching). When stitching lengthwise, every factor is critical. Sewing taut and loosening upper tension may be necessary.

Making a sample notebook

One of my most valuable machine-sewing references is a notebook that contains samples of all my favorite techniques. When I am planning a project, my notebook provides inspiration. And in the long run, keeping samples saves time. Each sample has the appropriate presser foot, stitch numbers, settings, and so on, written right on it; that way, I don't have to remember what I did the last time or retry all the possible variables for every technique.

I recommend that you stitch and save practice samples of any technique in this book that interests you. Use a ball-point pen to note thread, needle, presser foot, stitch number, stitch width and length, upper-tension adjustment, guiding aids, and so on, directly on the fabric pieces. I mark the stitch combinations I like best with a star. Include any information that will help you repeat this technique on your particular machine. Attach your practice pieces and notes to sturdy three-hole-punched paper or slip them into plastic pocket pages, and keep them in a three-ring binder. Add to your notebook as you experiment with other techniques on your machine. As it grows, it will become a valuable source of information.

A notebook containing practice samples is a valuable reference. All pertinent information should be noted directly on the fabric. You can star favorite combinations.

Often more than one thread is used on a single garment. For example, a fine machine-embroidery cotton thread might be used for the decorative stitching on a batiste or broadcloth blouse, while extra-fine cotton-wrapped polyester thread would be used to construct it.

Naturally, thread selection involves personal preference and is necessarily influenced by availability. The main threads used in machine sewing are cotton, polyester, and cotton-wrapped polyester; rayon, metallic, silk, and other specialty threads are also available. If you can't find them locally, you can order most of them through the mail (see Resources on p. 199).

COTTON THREAD

Cotton thread easily produces an attractive stitch (this is why most dealers use it to demonstrate sewing machines). It has some sheen but relatively little strength and stretch. Thread comes in various "sizes"—the higher the size number, the finer the thread. If there is a second number, it indicates the number of plies. Machine-embroidery thread is usually two-ply, and all-purpose cotton thread is three-ply. For example, 60/2 indicates a fine machine-embroidery two-ply thread and 50/3 a medium, all-purpose three-ply thread.

Machine-embroidery cotton thread is excellent for decorative stitching (including satin stitching for appliquéing and buttonholes) but is generally not strong enough for seaming. All-purpose cotton thread can be used to seam all-natural woven fabrics, but I rarely use it on garments since I find it too bulky for lightweight fabrics and not strong enough for heavier ones. It is often used for piecing quilts, though. Do not use cotton thread to seam swimwear or most knits.

Recommended brands of cotton thread include DMC, Madeira, Mettler, YLI Heirloom, and Zwicky.

POLYESTER THREAD

Polyester thread is strong and has some stretch. Good-quality (long-staple), fine polyester thread provides strength without bulk for seaming most medium- to heavyweight wovens, as well as knits and swimwear. Regular polyester threads, like those listed below, are not generally recommended for decorative stitching. (There are some new polyester threads, however, like Mettler Poly Sheen, that are especially designed with more sheen and less stretch for machine embroidery.)

Although a different sizing system is used for polyester thread (size 100 polyester is not as fine as size 100 cotton), the rule is still "the higher the number, the finer the thread." Polyester thread size 100 (or higher) is the fine weight usually preferred. If there is no size given on a polyester thread, unwrap a few inches and check the size visually.

Recommended brands of polyester thread for seaming include Gutermann, Metrosene Plus (from Mettler), Madeira Aerofil, and Molnlycke.

COTTON-WRAPPED POLYESTER THREAD

Cotton-wrapped polyester combines the nice sheen of cotton with the strength of a polyester core. It is available in all-purpose and extra-fine weights. No size numbers are given. The all-purpose weight can be used on heavier fabrics, where the bulk of the thread is not a problem. The extra-fine weight, such as Coats Dual Duty Plus Extra-Fine for Lightweight Fabrics (article #240—small spool with fuchsia and gold label), is ex-cellent for seaming light- to medium-weight fabrics and for blind hemming. Extra-fine white can be used on all light pastel colors.

SPECIALTY THREADS

Rayon threads (such as Madeira Rayon and Sulky) and metallic threads are for decorative stitching only. Some silk threads are recommended for hand sewing only, while others are designed for machine sewing. Buttonhole twist, topstitching thread, and cordonnet (on spools) are all different names for the same product. These heavy threads are used for topstitching, heavy-duty utility sewing, and some open (not dense) decorative machine stitching for a bold look on medium- to heavyweight fabrics. In fine machine sewing, these threads are used mostly for cording buttonholes or decorative stitching (as is pearl cotton) to add strength and a more finished appearance.

Many new special-purpose threads have become available in the last few years. Check thread labels and the information on thread displays for suggested uses for particular products.

Bobbins

For seaming, use the same thread on the bobbin as on the top. For decorative stitching, you can use a different thread on the bobbin for convenience and economy, as long as you adjust upper tension to compensate. For example, when decorative stitching with rayon thread, you might prefer a fine cotton thread for the bobbin in a color that matches the fabric, to save the time and expense of changing bobbins each time the top color is changed. Since it is desirable with decorative stitching for the upper thread to be pulled slightly to the underside,

TIP ✱ If the thread spool has a slit to hold the thread tail, put the spool on the machine with the slit to the right (toward the flywheel) on horizontal spool pins and down on vertical spool pins. This prevents the thread from catching on the slit.

✱ Thread the machine with the presser foot up so that the tension discs are not engaged. You can lower the presser foot when threading the needle, though. Many machines have a light color behind the needle to make threading easier.

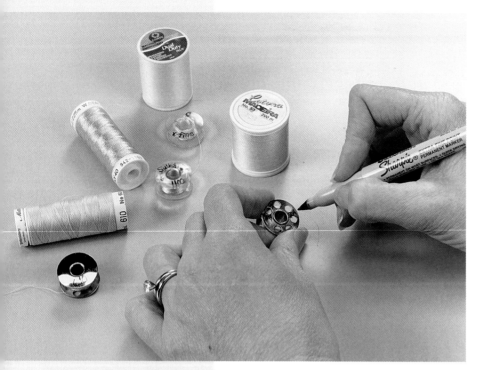

Labeling bobbins saves time and prevents the aggravation of not knowing what thread the bobbins hold. Abbreviate the thread type and size, and write the color number below.

you may have to loosen upper tension, depending on the type and weight of thread used.

When winding the bobbin with any thread that stretches, such as polyester, wind at a slow to medium speed to reduce potential puckering later.

I store each bobbin together with the thread spool from which it was wound. There are several easy ways to accomplish this. With most thread-spool racks, you can place the bobbin on a spool holder, then put the thread spool on top of it on the same holder. For taller thread spools, you can extend the length of the spool holder with a drinking straw cut to the desired length. If the bobbins will not fit over the straw, hammer a small nail near each spool holder for the corresponding bobbin. You can also buy plastic bobbin holders that fit on the center of most thread spools to hold the corresponding bobbin.

Even with these strategies, bobbins sometimes get separated from the spools. Therefore, I label bobbins with an extra-

fine permanent marker. (When necessary, the marking can be removed with alcohol.) Marking takes only a few seconds and saves the time and aggravation of having to guess. Abbreviate the thread type and size (for example, "Met 60" for Mettler size 60 cotton), and write the color number below. This information will fit between the holes on bobbins, if necessary, and is especially helpful when you have several different types and sizes of the same color thread, such as white. Avoid labeling bobbins with hole reinforcers or tape because either the label itself or its sticky residue can impede thread movement.

The following are some additional tips regarding bobbins that will help you avoid problems and ensure successful sewing:

✘ Use only bobbins recommended for that machine.

✘ Use only bobbins in good condition; don't use ones that are bent or that have rough spots.

✘ Invest in a good supply of bobbins, so you always have an empty one on hand.

✘ Make sure no loose threads or thread loops are hanging from the bobbin. (After you've begun winding a bobbin, stop and cut the thread tail close to the bobbin, then continue to wind.)

✘ Avoid winding one thread over another on a bobbin. The outside thread may not wind as evenly or as tightly as it should. Furthermore, when you get to the end of the outside thread, a tail from the inside thread can come loose and cause problems, such as jamming.

✘ Make sure to insert the bobbin into the bobbin case in the right direction and to "click" the thread into the bobbin-tension device. If you just drag the bobbin thread across the bobbin-tension slit, you may be sewing without bobbin tension.

✗ Don't use a metal tool to bring up the bobbin thread, as it can scratch the needle plate. Instead, pass a length of thread or a piece of fabric under the presser foot to catch the bobbin thread.

Needles

After you've made your thread selection, choose a needle appropriate for that thread and the fabric. You can find thread and needle charts in most sewing-machine manuals and machine-sewing books. In general, fabric, thread, and needle must all correlate: For a fine, lightweight fabric, for example, use a fine thread and a fine (small) needle. For some techniques, such as twin-needle stitching and hemstitching, you need special-purpose needles (see pp. 64-65 and pp. 78-79, respectively).

Use good-quality needles—ones manufactured by Schmetz or brands recommended by your machine dealer. A dull, damaged, or poor-quality needle will affect stitch quality and can also cause puckers and damaged fabric.

Needles with Universal points produce good results on most fabrics. (Happily, this is the least expensive needle type, and a good supply of Universals will cover most needs.) Usually, you need to switch to a needle with a special point or design—such as a Jeans (also called Denim), Stretch, or Embroidery needle—only when you have stitching problems with Universal needles, which can happen on certain fabrics or with special threads. For example, if fragile decorative threads are shredding with Universal needles, try Embroidery or Metallica needles from Schmetz or Metafil needles from Lammertz, which are designed for these threads.

With needles, the higher the number, the thicker the needle. Use the smallest-size needle in the range suggested for your fabric and thread. Too large a needle causes puckering, but the needle must be large enough for the thread to slide through the eye freely and to create a hole in the fabric big enough for the thread.

Most needles are now labeled with two numbers, such as 70/10. The first number is the size at the middle of the blade in hundredths of millimeters. (This is sometimes shown with "Nm" for "number metric.") The number following the slash is the American equivalent, based on Singer sizes used in the U.S. early in this century.

The needle types and sizes used most often for fine machine sewing are Universal size 70/10 for batiste-weight fabrics and Universal size 80/12 for broadcloth-weight fabrics. In this book, I will refer only to the metric size—for example, "70 Universal."

Generally you should replace the needle after stitching a major project. And whenever you have stitching difficulties, try a new needle. If a needle hits a pin, it is damaged and should be replaced. When you start a special project, put in a new needle to ensure the best possible results—a new needle costs very little considering your investment in fabric and supplies, not to mention your time. Be sure to insert the needle in the right direction (for most machines, the flat side goes to the back) and all the way into the needle bar.

The best way to store needles is in their original boxes. These boxes are de-

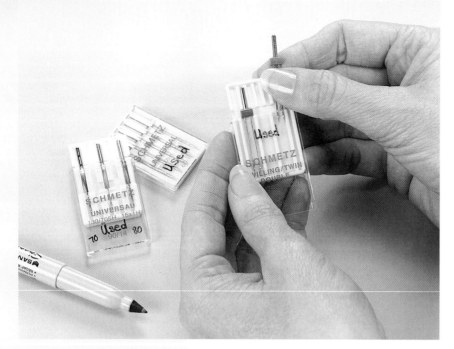

Empty needle boxes are good for storing slightly used needles. Mark the box "used," and include the type and size of the needle if different from the label.

signed specifically to protect the needles from the climate, to keep them from getting bent, and to protect the points.

Sometimes you need to replace a barely used needle with a different size or type. I store such used-but-still-good needles in empty needle boxes. I write "used" on the box with an extra-fine marker, plus the type and size of the needle if they are different from what the label states. When it is not crucial that the needle be new, use one of these slightly used ones again, then discard it. Some people suggest putting used needles back in their original box with the points up (toward the top of the box) to distinguish them from the new ones, which have their points down. However, I don't recommend this practice because the grooves in the box are shaped for points down and the needles can become bent.

Presser feet

For best results, the presser foot should hold the fabric as securely as possible. This is best accomplished with a foot that is metal, covers as much of both feed dogs as possible, and is flat on the underside. For most straight stitching, a basic metal zigzag foot adequately meets these criteria.

For any dense stitching, such as satin stitching, or any other raised effects, such as twin-needle pintucking or stitching over cord, a foot that is indented underneath is needed. Satin-stitch feet and their variations have grooves on the underside to let the raised stitching or fabric pass easily under the foot without becoming crushed. Do not use these feet for regular straight stitching because the indented area allows the fabric to flutter, which can cause puckering and skipped stitches. The photo at left shows zigzag and satin-stitch feet.

Unfortunately, the terminology for identifying presser feet is not uniform throughout the sewing industry. To identify the presser feet that go with your machine, you can always consult your sewing-machine manual. But understanding some of the basics about presser-foot design will help you identify feet and understand their uses, no matter what the feet are called.

Basic zigzag feet (left foot of each pair) are best for straight stitching. Satin-stitch feet (right foot of each pair) are best for dense stitching or other raised effects.

To some extent, presser feet are interchangeable from machine to machine. See the sidebar on p. 15 for specifics.

ZIGZAG AND SATIN-STITCH FEET

The basic zigzag and satin-stitch feet are by far the ones used most by sewers. The zigzag foot—also called a standard sewing foot—is usually the first foot (labeled "A" or "0") among the group that comes with the machine. It is basically flat underneath but may be partially indented behind the needle opening and/or at the back. The satin-stitch foot—also called an appliqué, embroidery, or fancy-stitch foot—may be metal, plastic, or a combination. It should have an indented area underneath.

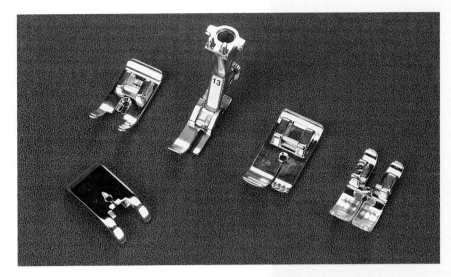

Straight-stitch feet, which are flat on the underside and have a round or very narrow opening for the needle, hold the fabric securely all around the needle.

STRAIGHT-STITCH FEET

Straight-stitch feet, shown in the photo above, are flat on the underside and have a hole or a very narrow opening for the needle. Thus, the only possible stitch with this type of foot is a straight stitch in center needle position. Because a straight-stitch foot holds the fabric around the needle more securely than does the basic zigzag foot, it will help reduce puckering and skipped stitches on lightweight fabrics, as well as offer more support for precision straight stitching near the edge of most fabrics. (Special straight-stitch feet for sewing $\frac{1}{8}$ in. or $\frac{1}{4}$ in. from an edge are discussed on pp. 30-31.)

If your seams on lightweight fabric are puckering and you do not have a straight-stitch foot, you can imitate its support when using a basic metal zigzag foot by changing the needle position to the far left or right, as shown in the photo at left (see also pp. 29-30). With the needle in this position, the fabric around the needle is held firmly on three sides. With the needle in center position, the fabric immediately to each side of the needle and sometimes in front (depending on the location of the open slit) is not

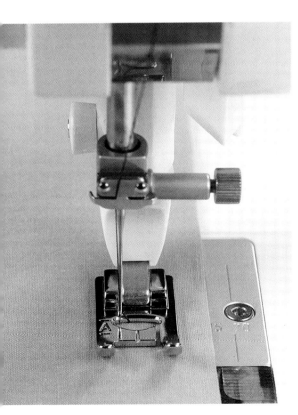

Moving the needle position to the far left or right when using a basic metal zigzag foot simulates the support of a straight-stitch foot and helps reduce puckering and skipped stitches on lightweight fabrics.

TIP For straight stitching, use presser feet that have flat undersides and cover both feed dogs. For dense stitching or other raised effects, feet that are indented underneath are best because the raised stitching or fabric passes easily underneath.

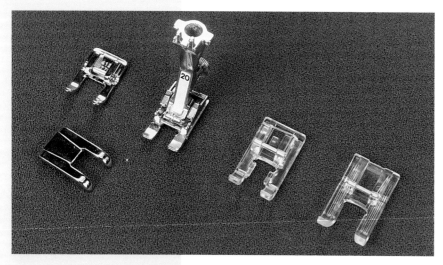

Open-toe feet provide excellent visibility during stitching but should be used only when the fabric is stabilized enough that it is not necessary for the presser foot to keep the fabric from fluttering.

underside allows additional movement or fluttering of the fabric as you stitch.

Open-toe feet should be used only for techniques where visibility is essential and where the fabric is already so sufficiently stabilized that the presser foot does not need to keep the fabric from fluttering. For example, you might use an open-toe foot for appliquéing when the fabric is in a hoop and/or has a stabilizer underneath. Unless the fabric is stabilized, puckering and tunneling are likely to occur.

OTHER USEFUL FEET

Special-purpose feet can be very helpful in certain situations. When choosing a special-purpose foot, take note of a foot's design, construction (metal versus plastic), and underside. If you keep in mind that the fabric will be held most securely by a metal foot, which provides the most surface covering the fabric and feed dogs, you will be able to choose the best foot for a task and to compensate when necessary.

The following are some special-purpose feet that are useful for fine machine sewing. When you need a foot for a special purpose, such as to guide fabric or cord in a certain position, consider using any foot that meets the need, as long as its underside is appropriate.

TIP On machines that sew up to a maximum width of only 4mm, the feed dogs and toes of the presser feet are closer together and hold the fabric more securely in the center than on machines that sew up to 9mm wide. If your machine has wide-set feed dogs, compensate when sewing lightweight fabrics by experimenting with different feet, needle positions, and guiding so that you are stitching where the fabric is held most securely.

held very firmly. Remember to adjust your guiding to compensate for the different needle position. (On Elna models through the Diva, use the sheer-fabric foot "Y," if you have it, since it is flatter underneath.)

OPEN-TOE FEET

Open-toe presser feet (see the photo above) are, as the name implies, completely open in front of the needle, providing excellent visibility as you sew. The drawback is that the only parts holding the fabric in front are the two "toes" extending on the sides. And since these are a variation of satin-stitch feet, the groove on the

Blind-hem feet and edging feet (like Bernina's foot #10 at right) can be used for techniques such as hemstitching lace, where their guides are helpful.

BLIND-HEM (BLIND-STITCH) AND EDGING FEET

The guide on a blind-hem foot or on an edging foot, which has a vertical guide similar to that on some blind-hem feet, is helpful for blind hemming as well as other techniques (see the bottom photo on the facing page).

BUTTONHOLE FEET

The two grooves under a traditional buttonhole foot (see the top photo on p. 16)

Interchanging presser feet

If a foot design you want is not available for your machine, the foot from another brand or a generic foot may work, especially if the shank length is the same. Most newer machines are short shank (also called low shank): the distance from where the shank screws onto the needle bar down to the needle plate (with the presser foot lowered) is about ½ in.

If your machine is not short shank, an adaptor may be available so that you can still use other short-shank feet. For example, the shanks on Bernina machines are unique, but if you want a foot not available for your Bernina, a short-shank adaptor for your particular model can be purchased from Bernina dealers. With the adaptor, you can use many short-shank feet or a short ankle and the corresponding snap-on soles. Sewing-machine dealers may also be able to help you find adaptors for other machines.

Both Clotilde and Nancy's Notions mail-order companies (see Resources on p. 199) have adaptors to enable high-shank machines (those that measure about 1 in. from the screw to the needle plate) to use short-shank feet.

If your machine has snap-on feet (the snap-on part is often called the sole), first check whether the sole from the other brand will snap onto your machine. If it does, lower the presser foot and carefully turn the flywheel toward you to lower the needle and then raise it to check the alignment (whether the needle hits the foot). If the sole does not fit your machine, or if it fits but the needle hits the foot, then try replacing your shank or ankle (the part that screws onto the needle bar) with an ankle from the other brand. Snap the sole onto the new ankle, lower the presser foot, and check the alignment. If this ankle works, you need to purchase only one, and you will be able to use all the soles

of that same brand and style. Some companies have more than one style of ankle, so if one does not work, another might.

Both the Elna 9000 and the Elna Diva have fixed ankles, but some other soles snap onto them and work fine. Elna's soles for these models (as well as for previous models) can be used on other brands. Several ankles are available to make a sole work on different machines.

Before stitching with a foot not designed for your machine, take the following steps:

1. Check whether the needle-hole opening is narrower than the maximum stitch width of your machine. For example, if your machine stitches 9mm wide and you try to stitch that width using a foot with a 4mm opening (designed for machines that do not stitch as wide as yours), the needle will hit the foot and break.

2. Lower the presser foot, and see how much of the sole covers the feed dogs. (Remember that for the best feeding and stitch quality, the sole should cover as much of the feed dogs as possible.)

3. With the needle in center needle position, check whether the needle is centered on the foot. When an Elna pintuck sole is used on some New Home machines, for example, the twin needles do not align with the center groove of the sole. Usually the needle position can be changed to correct this misalignment.

4. Finally, when you buy a foot (or any other sewing-machine accessory), make sure that, if you are not satisfied, it can be returned for a refund within a reasonable amount of time.

The two grooves under a traditional buttonhole foot can be used to guide cord or small corded piping.

TIP
Sewers who don't have an open-toe foot sometimes create one by cutting off the center front of plastic or semiplastic satin-stitch feet up to the toe. I would recommend doing this only if you need more visibility than the transparent front of a satin-stitch foot allows, and then only if you have another satin-stitch foot to use for all other satin stitching.

Multiple-cord feet have holes or slots to guide cord on top of fabric. These feet are especially useful to cord hemstitching and other decorative stitches.

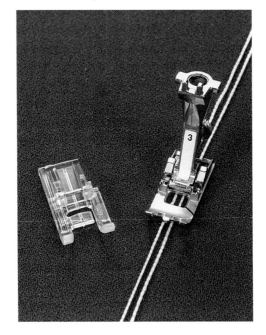

can be used to guide cord or small corded piping as well as to make buttonholes.

MULTIPLE-CORD FEET

Different configurations of holes or slots in multiple-cord feet (see the photo below) guide cord on top of the fabric. These feet are especially useful for cording hemstitching and other decorative stitches. They can be used without cord as metal satin-stitch feet.

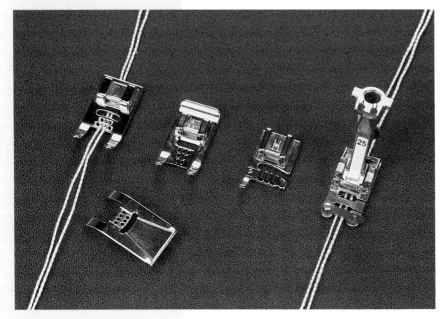

NARROW HEMMERS

Narrow hemmers (see the top photo on the facing page) are used to turn and stitch hems 2mm to 6mm wide. Some can be used only with a straight stitch, others are designed to align with a zigzag stitch (these are also called rolled or shell hemmers), and some can be used with either. An alternate use for these feet is for guiding cord to be stitched on top of the fabric; the cord is fed through the curl of the hemmer.

PINTUCK FEET

Pintuck feet (see the bottom right photo on the facing page) have grooves underneath to form twin-needle pintucks and to space them equidistantly. The grooves can also be used as guides for other stitching, including cords and corded edges. (Note: Pfaff uses the term "cording feet" for some of its pintuck feet.) I most often use pintuck feet with seven grooves (five grooves on Elna models through the Diva). The size and spacing of its grooves are perfect for pintucks on light- to medium-weight fabrics, as well as for corded edges and corded-edge fagoting. Try to find pintuck feet that do not have a wide center-front slit because fabric can be pulled up into this open space inconsistently.

Stitch settings

On lightweight or soft fabrics, a long stitch tends to cause puckering and a wide stitch tends to cause tunneling. You can compensate by shortening stitch length and narrowing stitch width. Stabilizing the fabric will also help eliminate these problems, as will loosening upper tension, as discussed on pp. 19-21.

LENGTH

For seaming lightweight fabrics, use a stitch length of approximately 2mm. If a long length is needed, as for gathering or basting, lengthen the stitch only as much as necessary, loosen upper tension, and stabilize by sewing taut. For example, to gather batiste, use a stitch length of only 3mm to 3.5mm for prettier gathers with less puckering. Loosen upper tension significantly—usually about two numbers. (The bobbin thread will be taut, which makes it easier to pull for gathering and removal later.) To sew taut (see the photo below left), put pressure on the fabric with one hand in front of and one hand behind the presser foot as you sew. Do not pull or stretch the fabric.

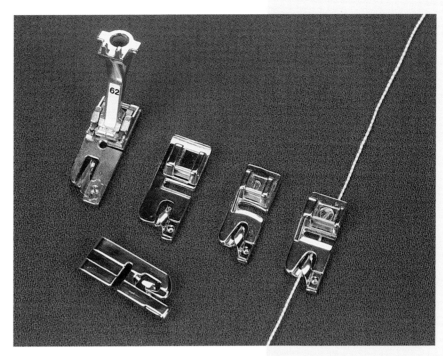

Narrow hemmers are for stitching hems 2mm to 6mm wide. They may also be used to guide a cord for stitching on top of the fabric.

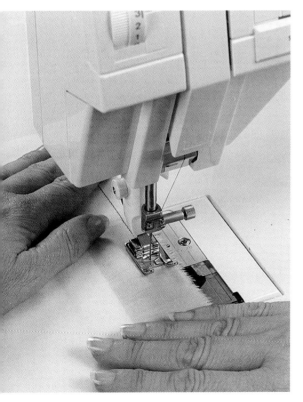

Sewing taut is one of the ways to compensate for the tendency of a long stitch to pucker. As you sew, hold the fabric taut with one hand in front of and one hand behind the presser foot; do not pull or stretch the fabric.

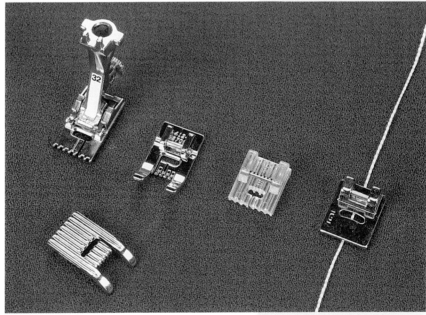

Pintuck feet have grooves underneath for forming twin-needle pintucks equidistantly spaced. The grooves can also be used to guide cord or corded edges.

Stitch Length in Millimeters	Stitches per Inch
1	25
2	12
3	8
4	6

Stitch lengths are given in millimeters throughout the book. If your machine is marked in stitches per inch, use the conversion chart above.

WIDTH

For any zigzag stitch, including most decorative stitches, use a stitch width no wider than necessary. If a very wide stitch is needed, compensate for the tendency of the fabric to tunnel by stabilizing the fabric and reducing upper tension. Spray-starching and pressing stabilize the fabric somewhat; a hoop can be used when appropriate, but generally a lightweight tearaway stabilizer should be used under any satin stitching, buttonholes, and most decorative stitching.

Stabilizers for lightweight fabrics

Thick and stiff stabilizers can distort delicate fabric or stitching when they are torn away. Lightweight fabrics call for lightweight stabilizers.

Fortunately, lightweight tearaway stabilizers have become much more readily available. Names to look for are Tear-Easy from Sulky, Jiffy Tear Away from Staple

Sewing Aids Corporation, Easy Tear from Graphic Impressions, Stitch & Ditch from Thread Pro, No Whiskers from Clotilde, and Armo Tear Away from HTC. You can use multiple layers of these lightweight stabilizers when more stability is required. If your favorite fabric store does not have any of these stabilizers, ask the owners if they'll consider carrying one. For mail-order sources of stabilizers, see Resources on p. 199.

Decorative machine stitchers used to use paper as a stabilizer all the time because that's all there was. Now, except for Stitch & Ditch, I would use it only if I had nothing else that would work. Feed dogs cannot grip and feed slick paper as well as they can the newer stabilizers. Although this deficiency may not be noticeable on some stitching, it is critical when precise feeding is important—for example, on buttonholes. Sewing through paper also dulls needles quickly; they need to be changed more frequently, and before you realize that the needles have become dull, the quality of the stitching may have already deteriorated. If you must use paper, use the lightest weight that will offer enough stability. (Use multiple layers, if necessary.) If the stabilizer has a smooth side and a rough side, put the rough side down for any techniques where accurate feeding is critical, so that the feed dogs can grip it.

Water-soluble stabilizers—such as Sulky's Solvy, Thread Pro's Kwik Solv, Aqua-Solv, and Madeira's Avalon—do not offer enough support for most decorative stitching, unless they are used in combination with a hoop. For light support, however, water solubles may be fused (using a press cloth) to the underside of fabrics before stitching. This op-

TIP ✱ Some stabilizers tear more easily in one direction than another. Check this before stitching to ensure easy removal, as well as to reduce distortion and whiskers.

✱ Put the tearaway stabilizer under the fabric before stitching. In some cases, it can easily be held in place. Otherwise, pin through the fabric and stabilizer from the right side, to keep it from shifting; remove pins as you stitch near them. Another option is to adhere the stabilizer in place with a temporary spray adhesive, such as Sulky's KK 2000. Lightly spray the stabilizer over a press cloth or paper, then apply it to the underside of the fabric.

tion is especially helpful for sheer (washable) fabrics, where more stability than spray-starching and pressing is needed but where whiskers left from tearaways would show through.

Either a heavier water soluble (like Sulky's Super Solvy) or multiple fused layers of regular-weight water solubles also work well for techniques such as fagoting, where other stabilizers would be difficult to tear away. You can fuse two or more layers together between press cloths to add needed body and stiffness. (Heavier and fused water solubles are easier to work with but will require longer soaking to remove all the residue.)

Viking distributes a product called America Sews Clear 'N Melt Stabilizer, which looks like clear plastic (like the water solubles) but disappears with low heat. (It leaves a nonsticky, bead-like residue that is easily brushed away.) This can be an advantage on projects that you do not want to wet after stitching. (See pp. 144-146 for instructions on using Clear 'N Melt for fagoting curved bias strips.)

In recent years, many new stabilizers have been introduced, including some fusibles, some paint-on and spray-on products, and some that disintegrate with the heat of a dry iron. All have unique advantages for appropriate applications, but sometimes there are also drawbacks. It is crucial to test a product thoroughly before using it on a special project, especially a delicate one, and to follow the manufacturer's instructions carefully.

Tension

Tension is one of the least understood factors in machine sewing. While it is true that upper tension rarely has to be adjusted for "normal sewing" (as the

When tearing away stabilizer, hold the stitching firmly between your thumb and index finger and tear up to your thumbnail, to protect the delicate stitching and fabric.

manuals usually say), there are many times upper tension should be changed on different fabrics and for certain techniques to get the best results. Furthermore, "normal" tension on any brand or model varies from machine to machine, because to a certain extent it has been set according to the judgment of the person setting the machine. If adjusting upper tension really weren't necessary, there would not be a numbered dial so accessible on every machine!

Tension is really not so mysterious. Think of it as a way to control the amount of thread fed into each stitch. When you want more thread fed into the upper side of the stitch, loosen upper tension by adjusting the dial to a lower number or toward "minus." This is the most common adjustment. For satin stitching, for example, it is desirable to loosen upper tension slightly to put more thread on top, creating a rounded look with no bob-

TIP Brand names for sewing machines sometimes vary by country (e.g., New Home is also known as Janome and Viking as Husqvarna).

For satin stitching, the top side of the stitch should be rounded, with no bobbin thread showing on the sides. The upper thread should be slightly pulled to the underside, as seen on the lower area that has been folded over. To accomplish this, loosen upper tension so that more thread is fed into the upper side of the stitch.

bin thread showing on the sides, as shown in the photo below. On some sewing machines the appropriate position for looser tension is marked on the dial (usually with a different color or the symbol for a buttonhole). And the computers on some machines automatically loosen tension in certain situations. But since the automatic adjustment is an estimate, you should still stitch a test sample and understand how to adjust upper tension yourself.

Adjust tension only after checking all the other factors. For example, if you are straight stitching on fine fabric, a dirty machine, thick thread, a bad needle, the wrong foot, or a long stitch length can all

cause puckering. Correct these conditions before adjusting the tension.

When tension adjustment is necessary, adjust upper tension, not bobbin tension. Once bobbin tension is set correctly, you should not have to adjust it regularly to balance the stitch. (For special effects, however, such as using thick threads on the bobbin, bobbin tension can be bypassed or loosened. See the question-and-answer section at the end of this chapter for more on bobbin tension.)

Tension-related problems include puckering, thread breaking, and an imbalanced stitch. With a straight stitch, the top and bobbin threads should interlock between the layers of fabric, and the stitches should look the same on both sides. If upper tension is too tight, too little top thread is being fed into the stitch; the top thread will look taut and the seam will pucker, as shown in the photo on the facing page. Loosen upper tension to feed enough thread into each stitch so that the stitch is balanced and puckers are eliminated. In general, adjust in increments of one-quarter to one-half, then test again. In other words, if the dial is set at 5 and you wish to loosen upper tension, turn the dial to $4^3/_4$ or $4^1/_2$. If upper tension is too loose, the bobbin thread looks taut, and loops from the upper thread show on the back side of the fabric. Correct the problem by tightening upper tension slightly.

For a standard zigzag or a utility-type zigzag variation, such as an overlock stitch, the sides of the stitches should interlock between the fabric layers. However, for satin stitching, buttonholes, and most decorative stitching, it is desirable for the upper thread to be slightly pulled to the underside. Slightly loosening upper tension accomplishes this, creates a

Tension controls the amount of thread fed into each stitch. When too little thread is fed into the upper side of a straight stitch, the top thread looks taut and the seam puckers, as in the sample at left. To correct this, loosen upper tension. The sample at right shows a correctly balanced straight stitch.

more rounded appearance on the right side, and reduces tunneling.

Understanding and using the upper-tension dial enables you to fine-tune your stitching according to the fabric and the application. Adjusting upper tension enables you to:

✗ get the best stitch balance without puckering, especially with lengthwise stitching on difficult fabrics (in most cases, loosen tension slightly; if you loosen too much, the upper thread will form loops on the underside);

✗ create more of a raised effect on twin-needle pintucks (tighten) or reduce puckering on them (loosen);

✗ with hemstitching, create holes that are more visible (tighten) or reduce puckering (loosen);

✗ eliminate the pulling of blind-hem stitches (loosen);

✗ keep the fabric flat when you are stitching two rows of lengthened straight stitching for gathering (loosen) or gather ruffles automatically (tighten);

✗ stitch fagoting that does not pull the two sides together (loosen).

Not taking advantage of this ability to adjust upper tension is needlessly limiting. Making it work for you will make your sewing much more enjoyable.

TIP Note that any additional guide through which a thread passes puts more tension on the thread. You can use this fact to your advantage to further increase or reduce tension on the top or bobbin thread. For example, if one side of twin-needle stitching appears loose and the other appears tight, feed the loose-side thread through an additional guide at the top of the machine or on the needle bar and bypass one of these guides with the tight-side thread.

Using the same principle, Bernina and Viking suggest threading the bobbin thread through a hole in the finger of the bobbin case (on models so equipped) for satin stitching and buttonholes. This increases drag on the bobbin thread, which pulls stitching to the underside.

Additional tips

The following are some additional tips for getting the best machine-sewing results:

✗ When beginning a line of stitching, always hold the thread tails toward the back of the machine for the first few stitches.

✗ Maintain a smooth, even stitching speed. Use a slow to medium speed for decorative and twin-needle stitching.

✗ If your machine allows for adjusting the pressure on the presser foot, consult the machine manual for the proper setting. There should be enough pressure to feed the fabric precisely but not so much as to mar or crush the fabric.

Sewing with lightweight fabrics

Lightweight fabrics, which are often used for fine machine sewing, can be tricky to sew. Here is a checklist for getting the best results:

✗ Clean the machine. Then oil it, if required for that model.

✗ Use good-quality, fine thread. For seaming most lightweight fabrics, use extra-fine cotton-wrapped polyester thread. Fine mercerized cotton can be used on all-natural wovens, if strength is not needed. For decorative stitching, use fine machine-embroidery thread, such as 50/2 or 60/2 cotton.

✗ Use a new, good-quality needle that is appropriate in size and kind for the fabric and thread, most often size 70 Universal.

✗ Use a stitch length of about 2mm for seaming and a stitch width that is no wider than necessary.

✗ For straight stitching, use the basic zigzag foot (with the needle in far left or right position, if necessary) or a straight-stitch foot. For dense stitching, use a satin-stitch foot.

✗ To stabilize straight stitching, sew taut with one hand in front of and one behind the presser foot. For decorative stitching or buttonholes, use a lightweight tearaway stabilizer under the fabric.

✗ Slightly loosening upper tension may be necessary, especially for lengthwise straight stitching or any decorative stitching.

✗ Press each seam flat, then press open or as desired.

✗ Test your stitching on scraps first.

BUTTONHOLES

Buttonhole-stitching problems are common on lightweight fabrics. Remember that a buttonhole is really two rows of satin stitching, so in general most of the rules for satin stitching apply.

✗ Use fine thread. Both good-quality size 50/2 or 60/2 machine-embroidery cotton thread and extra-fine cotton-wrapped polyester thread make attractive buttonholes on lightweight fabrics.

✗ Use a good-quality needle appropriate in type and size for the fabric and thread. It must be in good condition. If in doubt, use a new needle.

- Since interfacing is rarely used on sheer fabrics, you need a lightweight tearaway stabilizer underneath buttonholes. Carefully tear it away after stitching.

- If your machine has a sewing table, use it. The larger work surface will give you more control.

- Slightly loosening upper tension will create a smoother satin stitch and help reduce both puckering and tunneling.

- Use a smooth, even, slow to medium sewing speed. (Use the "slow" button if the machine has one.)

- Avoid making buttonholes thick and dense, especially on lightweight fabric. For more strength, cord buttonholes with buttonhole twist or pearl cotton rather than making them denser.

- Stitch several test samples with exactly the same conditions as exist on the garment, including grain direction, number of layers, interfacing or stabilizer, and so on. Follow instructions in your machine manual for any adjustments necessary.

- Keep in mind that any change in conditions can affect one or both sides of the buttonhole. For example, one buttonhole stitched over additional thicknesses of fabric (as on the seam allowance where a gathered skirt is attached to a yoke) might require additional adjustment. Always grade such areas to eliminate as much bulk as possible.

Questions

How can I keep from cutting through the ends of buttonholes when cutting them open?

Most experts cut buttonholes with a buttonhole chisel and a wooden block. To cut buttonholes smaller than the $1/2$-in. chisel, place one of the bar tacks just beyond the edge of the block.

If you do not have a buttonhole chisel, use a sharp seam ripper to cut carefully from one end of the buttonhole just to the middle. Then cut from the other end to the middle. As a precaution, you can put pins across each end of the buttonhole, just inside the bar tack.

Buttonholes made with fine machine-embroidery cotton thread (size 50 to 60) are attractive, but are they strong enough for stress areas, such as the shoulder on jumpers and jumpsuits? Should I use a heavier thread in these areas or stitch around the buttonhole twice?

Using heavier thread or stitching the buttonhole twice would add too much bulk and little strength. To add strength without bulk, simply cord buttonholes with pearl cotton, buttonhole twist, topstitching thread, and so on. Match the cord color to the thread color.

Many machine manuals have instructions for cording buttonholes. Either catch the cord over a prong and into the slits of a buttonhole foot designed for this cording, or lay the cord under the two grooves of other buttonhole feet, with the loop to the back in most cases. Position the fabric so that the loop is toward the outside edge of the garment (on jumpers, this is toward the top of the garment), and stitch the buttonhole over the cord.

After stitching, pull the cord tails until the loop is hidden. Then, using a needle threader, thread the tails into a hand-sewing needle with a large eye, take them to the underside, knot them together, bury a small length of the tails, and cut off the excess.

Whenever I try to stitch a satin stitch (such as for appliquéing or monogramming) or any satin-stitch shapes (such as filled-in scallops, flowers, leaves, hearts, and so on), the fabric won't feed and then the machine jams. What is wrong?

The most likely causes for this problem are using the wrong thread, presser foot, or stitch length.

Try a finer thread, such as cotton machine-embroidery thread size 50 or finer (higher number). Switch to a satin-stitch foot, which has a groove on the underside to allow the buildup of thread to pass underneath without being crushed. Finally, try a longer stitch length. If the stitch length is too short, the stitch will be too dense and the thread will build up, resulting in a jam.

Also, be sure the machine is clean, especially the bobbin area. Use a tear-away stabilizer under the fabric. Use a new, good-quality needle of the appropriate size and type. (With medium-weight woven fabric, use size 50/2 or 60/2 cotton thread and a size 80 Universal needle.) Slightly loosen upper tension (adjust tension mechanism toward a lower number).

What does "mercerized" mean on cotton-thread spool labels?

Mercerized thread has gone through a finishing process using a caustic-soda bath, which adds strength, luster, and dye affinity.

What is the difference between Denim or Jeans needles and Sharp sewing-machine needles? What are their uses?

Denim, Jeans, and Sharp needles are all the same. All Sharp needles are designed to penetrate densely woven fabrics more easily than Universal needles. Until a few years ago, Sharp needles were readily available only in the large sizes— 90/14, 100/16, and 110/18—and were called Denim or Jeans needles because that was their primary use. Now Sharps are available in smaller sizes, including 70/10 and 80/12. Schmetz has also added Microtex/Sharp needles in sizes 60/8 to 90/14; these are Sharps with a slimmer design for very fine, tightly woven, silky fabrics, such as microfibers.

Universal needles have a slightly rounded point, which deflects off fibers rather than piercing them. This deflection can occasionally make some stitches appear crooked, but there are very few instances when this would be noticeable. Universal needles work well on most wovens or knits.

Sharp-type needles actually pierce fibers. For this reason, they are not recommended for knits, where piercing the fibers would cause holes. They penetrate densely woven fabrics better than Universals and are also sometimes used when a perfect stitch is desired—for example, for topstitching.

Should a straight-stitch needle plate be used whenever a straight-stitch foot is used?

Not necessarily. A straight-stitch needle plate has only a round hole opening for the needle and offers extra support underneath the fabric, the same way a straight-stitch foot does on top of the fabric. It prevents the fabric from being pushed into the bobbin area. If you are experiencing that problem, first try a new, good-quality needle. Be sure it is the right size and type for the fabric and thread. If you must start stitching at the very edge of a soft, lightweight fabric, put the corner of a piece of lightweight stabilizer underneath and slightly pull the thread tails to get started. For a temporary straight-stitch plate, cover the oval needle opening of a standard needle plate with tape.

Straight-stitch needle plates are usually expensive. But if much of your sewing consists of straight stitching on soft, lightweight fabrics and you have persistent problems doing so, then a straight-stitch needle plate might be worth a try.

My friend has the same brand and model machine that I do, yet upper tension on my machine consistently needs to be set to a lower number than on hers. Is there something wrong with my machine?

Probably not. It is not at all unusual for tension settings to vary among individual machines. This is not a concern unless you have to go nearly to zero ("0") for regular sewing. If this is the case (assuming your machine is clean and all other factors are correct), I would recommend asking your dealer to adjust your machine. Take along some pieces of the fabrics you sew most often; otherwise, stiff demo cloth might be used to test-sew when setting the machine.

Should I adjust bobbin tension?

Once properly set for the thread you use most often, bobbin tension should rarely be adjusted. Apparent bobbin-tension problems can be caused by lint caught in the bobbin-tension device or by improper bobbin threading.

If your machine has a separate bobbin case, you can test bobbin tension by holding the thread and letting the case dangle. When you give the thread a jerk, the case should slip down. Occasional adjustments can be made by turning the adjusting screw to the right to tighten it or to the left to loosen it. Adjust the screw over a small box or a piece of fabric—the screw is tiny and easy to lose.

Some very attractive decorative effects can be created by sewing with the right side of the fabric down and with heavier threads (such as pearl cotton or ribbon thread) on the bobbin. Always bypass the bobbin-tension device or loosen tension when using these heavier threads in the bobbin. Check your machine manual to see whether bobbin tension can be bypassed. If it cannot, you can loosen and later reset the bobbin tension on your regular bobbin case, but doing so repeatedly can be tedious. If you plan to use this technique often, you may want to invest in a separate bobbin case. If you do, mark the case to distinguish it.

Easy Ways to Achieve Precision in Your Sewing

I am frequently asked how I achieve such even seam allowances, tucks, topstitching, and decorative stitching in my sewing. Accurate stitching is important not only for the look of the finished project but also for proper fit. Most sewers realize this, but many think precision requires more time and effort than they have to spend on their sewing. In fact, much of what is needed is just know-how. Some of the suggestions in this chapter may seem at first like extra work, but once you get used to them, they will actually save time, eliminate a lot of eyestrain and frustration, and make your sewing much more rewarding.

The look of delicate hand embroidery graces this white batiste blouse. Single-needle scallops frame briar-stitch fagoting and provide an attractive way to finish the raw edges underneath. Rows of folded tucks and feather stitching highlight the central motif. On the sleeve, tucks frame the fagoting as well as hiding the raw edges within. (Pattern adapted from Harbor Blouse, Creative Needle magazine, Sept./Oct. 1987.)

Cutting

Straighten the grain of your fabric. When a garment is cut off grain, the stitching can look "off" even if it was stitched correctly, especially once the garment has been washed.

For true crossgrain "cuts" on woven fabrics, clip through the selvage, and tear the fabric whenever possible instead of cutting. Tearing saves time and ensures accuracy. Always tear quickly; tearing slowly causes more pulls along the torn edge. On very delicate woven fabrics where tearing is risky, snip the fabric edge, pull a thread, and cut along the pulled thread.

When possible, do any decorative stitching on a piece of the fabric that is wider and longer than the pattern piece, then cut the pattern piece from the fabric. Since some stitching (for example, twin-needle pintucks) draws up the fabric, this sequence will ensure an accurate fit. In addition, if you work this way, the very beginning and ending of the decorative stitching—where it is difficult to achieve perfect stitching—will be cut off.

For accurate measuring, cutting, straightening, and blocking, use cutting boards, rotary cutting mats, and pressing surfaces with horizontal, vertical, and diagonal lines marked. Gridded ironing-board covers eventually become distorted; they should be checked occasionally and replaced when necessary.

Marking

Mark stitch placement directly on the fabric only when you cannot use the fabric design (such as a stripe, plaid, or repeated design) or guides such as markings on a presser foot, a needle plate, and so on. It is often possible to see the needle-plate edge or guides, such as tape, through the sheer fabrics commonly used for fine machine sewing. When marking is necessary, always test the fabric marker on a scrap of the fabric first, including following the instructions for removal. For accuracy, the marker must have a fine point.

On delicate woven fabrics (such as handkerchief linen or Swiss batiste), mark the placement for a row of stitching that is too far from an edge or a previous row to use other guides, by picking a thread at the fabric edge and pulling it enough to see it. You can press a crease along this line to make it more visible. (I usually have to pull a thread just once in a project, most often for the center-front stitch placement. I then plan the spacing for the other decorative stitching so that I can use guides, such as aligning the edge of the presser foot with a previous row of stitching.)

Pressing crease lines can be a time-saving alternative to measuring and marking. For a child's collar that called for tucks every 1 in., choosing an eyelet having a 1-in. design repeat made marking with crease lines easy. A blind-hem foot guides the stitching for accurate ⅛-in. tucks along each crease line.

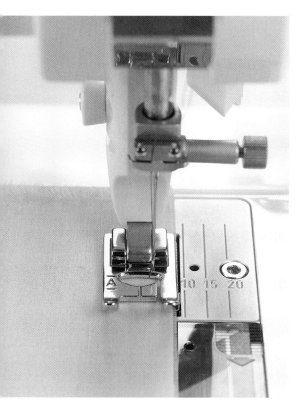

To sew close to a fabric edge while keeping the fabric over both feed dogs, move the needle toward the fabric edge instead of moving the fabric edge to the needle.

You can use crease lines for guiding, whenever it's more convenient than marking or if you want to avoid excessive marking. For example, for a child's collar that called for a long length of 5-in.-wide fabric to be stitched with ⅛-in. tucks every 1 in., I used crease lines instead of time-consuming marking, as shown in the photo on the facing page. I chose a 5-in.-wide eyelet with a 1-in. design repeat. (Eyelets fitting this criteria were not difficult to find.) Pressing crease lines at every design repeat was easy and eliminated marking.

Guides and guiding

The most accurate and even guiding is accomplished by using guides rather than by watching the needle. For most techniques, watch the needle only at the be-

ginning of the stitching to determine the best guides to use. Then learn to watch only the guide, checking your stitching periodically and adjusting, if necessary. Not only will your stitching be more consistent, but your eyes will not tire as quickly.

Sit directly in front of the needle. Most sewing-machine cabinets are designed so that the machine, rather than the needle, is centered in front of you. This machine position requires a person to lean left while sewing. This is not only less accurate for guiding but also hard on your back. Most cabinet tops can be raised (so that the machine sits at the same level as the top of the cabinet, rather than in a well), and you can then reposition your machine so that the needle is directly in front of you.

If your machine has a removable table for creating a larger stitching surface, use it whenever you do not need the free arm. The larger surface allows more control for guiding and allows more space for adding guiding aids. If your machine does not have a large sewing surface, a generic table (available through sewing-machine dealers or by mail order) may work.

NEEDLE POSITIONS

As discussed in chapter 1, the machine will do the best job of feeding the fabric evenly when the presser foot holds the fabric securely over both feed dogs. Changing needle positions allows you to use the best presser foot and fabric position for the job without compromising feed. For example, when sewing close to a fabric edge, rather than shifting the fabric edge close to the needle, move the needle instead so that the fabric stays over both feed dogs, as shown in the photo above.

TIP ✖ Mark with fine dots rather than solid lines, in case there is any unexpected difficulty with removal.

✖ Save your test swatches with notes in an envelope or in your notebook for future reference, so you will not have to test the same fabric again.

✖ A line of straight stitching can both hold a hem or facing in place and simultaneously mark the position for decorative topstitching. A normal or slightly lengthened stitch and fine thread usually will be covered by the decorative stitching and thus will not have to be removed.

Generally, for seam allowances or tucks wider than about $1/2$ in., guide the fabric edge along markings on the needle plate or other guide, and adjust the needle position, if necessary. For seam allowances or tucks between approximately $3/16$ in. and $1/2$ in. wide, guide the edge of the fabric even with the right edge of the foot, and move the needle to the best position for the correct spacing. Only when you are sewing closer than $3/16$ in. from an edge do you usually have to switch to a foot (such as an edging foot) that guides the fabric over just one feed dog. (For metric conversion, see the chart below.)

Note that when using a straight-stitch foot, the needle must be in center position. (With any other needle position, the needle would hit the foot and break.) Ideally straight-stitch feet should cover as much of the feed dogs as possible, but some feet that have guidelines for sewing $1/8$ in. and $1/4$ in. from an edge actually cover the feed dogs very little. The flat underside and small needle-hole opening on these feet compensate to some extent because they hold the fabric well. However, feed-dog spacing varies, so experi-

ment with these feet on your machine. The advantage of their readily apparent guides may outweigh the disadvantage of the fabric not being held by both feed dogs.

Most newer sewing machines allow the needle position to be changed. Some have only three needle positions, while others have almost unlimited positions. Some allow the needle position to be changed with straight stitches only, others with most stitches. Consult your machine manual for information on needle positions.

PRESSER FEET

When choosing a foot for a stitching task, consider not only the foot's function but also characteristics that can help with guiding, such as markings or notches on the foot, the foot's size, and so on (even its edges can be used as guides). Also bear in mind that presser feet with flat undersides are preferred for regular straight stitching, and those with indented undersides are best for satin stitching or other raised effects.

Presser feet can be used for purposes other than their names imply. For example, Bernina's jeans foot (#8) is a straight-stitch foot that can be used with fabrics other than denim. Elna's blind-stitch foot has a long adjustable guide that makes it a perfect adjustable edging foot. And the grooves of pintuck feet can be used to guide corded fabric edges for fagoting (see p. 138).

Many straight-stitch feet are designed so that the edges of the feet, toes, grooves, or markings can be used as guides for precision straight stitching close to an edge. These feet may be called quilter's, patchwork, or $1/4$-in. feet (see the top photo on the facing page).

TIP ✖ On many machines the needle position can be changed by selecting straight stitch, then using the width selector. If this moves the needle in only one direction, try engaging mirror image (if your machine has this feature) to move the needle in the other direction.

✖ On some machines, engaging the twin-needle option, whether or not you are using twin needles, may allow more needle positions.

Metric Conversion Chart

U.S. Measurement	Metric Equivalent
$1/16$ in.	1.5mm
$1/8$ in.	3mm
$3/16$ in.	4.5mm
$1/4$ in.	6mm
$3/8$ in.	10mm (1cm)
$1/2$ in.	13mm (1.3cm)
$5/8$ in.	15mm (1.5cm)
1 in.	25mm (2.5cm)

You can use an extra-fine permanent marker to help identify presser feet, as well as to add markings to help with guiding. For example, some Pfaff feet have helpful guidelines on the clear section in the center of the foot, but the marks do not go all the way to the front of the foot where it meets the fabric. I put additional marks at the front edge. Elna's multiple-cord foot can be used either with or without cord as a metal embroidery foot, but I add a mark to the center front of the foot for guiding. Marks can usually be removed with alcohol, but to be sure, test first in an inconspicuous place.

NEEDLE PLATE

Use needle-plate guideline markings as well as the edge of the needle plate. Unfortunately, most needle-plate guidelines are marked for millimeters, while (in this country) most instructions for seam al-

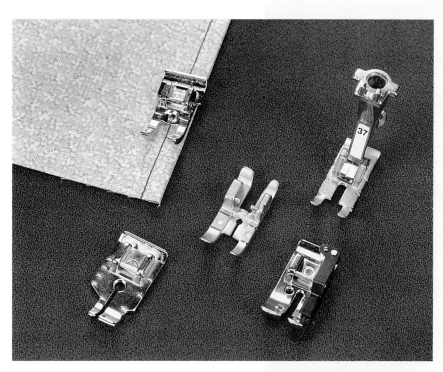

Presser feet can be used for purposes other than those implied by their names. Patchwork and quilter's feet are not just for quilters; they can be used as guides for any straight stitching ¼ in. or ⅛ in. from an edge.

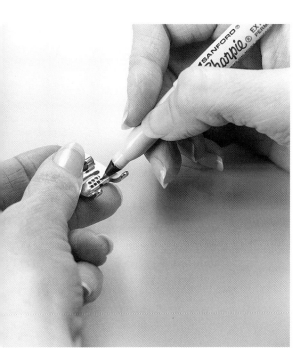

You can mark your own guidelines directly on presser feet using an extra-fine permanent marker. A center mark was added on this multiple-cord foot.

lowances are in inches. Millimeter guidelines can still be very helpful, though, especially when used in combination with different needle positions.

Consult your sewing-machine manual for suggestions on guiding with particular feet, guides, or the needle plate. You may find such information in sections on needle positions, pintucks, tucks, pleats, topstitching, or edgestitching.

You can also add helpful markings to your needle plate. On some Bernina models, the needle plates have guidelines calibrated in inches but not identified. I put an identifying mark at the front of the lines I use most often (¼ in. and ⅝ in.).

On some New Home machines, the needle plates have inch guidelines toward the back. I put a corresponding line near the front of the needle plate for the distances I use most often. (On New

> **TIP** To prevent needle breakage, the needle position on most machines can be changed only if the needle is up.

Stitching circles and arcs

You can stitch perfect circles or arcs (sections of circles), such as large scallops, by using a bent pin taped to the bed of the machine as a pivot. Bend a pin in half and tape it, point up, to the right or left of the needle, as shown in the top photo at right. The distance from the pin to the machine needle should be the radius of the circle. Stabilize the fabric well and impale it on the pin. Keep the center of the circle on the pin with a clean cork, eraser, or your fingers as you stitch (see the bottom photo at right). (A thumbtack taped point up is often recommended for this technique. But even if the thumbtack is

new, the point can damage many fabrics, so I don't recommend it.) Some Elna models have holes on their removable tables and a tack-like pivot for this technique. The table works well, but on more delicate fabrics, I recommend inserting a fine pin into the holes for the pivot.

(LEFT) To stitch perfect scallops or circles, tape a bent pin to the right or left of the needle. The distance from the pin to the needle will be the radius of the circle. (BELOW) An eraser stuck on the pin over the fabric helps control the fabric as it pivots.

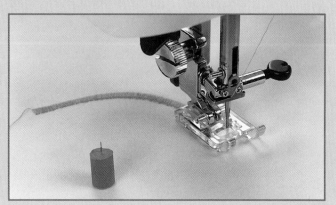

Home machines where the needle comes up automatically in the left needle position, the needle-plate guidelines measure from this position.)

SEAM GUIDES

There are seam guides that snap onto the needle plate or screw onto the machine bed for guiding an even distance from the fabric edge. These can be combined with different needle positions for narrower or wider spacing. For example, Elna has a snap-on cloth guide with a raised sliding guide that works very well for guiding 10mm to 75mm from an edge. It can be used with the 10mm line

and far right needle position to stitch as close as $1/4$ in. to almost $3^{1}/_{4}$ in. with the 75mm line and far left needle position.

Other guides, sometimes called quilting guides, slide into the needle bar behind the presser foot for even spacing from an edge or another row of stitching.

For stitching straight rows, long guides will give the best results. For curves, just use a point directly to the right or left of the needle as a guide. For stitching circles and arcs, see the sidebar above.

Avoid any guides that are wobbly and cannot be tightened. They are not accurate.

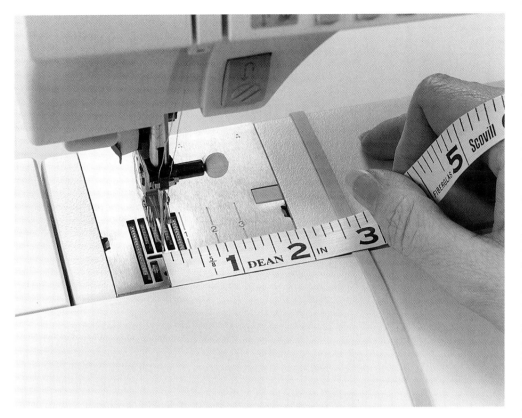

A rubber band placed around the free arm can serve as a guideline where there is none or can extend a short guide.

TIP Rubbing alcohol will usually remove any sticky residue that remains after you have removed tape or any other stick-on guide from the machine bed. If the residue is stubborn, try Goo Gone or Goof Off (both available at craft and hardware stores), but first test them in an inconspicuous spot.

TAPE

Masking tape or drafting tape, applied parallel to the presser foot on the machine bed, may be used as a guide. Even the sticky top edge of 3M's Post-it Notes can be used for a quick, temporary guide. You can create a raised guide by using several layers of tape or a pad of Post-it Notes.

RUBBER BANDS

A medium to wide rubber band that fits securely around the machine's free arm makes an easy temporary guide. If the machine has a removable table, you can create a longer guide by positioning a second rubber band around the front of the table so that it aligns with the one on the free arm.

CREATIVE GUIDES

In addition to these suggestions, be creative and try anything you think may be helpful. For example, a flat coffee stirrer or a picture-framing spacer affixed in front of the presser foot is great for maintaining an even space between two pieces of fabric for fagoting (see the photos on pp. 136-137). The spacers (plastic strips sold by the inch at framing shops) can also be used as temporary adhesive guides anywhere on the machine bed. Check for other guiding aids in catalogs and in notions displays at sewing-machine dealers and fabric stores.

TAKING MEASUREMENTS AND RECORDING THE RESULTS

I recommend measuring with an accurate flat ruler or graph paper to determine the best combination of foot, marking on the foot, needle-plate guideline, and needle position for the most common topstitching and seam allowances. Record the results on an index card (see the sidebar at right), and keep it near your machine so that the information is always just a glance away.

Starting, ending, and securing the stitching

When possible, start slightly in from the edge of the fabric so that the fabric is securely under the presser foot, especially for stitching techniques that are difficult to get started. The very beginning and end of the stitching will often be hidden in a seam or cut off anyway.

When you must start right at the fabric edge, slightly pull the thread tails to get started, as shown in the photo below. It is often helpful to put the edge of the fabric over the corner of a small piece of tearaway stabilizer.

Putting the corner of the fabric over a piece of tearaway stabilizer and slightly pulling the thread tails as you begin to stitch help to start difficult stitching at the very edge of the fabric.

Creating your index-card reference

An index card for your most-used machine setups will be immensely useful, since you won't have to keep re-creating them from scratch. Before taking measurements, though, make sure your needle is truly centered for a straight stitch in center needle position. If it's not, ask your machine dealer to adjust it.

Measuring with a flat ruler or seam gauge

To measure with a flat ruler or seam gauge, put the ruler on the bed of the machine beneath the needle. Manually lower the needle point to either the "0" or the 1-in. line, as shown in the top photos on the facing page. Then experiment with feet, guides, and needle positions to determine the combinations that give you the topstitching and seam-allowance widths you use the most. (You can use a tape measure if you have checked its markings for accuracy.)

Measuring with graph paper

To use graph paper as a measuring tool, insert an old machine needle in the machine. (No thread is needed.) Align a line on the graph paper with a guide, such as a presser-foot edge, as shown in the bottom right photo on the facing page. Then straight-stitch about 1 in. with the needle in whatever position is closest to the desired spacing. On the graph paper, note the guide used and the needle position. Repeat for other presser-foot guides and other presser feet.

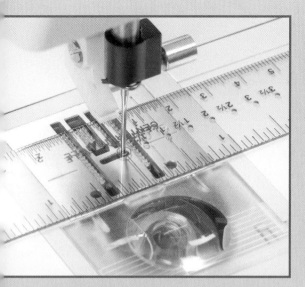

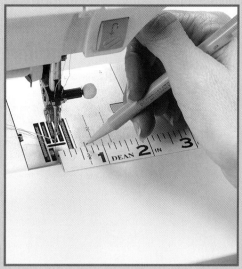

The 6-In. Design Ruler by Collins is a good measuring tool at the machine. Lower the needle (a large size—like a 120/19 Universal needle—will be most accurate) into the center hole of the ruler, then experiment with all the possible guides, needle positions, and markings for the best guiding combinations. Unless you want metric measurements, turn the ruler so that the inch markings are toward you.

To determine the best guiding combinations using guides on the machine bed, such as needle-plate markings, cut along a line on the graph paper. Use this cut edge to simulate a fabric edge, aligning it with the various guides and experimenting with different needle positions, as shown in the bottom left photo. The graph paper makes it easy to see which combinations give the desired measurements. Discard the needle when you are finished.

Recording the results on your index card

Once you find the best combinations, test them on fabric, then note them on an index card. Keep it handy for reference.

Guiding varies from person to person because you can align the fabric edge at the line, on the line, or over the line. Find combinations that work for you, and be consistent.

For example, here are my notes for the Elna Diva:

- ✗ 1/8 in.—Use left front edge of quilter's foot, or use blind-stitch foot (E) with guide at center and far left needle position.

- ✗ 1/4 in.—Use right front edge of quilter's foot, or use 10mm needle-plate line and needle far right.

- ✗ 1/2 in.—Use 10mm line, needle far left.

- ✗ 5/8 in.—Use 15mm line, needle near left.

- ✗ 1 in.—Use right edge of needle plate, needle near right.

- ✗ 2 in.—Use edge of removable sewing table, needle center.

Aligning the "o" position of a tape measure with the needle point helps determine the best foot, guide, and needle position for common seam allowances. On this machine (Pfaff 7550), when the needle is set two positions left of center, the machine's 1.5cm line marks a perfect 5/8-in. seam allowance.

Graph paper makes it easy to evaluate guiding/needle-position combinations. (BELOW RIGHT) Aligning a line of the 1/4-in. graph paper with the edge of the presser foot shows that with the needle set right of center, a perfect 1/4-in. seam allowance can be stitched. (BELOW LEFT) You can also cut along a graph-paper line and use that to simulate a fabric edge to determine what guiding to use.

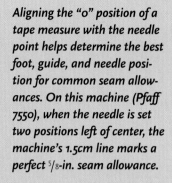

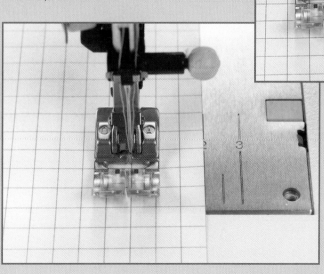

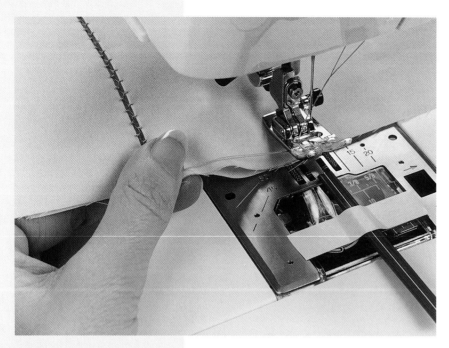

Pinching the threads as you pull the fabric away from the machine prevents the stitching at the fabric edge from becoming distorted.

TIP Maintain accuracy and save time when stitching several small pieces that have the same seam allowance by sewing one immediately after the other, rather than starting and ending each one separately. As soon as you get to the end of one piece, start the next one, without raising the presser foot. Cut the pieces apart afterward.

At the end of the stitching, gently pull the fabric out from under the presser foot, then pinch the threads at the end of the stitching as you continue to pull the fabric and threads away from the machine, as shown in the photo above. This prevents the fabric and stitching from becoming distorted, which often occurs when the threads are pulled too roughly at the end.

When it is necessary to secure straight stitching, the method to use depends on the weight of the fabric. On medium- to heavyweight fabrics, backstitch to secure the stitching. Start the stitching with the needle about $^3/_8$ in. in from the edge, stitch in reverse to the edge, then sew forward as usual.

Do not backstitch lightweight fabrics, because doing so causes an unattractive puckered area. If securing is necessary, shorten the stitch length to about 1mm for $^3/_8$ in. at the beginning and end of the stitching. (It is helpful to pull the thread tails slightly at the start.) Another option is to tie the top and bobbin thread tails to-gether on the underside or next to the fabric edge, then "bury" the tails.

To bury thread tails, cut the tails long. Take the top thread to the underside, and knot the top and bobbin threads together next to the fabric. Then thread both tails into the eye of a hand-sewing needle. Stitch into the seam allowance right next to the knot, then bring the needle out about $^3/_{16}$ in. away. Cut the threads close to the fabric, and the ends will disappear. Bury thread tails whenever they would show on the finished project—for example, at the end of topstitching.

When decorative stitching must be secured (for example, for individual flower motifs that do not tie off automatically), stitch in the same place several times. Most newer machines have a securing option or button for this. Or you can manually set the machine at "0" width and "0" length for several stitches.

Additional tips

The following are some additional tips for achieving accurate and precise stitching:

✘ Do not sew over pins. Remove them before they reach the presser foot. (Sewing over pins distorts stitching and risks damaging the needle.)

✘ Stitch with a smooth speed.

✘ Stop with the needle down when you need to adjust the fabric.

✘ In most cases, press after each step. Be careful not to stretch fabric or laces when pressing.

✘ Stitch test samples with exactly the same conditions (including grain direction, number of fabric layers, stabilizer, and so on) as on the project.

✗ Make notes, including guiding information, right on the fabric sample, and save it in your notebook for future reference.

Applications

Anything that ensures accuracy will improve almost any sewing technique. Keep in mind that you are more likely to use the best foot, guide, and needle-position combinations if the index card with your notes is always handy. Whenever you figure out other useful guiding information, add it to your card.

SEAMS

Accurate seam allowances are important for good fit. You can stitch precise seam allowances of any width if you use the appropriate guiding combination.

French seams (see the sidebar below) provide a professional-looking finish for very light- to medium-weight fabrics, especially sheer ones.

Most newer machines have several overlock-type stitches that are useful in certain seaming situations. The excess fabric is usually trimmed from the seam allowance after stitching. Consult your machine manual to see which ones you

French seams

For perfect French seams on medium-weight fabrics (such as broadcloth and most prints) with a ⁵⁄₈-in. seam allowance, follow these steps:

1. Stitch one ³⁄₈-in. seam with wrong sides together.

2. Press the seam flat, then open, then both seam allowances to one side.

3. Trim the seam allowance to ¹⁄₈ in.

4. Fold right sides together, and stitch a ¹⁄₄-in. seam enclosing the trimmed seam allowances.

As shown, the ³⁄₈-in. seam was sewn on a Pfaff 7550 using the right side of foot #0A, with two needle positions left. The ¹⁄₄-in. seam was stitched at the same guiding, with five needle positions right.

Note that the width of both the first and second seam allowances of a French seam will vary according to the width of the seam allowance provided for in the pattern as well as the weight of the fabric. On a very lightweight fabric, such as Swiss batiste, a finished French seam should be no wider than ¹⁄₈ in. to ³⁄₁₆ in.

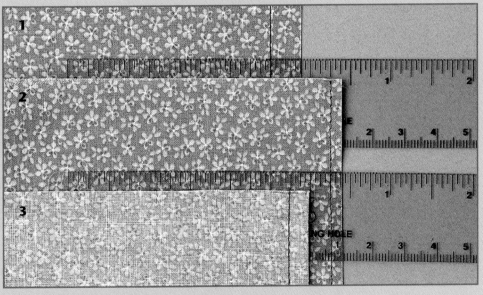

With a good guiding reference, French seams are easy.
1. With wrong sides together, stitch a ³⁄₈-in. seam.
2. Press seam flat, then open, then both seam allowances to one side. Trim to ¹⁄₈ in.
3. Fold right sides together; stitch a ¹⁄₄-in. seam, enclosing the first seam.

have and what their suggested uses are. Test for the best guiding combination to get a $5/8$-in. (or other width) seam allowance. Add this to your index card, noting the stitch width (since that will make a difference).

For example, on the Elna Diva the super overlock stitch (#9) is excellent for finished seams on light- to medium-weight fabrics where French seams are not appropriate. I often use this stitch to set in sleeves. The index-card entry might read: "$5/8$-in. seam allowance with stitch width 4.4mm—use 15mm line, needle far right."

TUCKS AND PLEATS

Guiding combinations will help you stitch perfect folded tucks and pleats with very little marking. For more on making folded tucks, see pp. 160-161 and the sidebar on pp. 134-135.

ROWS OF DECORATIVE STITCHING

Guiding aids enable you to stitch evenly spaced rows of decorative stitching—either an even distance from an edge or from another row—without marking. For example, using tape or a rubber band to guide the folded lower edge of a skirt will eliminate having to mark the stitching line for hemming from the right side with decorative stitches (see p. 73 and pp. 158-159).

TOPSTITCHING, EDGESTITCHING, AND UNDERSTITCHING

By taking advantage of the ability to move the needle left and right of center, you usually can topstitch, edgestitch, and understitch with the fabric edge aligned with the right edge of the presser foot

and over both feed dogs (see the discussion of needle position on pp. 29-30). This avoids many of the problems typically encountered when trying to guide evenly with the fabric over just one feed dog.

For stitching even closer to the edge, try an edging foot or a straight-stitch foot with guides, such as a quilter's foot.

PIPING

For precise and consistent application of piping, use a presser foot with one or more grooves—such as a standard buttonhole foot—to guide small piping. For stitching close to large piping, use a zipper foot. When making up the piping, set the needle to stitch one position away from right alongside the piping. Then when sewing the piping into the project, use the needle position closest to the piping. This prevents the common problem of having the first stitching visible.

GATHERING

Use a combination of guiding and needle position to make perfectly spaced rows of lengthened stitching for gathering a skirt, setting in a sleeve, and so on. For example, here is a way to gather any fabric where the needle will not leave holes (the seam allowance is $5/8$ in.):

1. Loosen upper tension and stitch one row of lengthened stitches $3/4$ in. from the fabric edge.

2. Stitch a second row $3/8$ in. to $1/2$ in. from the edge.

3. Pull up the bobbin threads to the desired fullness.

Preventing backache and eyestrain

To prevent backache, a high cutting table is essential. The best cutting-table height depends on your own height—just below hip height works well for me. Since my family rarely uses the table in our formal dining room, I have elevated it with several old books under each leg, and I use this for cutting fabric. If this is not an option for you, consider some of the very functional and reasonably priced cutting tables available at fabric stores and through sewing-machine dealers. For pinning and for cutting out small items, I use the ironing board adjusted to a comfortable height.

Setting up your sewing area

Invest in a rolling secretary's chair with adjustable height and backrest. Position the sewing machine so that the needle bar is directly in front of you (see p. 29). On many sewing-machine cabinets, the section on which the machine rests can be raised to be level with the rest of the cabinet, allowing you more leeway for positioning the machine. Devices that tilt your machine forward may help prevent neck- and backache as well as improve your vision of the area being stitched. Also experiment with different foot-pedal positions.

The importance of guides

To prevent eyestrain, learn to use guides. Watch the needle only when absolutely necessary—usually just at the beginning of each technique. Once the settings and guiding position are determined, force yourself to watch only the fabric at the guide. Check your work occasionally and adjust your guiding, if necessary. Using a guide is easier on the eyes (and back, because you do not have to lean over as much) and is also much more accurate than watching the needle. Although it may take some practice, using a guide definitely works.

Lighting

Your sewing area should have good general room lighting as well as task lighting for machine and hand work. For more direct light at the machine and for hand work, lamps with adjustable arms work well. They may be freestanding or clamped onto the cabinet or table. Just don't leave a hot bulb next to the machine for a long time; doing so could discolor or distort some machine cases.

Finally, take frequent breaks—at least long enough to stand up and stretch, and look off into the distance to rest your eyes.

4. To attach the gathered fabric, return the stitch length and upper tension to normal, and stitch ⁵/₈ in. from the edge, between the two gathering rows.

5. Remove the gathering stitches. (The loosened upper tension makes it easier to remove the bobbin threads before the top threads.)

A word about comfort

Aching backs and eyestrain are the bane of sewers everywhere (see the sidebar above). Take the time to assess your work area from an ergonomic point of view; a few minor adjustments could make a world of difference in your work as well as in your comfort.

Questions

How do you determine which fabric marker to use on a particular fabric?

Test fabric markers carefully on a scrap of the fabric. This takes some advance planning, but I have learned the hard way that not testing is risky. (Each pleat line I marked with an air-erasable pen on a teal faille moiré skirt—51 percent acetate, 49 percent cotton—is now permanently discolored to a light blue. The water-erasable pen markings I thought had been carefully removed with cold water on a Swiss cotton piqué blouse kept reappearing whenever it was ironed, often leaving a brownish-colored residue.) Always mark a scrap of the fabric with any markers you are considering, then follow the removal method (usually rinsing) recommended on the package. Let the fabric dry, press it, and note the results. If you are testing a pencil mark, wash the fabric scrap as you intend to wash the completed project.

Write notes directly on the fabric scrap, such as "Italian organdy—not prewashed; blue water-erasable marker reappeared twice when ironed; purple air-erasable marker caused no problems." Also note other variables, such as "prewashed, spray-starched, and pressed before marking."

Keep the fabric scraps and notes in a file, an envelope, or a pocket page in your sample notebook, along with the package instructions for each marker. This is valuable for future reference, so you will not have to test the same fabric again. Even with a successfully tested marker, it is wise to mark very sparingly.

Do you have any tips for sewing over thick seams, like those on a jeans hem? My machine keeps stitching in one place and jams and/or jumps off the thickness, leaving a space with no stitching.

First, eliminate as much bulk as possible. On jeans, I often serge or overcast the raw lower edges and then turn them up only once for stitching. The once-folded hem is easier to stitch and is a good option—unless, for some reason, the underside will show or the wearer specifically wants the traditional double-fold jeans hem. With the right tools, though, you can handle the thickness of even a traditional jeans hem.

Use a Denim needle appropriate in size for the fabric (I use size 90 most often). The sharp point will help pierce the thick fabric. When the presser foot starts onto a thick seam and angles up, stop (with the needle down), raise the presser foot, and put a shim under the back of the presser foot to make it level. The shim can be the plastic box for sewing-machine needles; folded-up fabric, paper, or cardboard; or a notion that is specifically designed for this purpose. Lower the presser foot, and continue stitching.

As you stitch off the thick seam, slightly lift the fabric behind the presser foot to allow the foot to roll off the thickness rather than jump off, skipping stitches. If the seam is exceptionally thick, a shim may be needed in front, too. In this case, when the front of the presser foot goes off the thick seam, the foot angles down. Stop (with the needle down), raise the presser foot, and put a shim under the front of the foot (in front of the needle). When the back of the foot clears the thick seam, gradually pull the shim out toward the front as you stitch.

What is directional stitching?

Directional stitching refers to the practice of stitching in the same direction for like applications, in order to avoid distortion of the fabric. For example, when applying a centered zipper, it's best to stitch each side across the lower edge and then up, rather than down one side, across, and up the other. In general, seams should be stitched from top to bottom (there are sewers, however, who recommend stitching from the wide end toward the narrow end). In any case, after you have found what works best for you, the most important thing is to be consistent. If you stitch one side seam from top to bottom, stitch the other side seam from top to bottom as well. Fabrics with a nap should be stitched "with the nap" (the way the pile feels smooth when stroked). If there is any doubt about the best direction to stitch a fabric, do some test-stitching on scraps.

I am having difficulty getting two rows of scallops to mirror and match each other exactly. What would cause this problem? Could stitching speed be a factor?

Yes, it is possible that speed could slightly affect stitch density. The difference would hardly be noticeable except when two rows of stitching must match exactly, as in the situation you describe.

I tested the effect of stitching speed by stitching three rows of 10 baby scallops, each at a different speed. The row stitched at a medium speed (using the "slow" speed button) was 80.5mm long. The row stitched at a fast speed measured 82.5mm. The third row, which was stitched while varying the speed from slow to fast, was almost 83mm long.

For decorative stitching, the best results are obtained with a slow to medium speed and smooth, even stitching. For this reason, some of the newer machines automatically switch to a slower speed with this kind of stitching.

The problem you describe can have other causes. For example, the stitching may be too dense. In this case, use finer machine-embroidery thread (and an appropriate new needle), and lengthen the stitch slightly. Using the wrong presser foot can also cause uneven satin stitching; use a satin-stitch foot, which has a channel underneath to allow the stitching to pass under the foot easily. If the presser foot rides over part of the previous stitching, the stitching will be affected. Unfortunately, this sometimes cannot be avoided. Always stitch a sample, and if necessary, adjust the second row of stitches to match the first using the balancing feature (also called elongation or fine-tuning) or the stitch-length adjustment. Any other difference between one row and the next, such as more or fewer layers of fabric, different grain direction, mirror-image stitching, or stitching in the opposite direction, could also slightly affect the stitch and require adjustments when an exact match is required.

If the fabric is not adequately stabilized, the lengths of motifs can be affected. For decorative stitching, most fabrics should be prewashed and spray-starched, and then stitched with a tear-away stabilizer underneath. (A lightweight stabilizer should be used under lightweight fabrics.) After stitching, gently tear away the stabilizer.

Finally, a flat sewing surface will also help. If your machine has a sewing table, use it whenever the free arm is not needed.

Decorative Edges and Creative Appliqué

In garment sewing as well as sewing for home decorating, there are many edges that need to be finished. Consider these: the neck, armhole, and lower edges on slips, nightgowns, and baby garments; the edges of ruffles; sleeve edges (especially on little girls' garments); tablecloth, placemat, and napkin edges; and for smockers, smocked sleeve edges and ruffled edges on smocked skirts, pinafores, sundresses, and pockets. You can create outstanding decorative edges for these applications using variations of common utility and decorative stitches. The same stitches can also be used for creative appliquéing.

The colors of this cheerful tulip print are repeated in the ribbons that decorate the collar. The stretch blind stitch embellishes the ribbons and appliqués them to the blouse at the same time. The ruffled edges of the sleeves and skirt are finished with a picot edging, using the same stretch blind stitch. (Pattern adapted from Children's Corner #81, designed by Carol Laflin Ahles.)

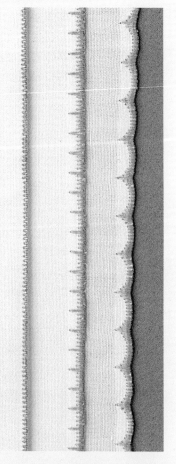

Three easy decorative edges are a corded edge (left), a picot edge (center), and a "no-trim-around" scalloped edge (right).

Decorative edges

When you want something more decorative than a plain, narrow-hem-type finish, you can easily create a corded, picot, or scalloped edge using any of several common machine stitches. For these edge finishes, the stitching is done on a folded edge, which makes it much more secure than stitching done on a raw edge. An additional advantage to stitching on a folded edge is that on the underside you simply trim away the excess fabric up to the stitching, rather than having to trim meticulously around the stitching on the right side, as is required with most other decorative-edge techniques. (Eliminated is the tedious job of trimming around traditional scallops closely enough to remove whiskers without cutting the stitching itself!) And it's easy to add a touch of color by using contrasting thread.

The specifications that follow apply to corded, picot, and scalloped edges:

Fabric: Usually light- to medium-weight wovens. For the corded-edge and baby-edging scallop, additional suitable fabrics include tulle and tricot.

Thread: Machine-embroidery cotton (DMC, Madeira, Mettler), usually size 50/2 or 60/2. Also experiment with other decorative threads as appropriate for the application, such as rayon or metallic thread for a Christmas tablecloth. Thread color can match or contrast with the fabric.

Needle: 70 or 80 Universal (or size and type appropriate for the fabric and thread). If fragile decorative threads are shredding with Universal needles, try Embroidery or Metallica needles from Schmetz or Metafil needles from Lammertz.

Upper tension: Loosen (decrease) slightly.

PREPARATION FOR CORDED, PICOT, AND SCALLOPED EDGES

To prepare for stitching any of the decorative edges, spray-starch and press under the raw edge about 1/2 in. (1/4 in. on curves). (With tulle or tricot, just finger-press under 1/4 in. to 1/2 in.) If necessary on sharp curves, clip along the underside of the pressed-under edge.

If you are edging a ruffle on fabric that will be smocked (for example, for a smocked sleeve edge or smocked skirt, pinafore, or sundress), pleat the fabric for smocking first. Start the first row to be smocked the distance of the depth of the ruffle plus 1/2 in. from the edge. Leave long pleater threads. Press the pleated area flat, then press the raw edge under 1/2 in.

CORDED EDGE

The corded edge is the simplest of the decorative edges (just a zigzag stitch over cord along a fold), but it makes a very pretty edge. It is similar to the "roll and whip" (zigzag over a cut edge) technique from heirloom sewing, except that because you stitch over a cord and a fold, you end up with a stronger, more finished edge. This is also a very practical way to finish fabric edges for fagoting— used with a pintuck foot, the corded edges make guiding especially easy (see p. 138).

If the excess fabric will be trimmed from the underside of the stitching (as is usually the case), this finish is not recommended for a loosely woven fabric or for a garment that will get rough wearing and washing. Both the picot edge and the scalloped edge are sturdier, and therefore better choices, because of the wider

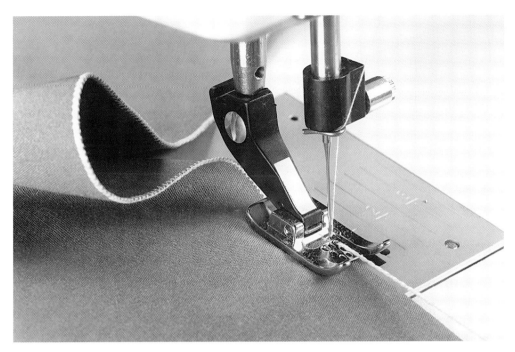

For the corded edge, a foot with holes or grooves helps keep the cord right next to the folded fabric edge. The stitch goes into the fabric on the left and just over the cord on the right.

zigzag in at least part of their stitch patterns.

Cord: Pearl cotton in size 5 for a heavier look, size 8 for a more delicate look. Other options for a delicate look include crochet cotton, buttonhole twist/topstitching thread, and so on. The cord size should be appropriate to the fabric and the look desired. Cord color should match thread color as closely as possible.

Foot: To guide the cord, a foot with one or more holes (like a cording foot or Bernina's embroidery foot with the hole in front) or grooves (like a buttonhole or pintuck foot) is helpful. On some machines and with certain stitches, the needle position can be moved so that you can use a foot with an off-center groove, such as a buttonhole foot, and adjust the stitch to align with the groove. Be creative. Sometimes even the curl of a narrow hemmer is very useful for guiding cord. If necessary, use a satin-stitch foot

and hold the cord next to the fold with your hands.

Stitch: Zigzag.

Width: 2mm to 2.5mm (just wide enough for a secure "bite" into the folded fabric).

Length: About 0.8mm (a little longer than a satin stitch).

With the cord next to the folded edge of the fabric, stitch so that the left side of the stitch goes into the fabric and the right side goes just over the cord. (The stitch must clear the cord, not go into it.) When using a foot with grooves, lifting the cord in front as you stitch helps to keep it in the groove. If you plan to trim the excess fabric up to the stitching on the underside, it is important that you make the stitch wide enough to be secure but not so wide that it is unattractive. Adjust guiding and/or stitch width as necessary.

Zigzag stitch

Stretch blind stitch

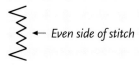

← *Even side of stitch*

Stretch stitch

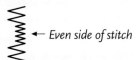

← *Even side of stitch*

For the picot edge, the even side of the stitch goes over and just off the folded edge. The side of the stitch that has the wide stitches goes into the fabric. Using a strip of lightweight tearaway stabilizer underneath produces a more tailored look.

PICOT EDGE

The stretch blind stitch is usually recommended for blind hemming knits. However, if you shorten the stitch to the length you would use for a satin stitch, the stretch blind stitch makes a beautiful edging or appliqué stitch. (The shortened version of this stitch and the Parisian hemstitch can both resemble a blanket stitch. See pp. 60-61.) The wider stitches within the stitch pattern create a picot appearance. On stabilized fabric, the edging has a tailored look; on a lightweight, unstabilized fabric, it has a more delicate look, resembling baby scallops. (Note: Stitch numbers and settings for some machines are given on pp. 195-197.)

Foot: Satin stitch.

Stitch: Stretch (or elastic) blind stitch. (On Berninas, use the stretch stitch; it takes two wide stitches rather than one.)

Width: 4mm to 5.5mm.

Length: About 0.5mm or less (as would be used for a satin stitch).

Stabilizer: Spray-starching and pressing may be all that is needed for fabrics with body, especially if you want a delicate look. Otherwise, use a strip of lightweight, tearaway stabilizer underneath.

Stitch with the right side of the fabric facing up. Position the fabric so that the even or straight side of the stitch goes completely over and off the folded edge. Always test on a scrap of your fabric. If on your machine the even side of the stitch is on the right (as in the drawings at left), the folded edge of the fabric will be to the right. (This is the case with most models of Elna, Kenmore, New Home, Pfaff, and Viking.)

If on your machine the even side of the stitch is to the left and the stitch cannot be mirror imaged, the folded edge of the fabric must be to the left. (This is the case with the stretch stitch on models of Bernina that cannot mirror image.)

For a more delicate look, do not use stabilizer other than the basic spray starch and pressing; allow the widest zigzag in the stitch pattern to pull the fabric, creating a slight scallop effect. Sew taut, holding the fabric with your hands in front of and behind the presser foot. Adjust the stitch width and length, if necessary. If there is puckering, experiment with loosening upper tension a little more and/or applying more spray starch and pressing along the fold before stitching.

If you want the decorative edge to appear straighter and more tailored, stitch with a strip of lightweight tear-away stabilizer under the fold, extending at least $1/2$ in. from the edge. You can use a shorter stitch length when you use a stabilizer. After stitching, gently tear away the stabilizer.

On the wrong side, trim away excess fabric. Trim straight across, getting very close to the widest stitches using appliqué scissors or small scissors. The fabric will not ravel if it is trimmed closely and carefully. (Although it is possible to finish the raw edge of the fabric with overcasting or serging before pressing it under and stitching the decorative edging, this is really unnecessary.)

For some applications, you can narrow-hem the edge before or possibly at the same time as you stitch the edging (see pp. 190-191).

Picot edging can be corded. The technique is the same as for the corded edge described earlier, except that the stretch blind stitch is used instead of the zigzag stitch. With the cord next to the folded edge, stitch so that the straight side of the stitch goes over the cord. A stabilizer may still be needed.

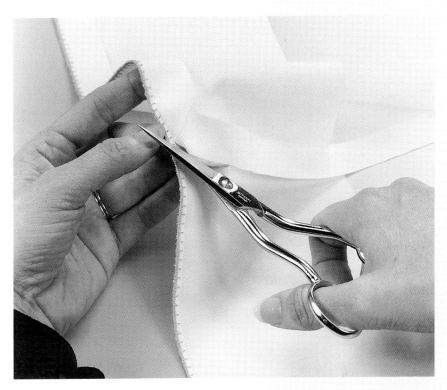

After stitching a decorative edge, trim excess fabric from the underside, straight across just up to the widest stitches.

"NO-TRIM-AROUND" SCALLOPED EDGE

Many machines have an edging scallop—a variation of a scallop stitch—which makes a lovely shaped edging when you stitch it over a folded edge. When you use the edging scallop on the folded edge of a lightweight fabric, the wider zigzag stitches in the pattern actually pull in the fabric to create the scallops. The unique beauty of this version of scalloped edging is that you do not have to trim around every scallop on the right side; you need only trim up to the stitching on the underside. As with corded and picot edging, stitching over a fold creates a stronger, more finished edge.

The size of the scallop varies from machine to machine—from a tiny baby scallop suitable for children's garments or lingerie to a very large scallop suitable for bed linens. Some machines allow you to adjust the length of the scallop without

The stretch blind stitch or Bernina's stretch stitch can create a delicate scalloped effect similar to the baby edging scallop (left) when stitched over a light- to medium-weight fabric without stabilizer (upper portion at right). When a stabilizer is used (lower portion at right), the straighter and more tailored look of picot edging is created.

Edging scallop

altering stitch density. Even if your machine does not have this feature, using a slightly finer or thicker thread provides a little flexibility in the size of the scallop. For example, using a finer thread will allow you to shorten the scallop for a particular application, such as a baby garment. If the scallop is still too large or if your machine does not have the edging-scallop stitch, use the stretch blind stitch. As shown in the samples at left, on an unstabilized lightweight fabric the stretch blind stitch creates an effect very similar to a baby edging scallop.

Specifications are the same as for the picot edge with the stretch blind stitch (see p. 46) except for the following:

Stitch: Edging scallop. If necessary, use the mirror-image function, so that the straight side of the stitch is to the right and the curved side is to the left, as illustrated.

Stabilizer: To form the scallop, the wide zigzag must be able to pull the fabric, so spray starching and pressing usually provide adequate stability. Occasionally on larger scallops, a very lightweight tear-away stabilizer is helpful. If the stabilizer is too stiff, the edging will be decorative, but it will not be pulled into scallops.

Stitch with the right side up and the folded fabric edge to the right. Position the fabric so that the even or straight side of the stitch goes totally over and off the folded edge.

Hold the fabric taut with your hands in front of and behind the presser foot. If there is puckering, experiment with loosening upper tension a little more and/or applying more spray starch and pressing before stitching.

Trim away the excess fabric on the wrong side after stitching. Trim straight across, very close to the widest stitches using appliqué scissors or small scissors.

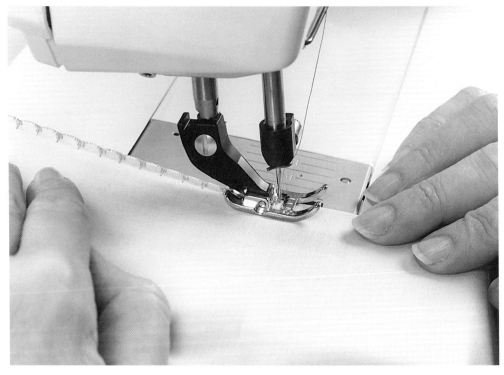

The edging scallop stitch is used for "no-trim-around" scallops. Hold the fabric taut with your hands in front of and behind the presser foot.

The fabric will not ravel if trimmed very closely and carefully.

Note that this edge can also be narrow-hemmed in advance or possibly at the same time as the edging is stitched (see pp. 190-191).

This stitch can also be corded. The cord lies alongside the folded edge, and the straight side of the stitch passes over the cord. The technique is the same as for the corded edge (see pp. 44-45), except for the stitch used and possibly the presser foot: Since the cording will have to curve with the shape of the scallop, a foot with straight, narrow grooves, like a pintuck foot, may keep the cord too

straight. If so, use one of the other feet suggested for cording or use a satin-stitch foot.

Creative appliqué

You needn't limit yourself to the traditional satin stitch for appliquéing! Attaching appliqués is an area where you can easily and effectively use your creativity to experiment with other machine stitches. For example,

✘ the same shortened stretch blind stitch used for the picot edge also makes a very pretty and different appliqué stitch. As

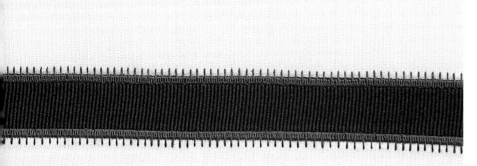

Grosgrain ribbon appliquéd with the stretch blind stitch appears to have a picot edge.

with the edging, the wide stitches in the pattern create a picot effect. (When I use this stitch to attach grosgrain ribbon to square collars, I am frequently asked where I found that wonderful grosgrain ribbon with picots!)

✗ The edging scallop stitch (used for the "no-trim-around" scalloped edge) was perfect for appliquéing the strip of yellow linen onto grosgrain ribbon for the belt in the photo below since it echoed the scallop shapes on the dress collar and hem.

Dense, satin-type stitches, such as the shortened stretch blind stitch and the edging scallop can be used for most appliqué projects, including those where raw edges must be covered. Open or running-type stitches, such as the feather stitch, blind-hem stitch variations, and the Parisian hemstitch (illustrated on pp. 60-61), are more appropriate for attaching appliqués with finished edges, such as ribbon, trims, purchased medal-

A strip of yellow linen appliquéd onto grosgrain ribbon with the edging scallop stitch creates a belt that echoes the scallop shapes of the hem and collar border. See details of dress on p. 160.

lions, and faced or turned-edge appliqués (like those used for Madeira appliqué).

Fabric: Most weights of cotton or cotton-blend wovens are traditional for appliquéing, but in fact very few fabrics should be rejected without at least being tested. With adaptations in thread, needle, settings, tension, stabilizer, and so on, almost any fabric appropriate for the project—including knits, ribbons and trims, lace, felt, lamé, and Ultrasuede—can be considered.

If the finished project will be washed, prewash the backing and appliqué fabrics if any of them could shrink or bleed. Prewashing to remove the sizing also makes many fabrics easier to stitch. Soft or stretchy fabrics may need spray starching and pressing or a fusible interfacing to make them manageable.

Grain direction: Large appliqués should match the background fabric grain, but with small appliqués, consider practicality and your own personal preference.

Thread: Machine-embroidery cotton or rayon. Experiment with other decorative threads, such as metallics, as appropriate for the application. The size of the thread should be appropriate for the fabric; 50/2 or 60/2 cotton (40 in rayon) is usual for light- to medium-weight fabrics; 30/2 cotton (also 30 in rayon) for heavier fabrics. Thread color can match or contrast with the fabric.

For the bobbin thread, you can use a fine thread (usually cotton) in white or a color to match the background fabric when decorative threads are used on the top. This saves the time and expense of changing the bobbin every time the top thread color is changed.

Needle: 70 or 80 Universal (or needle appropriate for the fabric and thread). If fragile decorative threads are shredding with Universal needles, try Embroidery or Metallica needles from Schmetz or Metafil needles from Lammertz.

Foot: For dense stitching, use a satin-stitch foot. For more open, running-type stitching, the basic metal zigzag foot will hold the fabric more securely. If more visibility is needed during stitching, you can use an open-toe satin-stitch foot, but be sure that the fabric is well stabilized and/or in a hoop.

Stitch: Consider the following factors when choosing stitches for appliquéing:

✗ Stitches should cover raw edges. Relatively dense stitches with a width of 2mm or more and a length of 0.5mm or less should generally be used.

✗ Finished edges (like those on ribbon and turned-edge appliqués) will not

Many machine stitches are effective for appliquéing. Satin-type, dense stitches (as seen on pp. 49–50) can be used on raw as well as finished edges; open or running-type stitches, like the blind-hem variation (upper sample) and the Parisian hemstitch (lower sample), should be used only on folded or finished edges.

For this double ribbon trim, the edges of the narrow ribbon were appliquéd with the stretch blind stitch, securing both it and the wider grosgrain ribbon to the background fabric at the same time.

ravel, so they do not have to be completely covered with stitching.

✗ Some stitches that work beautifully on straight edges become distorted on curves. Therefore, the shape of your appliqué also determines stitch choices.

Width: Varies with application, but usually 3mm to 5mm for satin-type stitches. Small appliqués with detailed shapes are more attractive and easier to stitch with a narrower width (2mm to 3mm). With the running stitches, the width will vary with the look desired.

Length: Varies with stitch and application, but usually 0.5mm or less for satin-type stitches and 2mm to 3mm for running stitches like the Parisian hemstitch and feather stitch. Don't make the stitching too dense on lightweight fabrics.

Upper tension: Loosen (decrease) slightly. (Some Bernina and Viking models have the option of threading the bobbin thread through the hole in the finger of the bobbin case, which increases bobbin tension and creates more pull to the underside.)

Stabilizer: To prevent puckering and tunneling, a stabilizer is needed with any dense or wide stitching, including most appliquéing. Use a tearaway stabilizer, appropriate in weight for the fabric, under the backing fabric. When more stability is needed, I prefer to use multiple layers of a lightweight tearaway rather than a single layer of a very heavy one. After the stitching is complete, gently tear off the stabilizer.

Prewash, spray-starch, and press the fabric, if appropriate for the fabric. Fuse, temporarily adhere (with a temporary spray adhesive, like Sulky KK 2000),

or pin (with a few pins on the right side) a piece of lightweight stabilizer to the wrong side of the background fabric. Then position the appliqué. As always, stitch a test sample and make any necessary adjustments before stitching your project.

Experiment with both utility and decorative stitches, keeping in mind the stitch specifications above. With some stitches, mirror imaging or stitching from the opposite direction will produce a completely different look. For example, when appliquéing with the shortened stretch blind stitch, the look is different depending on whether the wider stitches within the pattern go into the fabric or the appliqué. Also experiment with matching as well as contrasting thread.

CORDING

Many appliqué stitches can be corded as they are stitched to give them more dimension. For the cord, use pearl cotton, crochet thread, buttonhole twist/topstitching thread, and so on. The cord size should be appropriate for the fabric and the look desired. The color of the cord should match thread color as closely as possible.

A foot with one or more holes (such as a cording foot or Bernina's embroidery foot with the hole in front) to guide the cord is helpful. Feet with narrow, long, straight grooves (like some pintuck feet) work well if the appliqué shape does not require sharp curving. Test on scraps. If necessary, use a satin-stitch foot (open-toe, if visibility is needed), and hold the cord in place with your hands.

The fabric photo appliquéd onto the wedding-album cover has a two-step stitch treatment: a fine corded satin stitch followed by a feather stitch. To make the appliqué, the photo was copied onto fabric. Photos may be copied or printed directly onto backed fabric sheets (June Taylor and Canon are two of the many brands available) or onto special paper (such as Dragon Threads' Image Transfer Paper) that is then pressed onto fabric. A fusible interfacing was applied to the back of the fabric photo to give it body, and the appliqué shape was cut out. It was first appliquéd in place with a fine corded satin stitch to finish the raw edges. (Zigzag length about 0.7mm to 1mm, width about 1.5mm to 2mm, with an open-toe foot, positioning size 8 pearl cotton just onto the photo appliqué while zigging into the photo fabric and zagging over the cord and into the background fabric.) A decorative feather stitch was then stitched over the fine corded satin stitch. (Narrow and shorten the feather

A combination stitch treatment was used to appliqué a fabric copy of Emily's bridal portrait onto this parents' memory album cover. First, it was satin-stitched in place over size 8 pearl cotton to finish the raw edges. On the second pass, it was feather-stitched to give it an antique heirloom look in keeping with the keepsake lace and ribbon pieces surrounding it.

(Wedding photo by Dale Guillory Photography, Houston, Texas.)

Salvaged bits of antique handkerchiefs, tea napkins, and other vintage textiles were combined with new fabric to create this heirloom version of a snowball quilt. The hearts and small squares were faced with batiste and appliquéd with a feather stitch. Embroidery floss woven in and out of the Venetian hemstitched holes around the nine quilt "squares" both hand-quilts and embellishes at the same time. Machine stippling and free-motion quilting finish this beautiful vintage/new quilted wallhanging. (Designed and stitched by Janice Ferguson.)

TIP With any method for turning appliqué edges, start with simple designs. Small appliqués are more difficult and will be easier after practicing with larger designs.

from the automatic settings. One side of the feather is on the appliqué and the other side on the background fabric.)

TURNED-EDGE APPLIQUÉS

At the International Quilt Festival in Houston a few years ago, I was impressed by the way quilt expert Karen Kay Buckley prepared absolutely perfect turned-edge appliqués. She dampened the appliqués' raw edges with starch, then pressed them over heat-resistant templates cut from a product called Templar. When the templates were removed, there were perfectly formed turned-edge shapes ready to be appliquéd in place. I started experimenting with Templar for other turned-edge applications, such as appliquéd scalloped hems, borders, and Madeira appliqué, and found that it made accurate and even turned edges easy to accomplish!

Another of my favorite ways to prepare turned-edge appliqués is to straight-stitch the appliqué fabric to a facing, right sides together. When you slit the facing and turn the appliqué right side out, the appliqué's raw edges are neatly enclosed.

As with many other tasks, it is helpful to know several ways to turn appliqué edges. One may work better than another in certain situations, the products needed for one method may not be on hand, or you may simply prefer one method over another.

Cotton and linen are the easiest fabrics on which to turn edges, but one advantage of using Templar or facing the appliqué is that some blends and other fabrics that would be almost impossible to turn by hand may be usable. As always, test first.

You can use any of these techniques to prepare appliqués whether you choose to stitch them by hand or machine. But there are stitches available on most sewing machines that can be made to closely resemble hand-appliqué stitches such as feather, blanket, and pin stitch.

Preparing turned-edge appliqués using heat-resistant template products Templar, from Heirloom Stitches, comes in $8^1/2$-in. by 11-in. sheets. Other heat-resistant template products include: Perfect Shape No Melt Templates (9 in. by 12 in., from The Stem Emporium), No Melt Mylar Template Plastic Sheets (9 in. by 12 in., from Worldwide Template Products and available from Viking dealers), and Heat Resistant Mylar (two sizes: 10 in. by 12 in. and 13 in. by 18 in., from Quilter's Rule). To use these products for turning appliqué edges:

1. Lightly trace the appliqué (without seam allowance) onto the dull side of Templar (or other heat-resistant template sheet with a dull side) using a sharp regular pencil, or onto the shiny side of Templar or any other shiny product using a template pencil.

2. Cut out carefully, cutting off as much of any regular-pencil marking as possible. Remove template-pencil markings with a damp cloth. Smooth any rough edges with an emery board.

3. Trace the shape onto the wrong side of the appliqué fabric using the cut Templar as a template.

4. Cut out the appliqué, adding approximately $3/16$-in. seam allowance. (Just estimate the seam allowance as you cut.) Several multiples may be cut at one time by putting

Trace the appliqué shape onto the Templar, and cut out carefully.

TIP I have had very little trouble with regular-pencil marking on the Templar coming off onto the fabric, but pencil lead and starch vary. If using white or very light-colored fabric, you may want to erase any remaining pencil marking from the Templar and then test with a scrap of your fabric.

TIP It is important that the appliqué shape is cut carefully from the Templar because any imperfections will be repeated every time an appliqué is pressed over it. The appliqué shape with the added seam allowance cut from the fabric is not as critical. It will take the shape of the Templar template it is pressed over.

Trace around the Templar template to transfer the shape onto the wrong side of the appliqué fabric. Cut out the appliqué estimating a 3/16-in. seam allowance around the traced shape. Several multiples may be cut at one time.

TIP When preparing appliqués, be aware of the direction the appliqué will be when it is right side up. When working from the wrong side of the fabric, some shapes may have to be mirror-imaged to be the correct direction on the right side.

several layers of fabric under the piece with the traced design.

5. Clip deep curves about halfway into the seam allowance and inside points ("V" shape) to one or two threads from the design.

6. Protect the ironing-board cover with a piece of muslin or similar fabric. Center the cut Templar shape onto the wrong side of the cut fabric shape.

7. Lightly dampen one section of the seam allowance around the Templar with spray starch using a stencil brush or Q-tip. (Faultless Heavy and Spray 'n Starch brands both work well. I spray a small amount of starch into the spray-can lid or a small bowl and work from that.)

8. Guide the seam allowance over the Templar with an iron. (See details in the sidebar on the facing page.)

9. Use glue stick, a temporary spray adhesive (such as Sulky KK 2000), or pins to hold appliqués in place for stitching.

Preparing faced turned-edge appliqués Another easy way to prepare turned-edge appliqués is to stitch the appliqué to a facing, right sides together, then slit the facing to turn the appliqué right side out.

The appliqué's seam allowances are then neatly enclosed. Some facing materials are dissolved after the shape is appliquéd to the background fabric, while others are permanently left in place, giving you many options.

Facings made from a water-soluble stabilizer can be dissolved by soaking in water after the appliqué has been stitched to the background fabric. The fabrics must be washable, of course, but there is no problem with added stiffness (if the project is soaked long enough) or with

Center the cut Templar shape onto the wrong side of the cut fabric shape. Use a brush or Q-tip to lightly dampen one section of the fabric around the Templar with starch, starting with any inside curves or inside points.

the facing showing through sheer-fabric appliqués.

There are many other facing-material options, including lightweight fusible interfacings, permanent (leave-in) lightweight stabilizers, and fabric. (The hearts on Janice Ferguson's quilted wallhanging shown on p. 54 and p. 58 were faced with batiste.) Some facing materials can add loft to the appliqué, which can be desirable for some projects. It is fun to experiment. Just remember that generally the facing material should be very lightweight to be suitable for lightweight fabrics. Test on scraps to be sure that a leave-in facing will not show through or add unacceptable stiffness. It is easier to get neatly turned edges if the fabric and facing have body. Spray-starch and press the appliqué fabric before stitching. I look for facing materials that have some stiffness but not too much or to which I can add stiffness by pressing.

Still another possibility is to use any facing material that will make the appliqué easy to turn, and stitch the appliqué to the facing using a water-soluble basting thread top and bobbin. After the facing is slit and the appliqué is turned

Using heat-resistant templates

To press appliqué seam allowances over heat-resistant templates:

✗ Use a dry iron (no steam), set at medium heat (wool-cotton, but test setting).

✗ Dampen (do not saturate) with starch, and press one area at a time. Leave iron in place without pressure until the fabric is dry each time.

✗ Start with any inside curves or inside points, then work around the shape.

Use a dry iron, medium heat, to guide the dampened seam allowance over the Templar. Leave iron in place without pressure until the fabric is dry on each section before moving on around the shape.

✗ As much as possible, use the sides of the iron and keep the iron on the fabric rather than on bare Templar.

✗ To form neatly folded points, press the seam allowance over the Templar along one side of the point until dry, then press the other side. If any fabric extends beyond the point (as happens with sharper points), dampen it with spray starch, fold it in where it will not show, and press.

✗ If you make a mistake, simply dampen that area and press it over the Templar again.

✗ To avoid warping the Templar, do not use a very hot iron setting and do not press down on the iron.

✗ Gently remove the Templar, disturbing as little of the appliqué as possible.

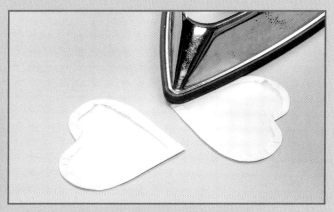

For neatly folded overlapping points, press one side of the point over the Templar using the side of the iron. When dry, press the other side over the point.

Another way to prepare turned-edge appliqués is to stitch the appliqué to a facing, right sides together, then slit the facing to be able to turn the appliqué right side out. There are many facing-material options. The hearts on this quilted wallhanging by Janice Ferguson were faced with batiste.

right side out and pressed, spritz along the edge with water. The basting thread will dissolve, and you will have an unfaced appliqué with its raw edges neatly turned under. You may be able to keep using the same slit facing piece(s) for multiple appliqués of the same shape. For some simple shapes you may be able to prepare two appliqués at once: Stitch them right sides together, leaving a small area unstitched so that you can turn them right side out without having to slit one. Choose a relatively straight area to leave open to make it easy to go back and press under at that one place.

Test on scraps any facing choices you are considering before starting your project.

1. Cut pieces of the appliqué fabric and the facing material at least ¼ in. larger than the appliqué. Spray-starch and press the fabric and facing, if appropriate for those materials.

2. Trace the appliqué shape onto the facing material or onto the wrong side of the appliqué fabric. (With transparent water-soluble stabilizer facings, you can trace the design onto the right side of the appliqué fabric, lay the water-soluble stabilizer on top, and stitch.) If facing with a lightweight fusible interfacing, trace the design onto the nonfusible side.

3. Straight-stitch the appliqué and facing right sides together following the traced shape. (Stitch length 1.5mm with slightly loosened upper tension.) If facing with a lightweight fusible interfacing, stitch with the fusible side to the inside, so that after turning it will be to the outside, allowing you to fuse the appliqué in place.

4. Trim the seam allowances to about ⅛ in. to 3/16 in. Clip deep curves about halfway into the seam allowance and inside points ("V" shape) to one or two threads from the design.

5. Cut one or two (intersecting) slits or a small hole in the facing after stitching it to the appliqué fabric. Carefully turn the appliqué right side out, gently forming the curves and points.

6. Press the appliqué from the fabric side. (If a fusible interfacing was used, press over a Teflon pressing sheet.)

7. Fuse, temporarily adhere, or pin appliqué in place. With water-soluble stabilizer facings, lightly spray-

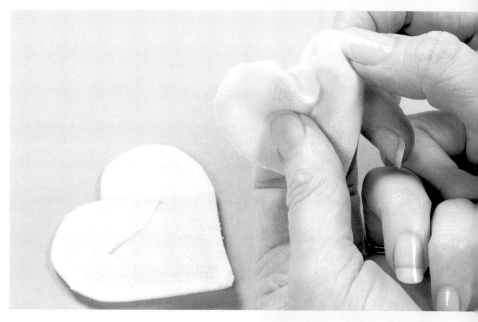

Cut one or two (intersecting) slits or a small hole in the facing. Carefully turn the appliqué right side out, gently forming the curves and points.

starch the background fabric, position an appliqué, and press. This will temporarily fuse the appliqué to the background fabric. For fusible interfacing facings, follow the instructions that came with the interfacing to fuse the appliqué in place. For fabric or other non-fusible facings, use glue stick, a temporary spray adhesive, or pins to hold the appliqué in place for stitching.

8. After stitching, water-soluble stabilizer facings may be dissolved by soaking in water.

MACHINE STITCHES TO RESEMBLE HAND-APPLIQUÉ STITCHING

Most sewing machines have stitches that can closely resemble hand-appliqué stitches, such as feather, blanket, and pin stitch (as used for Madeira appliqué) as well as "invisible" appliqué stitching. Fabric, thread, needle, and settings choices can make the same stitch appear bold, like those used for crazy patch, or delicate, resembling appliquéd antique handkerchiefs or linens.

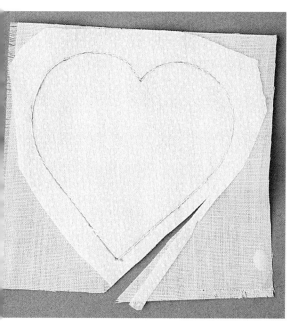

To prepare turned-edge appliqués using a facing: Trace the appliqué shape onto the facing or onto the wrong side of the appliqué fabric. Straight-stitch the appliqué and facing right sides together following the traced shape. (If facing with a fusible, stitch with the fusible side to the inside.) Trim the seam allowances to about ⅛ in. to 3/16 in., and clip into any deep curves or inside points.

TIP Tips for stitching appliqués:

✖ Use an open-toe (appliqué) presser foot so that the edge of the appliqué is visible.

✖ Start stitching on a straight or slightly curved area, not on a point.

✖ Try to anchor points securely with a stitch on or near the tip. This may take some experimentation with the stitch pattern.

✖ To reduce puckering, slightly loosen (decrease) upper tension, and apply more spray starch and pressing and/or add an additional layer of a lightweight tearaway underneath.

Machine versions of hand-appliqué stitches include (from left to right): a variation of a blind-hem stitch, a blanket stitch (Parisian hemstitch with regular needle and heavier thread), and a pin stitch (Parisian hemstitch with large needle and very fine thread).

Feather stitch and variation

The specifications on pp. 51-52 for creative appliquéing also apply to turned-edge appliqués with these modifications:

Fabric: Wovens with a high percentage of cotton or linen will give the best results for the pin stitch (using the Parisian hemstitch with a large needle). With the other stitches, there is more room for experimentation with blends and other fabrics, but as always, stitch test samples first.

Thread: Most often machine-embroidery cotton. Options: decorative threads (such as rayon) and, for "invisible" appliqué, fine monofilament. The size of the thread should be appropriate for fabric, technique, and look desired:

✘ medium to medium/heavy, to resemble a blanket stitch (Mettler 30/2 or 50/3, Madeira 30/2 or 50/2);

✘ fine to very fine, for more invisible stitching (Madeira 80/2, YLI Heirloom 70/2 or 100/2, Zwicky 70/2, Mettler 60/2, DMC 50/2, or fine monofilament such as Madeira Monofil, Sulky Invisible, or YLI Wonder Invisible Thread);

✘ very fine, for pin stitch (Madeira 80/2, YLI Heirloom 100/2, Zwicky 70/2, or Mettler 60/2).

Needle: Appropriate for the fabric, thread, and technique. With most stitches, use 70 Universal for fine fabric and thread and 80 Universal for medium-weight fabric and thread. With the Parisian hemstitch (pin stitch), use 120, 110, 100, etc., Universal (rarely wing).

Presser foot: Open-toe (appliqué) foot is helpful so that the edge of the appliqué is visible. Edging, adjustable blind-hem, or other foot with guide helpful if folded edges are mostly straight.

Stabilizer: In most cases, spray-starch and press fabric before stitching (several times before hemstitching). A lightweight tearaway stabilizer is often necessary under soft, lightweight background fabrics to prevent puckering.

Stitch: Feather stitch and variations; Parisian hemstitch (pin stitch), picot stitch, and variations; blind-hem stitch and variations.

✘ Feather stitch and variations—One side of the feather goes into the appliqué and the other into the background fabric. Choose thread according to the look desired. Stitch settings will usually be shorter and narrower than automatic settings, especially if turning is required (for example, for appliqué shapes with sharp curves or points). Experiment with turning on a scrap of the fabric. If your machine has an "end of pattern" option, try using it for turning. There are many variations of the feather stitch. Do some test stitching to determine the settings and alignment you like.

✘ Parisian hemstitch, picot stitch, and variations to replicate hand pin stitch (as used for Madeira appliqué) or hand buttonhole and blanket stitches— Forward and back straight stitches are on background fabric, and the zigzag catches the appliqué.

For the pin stitch, choose fabric appropriate for hemstitching (see p. 78 for more detail), very fine thread, and a large (120, 110, 100, etc.) Universal needle. (Most common settings for the pin stitch: width 1.5mm to 2mm, length 2mm to 2.5mm.)

To replicate hand buttonhole or blanket stitch, choose thread weight according to the look desired, then choose an appropriate needle. On antique samples of the hand version, a more visible heavier cotton thread, sometimes black, was commonly used. Use wider and possibly longer settings than those used for the pin stitch.

✘ Blind-hem stitch (or variation) for "invisible" appliqué stitching—Align so that the straight stitches are on the background fabric and the zigzag swings just wide enough to catch the appliqué. Choose fine machine-embroidery cotton thread or fine monofilament thread. Settings will be much shorter and narrower than for blind hemming.

Questions

When I try to cord stretch blind-stitch picot edging, the cord won't stay at the edge of the folded fabric. Can you help?

On some machines, it is difficult to keep the cord right next to the fabric edge—it rolls over or under the fabric. If the cord consistently and evenly rolls over the fabric and you like the look, that's fine. However, if you want it to stay alongside the folded edge, try any foot you have with one or more holes or grooves to guide the cord. If none of these works, try a satin-stitch foot and firmly hold the cord next to the fold with your hands. If the problem persists, do not use the cord. The effect of this edging is pleasing, uncorded as well as corded.

I use glue stick to hold fabrics in place for stitching. Is there any reason to use fabric glue stick rather than multipurpose glue sticks from an office-supply store?

To answer your question, I compared several kinds of multipurpose glue stick and fabric glue stick by testing them on the fabrics I use most often. I got excellent results with all of them.

Just be sure the label lists fabric as one of the suggested uses and says that the glue is either water soluble or washes out. Even though some of these glues are now acid free, I would be cautious about using glue stick on an unwashable project that I planned to keep indefinitely, because of possible unknown long-term effects such as discoloration.

One of my favorite uses for glue stick is to hold buttons in place for sewing by hand or machine. However, before using any product on a project, it is always best to test it on that particular fabric.

TIP ✘ For almost invisible stitching on very small appliqués, a tiny zigzag with very fine thread will be easier to manage than the blind-hem stitch.

✘ Mirror-image the stitches below if that direction is more comfortable for you.

Parisian hemstitch and picot stitch

Blind-hem stitch and variations

Twin-Needle Stitching

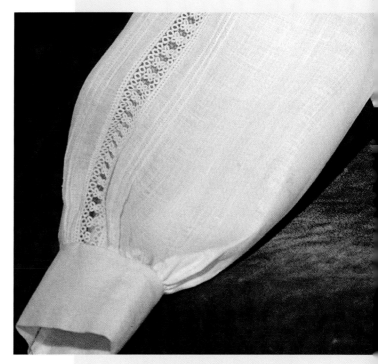

4

Stitching with twin needles opens many practical as well as creative possibilities. Twin needles allow you to:

✗ stitch two perfectly even rows of topstitching or decorative stitching at the same time;

✗ stitch both sides of a narrow ribbon or trim at the same time;

✗ add texture and/or color, especially when the stitching is corded;

✗ creatively hem a garment or disguise the crease line when letting down a hem;

✗ create pintucks on light- to medium-weight fabrics for a classic heirloom look;

✗ embellish sheer fabrics with a shadow-work effect.

Delicate tatted insertion on this handkerchief linen blouse is highlighted with twin-needle corded pintucks. The tatting is sewn to the linen with a Venetian hemstitch, then the linen underneath is trimmed away. The motif is repeated on each of the sleeves.

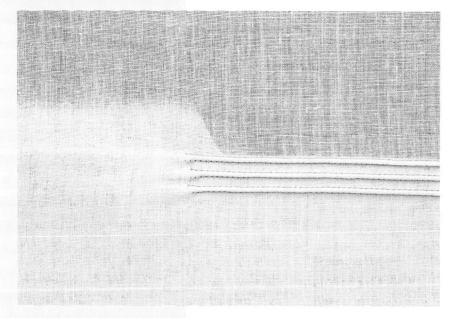

One use for twin needles is decorative hemming. This sample shows how three rows of corded twin-needle straight stitching can both stitch and embellish the top edge of a hem.

TIP Some machines, particularly older models, had twin needles designed specifically for them. Special Schmetz needles for mechanical Elnas prior to the 7000 had a maroon bar and those for unmodified Elna 7000s had a black bar, to give two examples. (The needles angle differently for the best alignment.) Some of the nonstandard twin needles are now difficult to find, but many of these machines can stitch with standard twin needles. Just avoid needles that are widely spaced, and keep the stitching narrow. (See the needle test explained on the facing page.)

Stitching with twin needles is easy. But to get the best results and the effects you want, it is important to know something about the needles themselves.

Twin needles

Twin needles (sometimes called double needles) will work in most zigzag sewing machines, except for those with a side-loading bobbin. Twin needles can be most easily distinguished by the color of their connecting bar near the top. The Schmetz Universal twin needles that fit the greatest number of machines, including almost all recent models, have a red bar.

Specialty twin needles such as Stretch, Jeans (Denim), and Embroidery twin needles are also available for use on certain fabrics or with fragile decorative threads. Some, but not all of these, have a different color connecting bar to help distinguish them. (Returning them to their original box is the best way to know

what they are.) Try these if the standard Universal-point twin needles do not give satisfactory results.

Triple needles are also available. They have three needles joined to one bar and shank. (For the third thread, you can wind a bobbin with the same thread and place the bobbin under one of the thread spools.) Like twin needles, triple needles can be used for topstitching, hemming, and decorative stitching with various machine stitches, but they do not really give the look of traditional pintucks.

Double wing needles have one Universal needle and one needle with wide metal "wings." They are used for a method of hemstitching (see pp. 80-81).

New Home/Janome machines and Elna models after the 9000/Diva, which come with Organ black-bar twin needles, can use Organ-brand needles or Schmetz needles for the techniques covered here.

If your machine came with twin needles, record in your manual the brand, color of the bar, and any identifying markings. To find out which twin needles should be used in your machine, check your machine manual, ask your dealer, or if necessary, perform the simple test described in the sidebar on the facing page.

TWIN-NEEDLE SIZES

Twin needles are labeled with two numbers separated by a slash. The first number is the distance between the two needles in millimeters; the second is the size of the needles. For example, 2.0/80 means size 80 needles, 2mm apart. Twin needles that are relatively close typically have finer needles for use on lightweight fabrics, and those spaced farther apart have larger needles for heavier fabrics. Accordingly:

- ✗ needles spaced 1.6mm to 2mm apart are for pintucks and decorative stitching or for hemming on lightweight fabrics;

- ✗ needles 2.5mm to 3mm apart are for decorative stitching, hemming, or a pintuck/texturing effect on medium-weight fabrics;

- ✗ needles 4mm apart or more are for topstitching or hemming on medium- to heavyweight fabrics.

General specifications for twin-needle stitching are as follows:

Fabric: Light- to medium-weight wovens for pintucks; most weights of wovens or knits for decorative stitching, topstitching, texturing, and hemming.

Twin-needle stitching that creates a raised effect (such as pintucks or texturing) draws up fabric. For areas where garment fit could be affected, stitch on an oversized piece of fabric, then cut out the pattern piece(s). For example, the top right photo on p. 67 shows a rectangle of organdy embellished with fagoting, twin-needle shadow work, and corded pintucks. From this, a piece for the front of a

Needle test

Whenever you are in doubt about using a needle in your machine, do the following test:

- ✗ With the machine set on straight stitch, turn the flywheel toward you to lower the needle and raise it again. Watch and listen for any indication that the needle is hitting or grazing anything, and if it is, do not use it.

- ✗ Next run the machine at a slow speed. If you hear a clicking sound, the needle is hitting something (usually the needle plate or the bobbin hook) and should not be used.

- ✗ If a wider stitch is desired, increase stitch width cautiously so that the needles will not hit the foot, needle plate, or bobbin hook as they cycle all the way to the right and left. If you hear clicking, narrow the width.

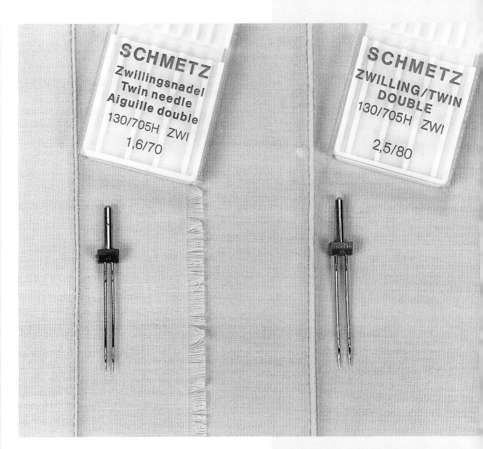

Twin needles come in various sizes and spacings. In general, the closer the two needles, the finer they are. The twin needles on the left are size 70, and the two needles are spaced 1.6mm apart; these would be used for pintucks on lightweight fabrics. The heavier, more widely spaced needles on the right are for medium-weight fabrics.

or contrast with the fabric. For decorative stitching, you can also use a different color in each needle.

Cord: Pearl cotton, crochet thread, buttonhole twist/topstitching thread, and so on, in a size appropriate for the fabric, the look desired, and the space between the two needles. The cord may match the fabric in color or, for a shadow effect on sheers, may contrast with the fabric.

Cording twin-needle stitching adds dimension and stability. (The cording is underneath the fabric, caught in the zigzag formed by the bobbin thread.) Methods for cording twin-needle stitching are explained on pp. 69-70.

Foot: Pintuck foot, zigzag foot, satin-stitch foot. Use a pintuck foot for stitching pintucks or straight rows of texturing. (If more than one pintuck foot is available for your machine, generally choose one with narrower grooves for pintucking on lightweight fabrics with closely spaced twin needles, and one with wider grooves for texturing with the more widely spaced twin needles.)

Use a basic metal zigzag foot for less dense stitching when you want the fabric to stay flat.

Use a satin-stitch foot for dense stitching, to encourage a raised effect other than straight rows or when a pintuck-type foot is unavailable for straight rows.

Width: When using any stitch other than a straight stitch with twin or triple needles, test the stitch width very carefully to avoid having the needles hit the presser foot and break. Test by stitching slowly through the stitch pattern. When approaching the farthest right side of the pattern, turn the flywheel by hand to be sure the needles clear the foot. Also test all the way to the left since many patterns are not centered as stitched.

Perfect for a wedding or any special occasion are the organdy pinafore-style bib (ABOVE) and pillow top (BELOW) cut from rectangles of decoratively stitched organdy. The ruffles on both were narrow hemmed and hemstitched. The satin ballet shoes (BELOW) were dyed in coffee, then trimmed with ribbon bows and rosettes attached with hand stitching.

pinafore-style bib or a pillow top (like those shown above and left) could be cut.

Always stitch a test sample with the same grain direction as on the project. Lengthwise stitching (parallel to the selvage) on some wovens is more likely to pucker than crossgrain stitching.

Thread: Machine-embroidery cotton, rayon, or other decorative threads for decorative stitching; fine machine-embroidery cotton for pintucks; polyester, cotton-covered polyester, or other appropriate thread with strength and stretch to hem knits.

Thread size should be appropriate for the fabric. For example, use fine thread for a fine fabric. Thread color may match

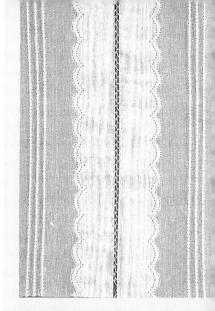

To help prevent twin-needle breakage, some machines have a twin-needle button or option to limit the stitching width. This feature works differently on different machines. On some the stitch width is cut in half, on some it is narrowed by 2mm, and on some you can select the amount the width should be narrowed, based on the twin needles you are using. When using twin needles and stitch patterns with a width, such as scallops, it is prudent to test the width carefully even when using this option. If this feature limits the width too much (for example, if it limits width to the point that only very shallow scallops can be stitched), then disengage it, but test the width very carefully yourself.

Upper tension: Increase upper tension (adjust to a higher number) to create more of a raised effect. Loosen upper tension (adjust to a lower number) to keep the fabric flat or to reduce puckering. (Most necessary adjustments can be made with upper tension alone, but loosening or bypassing bobbin tension will also keep uncorded twin-needle stitching flat.)

This organdy panel was embellished with fagoting, twin-needle shadow work, and corded pintucks. The shadow work was stitched through both the top layer and the organdy folded under for the fagoting. The excess organdy on the underside was trimmed up to the stitching for an attractive, clean finish.

TIP A centered stitch pattern allows the widest stitch without breaking a needle. On some machines, a stitch may be centered with the twin-needle width limit or by changing the needle position.

The hem of this delicate organdy pinafore is adorned with twin-needle corded pintucks, shadow-work scallops, and folded tucks embellished with the feather stitch. Fagoting is an additional detail added to the bib.

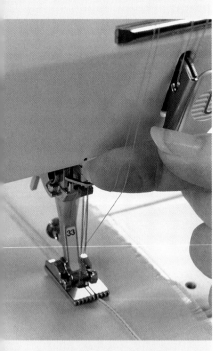

When using twin needles, make sure that the two threads are not twisted, especially directly over the needles.

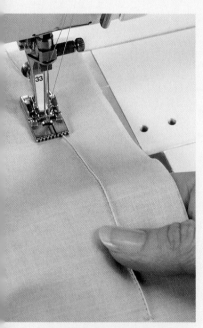

The best way to maintain even spacing with pintucks is to guide an adjacent, already stitched pintuck into another groove of the pintuck foot. Slightly lifting the fabric helps keep the pintuck in the groove.

Stabilizer: A stabilizer (other than spray starching and pressing) is usually not used for pintucks or texturing because it would keep the fabric flat, or for shadow work because it would be caught in the stitching and show through the sheer fabric. Unless the area is interfaced (as are collars, cuffs, lapels, and so on), a light-weight stabilizer may be needed to keep other twin-needle stitching flat, especially lengthwise stitching on wovens.

Threading: Check your sewing-machine manual for a diagram or instructions on threading for twin-needle stitching. Arrange the spools to avoid having the two threads rub together. (With two vertical spool pins, the thread should come off the back of one spool and the front of the other.) Usually the two threads are separated at the tension disc and over the needles. It is important that the two threads not be twisted together, especially directly over the needles (see the top photo at left).

Twin-needle pintucks

Twin-needle pintucks add a classic heirloom look to bodices, yokes, skirts, and sleeves, as well as to table or bed linens and home-decorating items. Since they have a tailored look, they are appropriate when other heirloom embellishments would be too frilly—for example, on women's or older girls' garments and on little boys' dress shirts. Pintucks alone can make a plain garment extraordinary.

You can experiment with different designs for stitching pintucks, such as stitching them in groups of three or more rows, stitching crossed rows for a waffle or diamond effect, or stitching shapes. Twin-needle pintucks are also an easy, attractive way to re-hem and hide the

crease line at the same time when you are letting hems down. It's best to make several rows of tucks, one of which is over the crease (see the photo on p. 64).

Fabric: Light- to medium-weight wovens. Always stitch a test sample on a scrap of the fabric with the grain direction the same as on the project (see pp. 70-71).

Thread: Fine machine-embroidery cotton, such as Mettler 60/2, Madeira 50/2, or DMC 50/2. Coats Dual Duty Plus Extra-Fine may be used, but because of its polyester core, upper tension may need adjustment to prevent puckered pintucks. Color may match or contrast with the fabric.

Needle: Twin needles 1.6mm, 2mm, or 2.5mm apart with size 70 or 80 needles, as appropriate for the fabric and thread. Ideally, the finer the fabric, the closer the needles and the smaller the needle size— for example, 1.6/70 for Swiss batiste.

Foot: A pintuck foot with multiple grooves on its underside will help make the tucks raised and equidistant. (If your machine has several pintuck feet available, the one with seven grooves is a good choice for most pintucks.)

If you do not have a pintuck foot and your machine has changeable needle positions, try a traditional buttonhole foot (or similar foot with grooves) and move the needles to align with one of the grooves, making sure the needles will not hit the foot. Otherwise, use a satin-stitch foot.

Stitch: Straight.

Length: About 2mm.

Upper tension: Normal to slightly loosened. Test.

MARKING AND MEASURING

It is usually necessary to use a wide guide or to measure and mark (pull a thread, press a crease, and so on) for only the first pintuck. For subsequent pintucks on the project, you can guide the first pintuck into another groove of the pintuck foot or alongside the foot to keep the spacing even between tucks, as shown in the bottom photo on the facing page. Slightly lifting the fabric will help keep the pintuck in the groove.

CORDING

Cording pintucks can be a real problem solver. On stiff fabrics, such as organdy, it is difficult to get raised pintucks without tightening tension almost to the point of perforating the fabric along the stitching. Simply cording the pintucks and stitching with normal tension easily creates raised pintucks. Cording also stabilizes, thereby reducing puckering. On sheer fabrics, the cord can be used to add color as it did on the organdy panel, pinafore-style bib, and pillow on pp. 66-67.

There are many methods for cording pintucks. Some machines have a hole in the needle plate (Bernina, Pfaff) or a guide that snaps onto the needle plate (Viking) through which the cording can be threaded. A dental-floss threader is often helpful for threading the cord, especially for threading cord up through Bernina needle plates. (On Bernina 1630 machines, threading may be easier if you tip the machine back slightly.)

If you are comfortable bypassing bobbin tension (this is especially easy to do on most Elna models through the 9000/Diva), you can wind the cord onto the bobbin. Then thread the cord through the bobbin-tension bypass hole, rather than into the usual tension slit; it will be caught in the pintuck as you stitch with the twin needles. Upper tension may have to be tightened.

Dental-floss threaders

Dental-floss threaders are designed for threading dental floss through orthodontics and bridgework, but they work well as long, flexible plastic threaders for sewing. Use them to:

✗ thread cord up through the hole in Bernina's or Pfaff's needle plate or through Viking's raised seam plate for corded twin-needle stitching (see the photo below);

✗ thread cord between the two needles to cord twin-needle pintucks on any machine (see the top photo on p. 70);

✗ thread cord through the hole of a presser foot, such as Bernina's embroidery foot or Viking's, Elna's, and Pfaff's multiple-cord feet (see the top photo on p. 90);

✗ thread cord or ribbon thread through the hole in the finger of Bernina's or Viking's bobbin case;

✗ thread sergers.

You can purchase dental-floss threaders at drugstores. A package of 20 costs about $2. If you can't find them—they are usually displayed by the dental floss—check several drugstore chains or ask your dentist for a source.

Dental-floss threaders work well as long, flexible plastic threaders for sewing. One of their many practical uses is to thread cord up through the hole in Bernina's needle plate to cord twin-needle pintucks.

A simple method to cord twin-needle stitching on any machine is to take a few stitches and stop with the twin needles just into the fabric. Then raise the presser foot, lift the fabric, and use a dental-floss threader to thread cord between the needles.

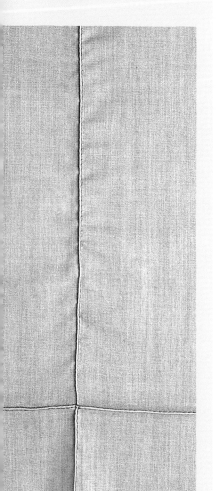

Uncorded lengthwise pintucks on lightweight fabric with no changes in thread, needles, and settings are likely to pucker, while cross-grain pintucks on the same fabric look fine.

An easy and effective way to cord twin-needle stitching on any machine is to use a dental-floss threader.

1. Take a few stitches, and stop with the needles down.

2. Raise the presser foot, and lift the fabric.

3. Thread the cord under the fabric between the two needles (front to back) using the dental-floss threader. Keep the floss threader flat on the bed of the machine as you guide it between the needles and toward the back, as shown in the photo above. (If you aim down, it may go into a hole in the needle plate.)

4. Lower the presser foot.

5. Check that the cord is under the center groove of the foot. As you stitch, slightly lift the cord to keep it in this groove.

Pfaff has "cording tongues" in two sizes that snap onto the needle plate. They lift the fabric in front of the center groove of the pintuck foot. (Note: Pfaff calls a pintuck foot a "cording foot" in some manuals). You can experiment with these cord-

ing tongues to put more fabric into the pintuck without using cord.

WORKING WITH DIFFICULT FABRICS

Some fabrics present special challenges for twin-needle stitching for which you may need to compensate and/or compromise. With challenging fabrics, every factor is critical and must be as close to the ideal as possible.

For example, on very fine, soft fabrics, such as Swiss batiste, it is difficult to get crisp lengthwise uncorded pintucks without any puckering. However, there are a number of things you can do to compensate:

✗ spray-starching and pressing the fabric first;

✗ using new needles that are as close as possible to the ideal size (1.6/70), fine machine-embroidery cotton thread (such as Mettler 60/2 or DMC 50/2), and if you have a choice, a seven- or nine-groove pintuck foot;

✗ shortening the stitch length;

✗ loosening (lowering) upper tension;

✗ sewing taut with a smooth, slow to medium speed.

Make sure the machine is clean. (Lint can cause tension problems.) If there is still a problem, then you may have to compromise, either by loosening upper tension a little more and accepting a flatter tuck in order to prevent the puckering, or by cording the tuck with a fine cord, such as size 8 pearl cotton.

On polyester/cotton broadcloth, lengthwise rows of pintucks are especially difficult. Prewash, then lightly spray-starch and press the broadcloth. Follow the same guidelines as for Swiss batiste, except use

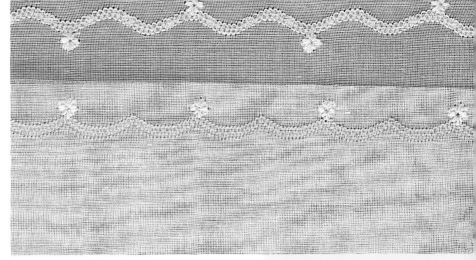

new 2.0/80 twin needles with a five- or seven-groove pintuck foot and a medium-size cord, such as size 5 pearl cotton.

On some fabrics, including some broadcloth, it is virtually impossible to get acceptable, unpuckered lengthwise pintucks (be thankful you found out on your test sample!). The bottom photo on the facing page shows how different a lengthwise and crosswise pintuck can look. On a craft project, such as a pillow, you can change the grain direction when cutting the pattern so that the pintucks will be stitched crossgrain (assuming that on a test sample the crossgrain pintucks were fine). However, changing the direction a garment pattern piece is cut (for example, cutting a blouse so that pintucks down the blouse front would be crossgrain) is not recommended because the fit and hang of the garment could be affected. So it may be necessary to change either your fabric choice or your design plan. Folded pintucks stitched with a straight stitch and a single needle might be successful even when twin-needle pintucks are not, but test to be sure.

Twin-needle shadow work

You can take advantage of the fact that the thread on the underside of twin-needle stitching zigzags between the two rows to create a shadow-work effect on sheer fabrics. This type of shadow work is effective around a skirt (or even for hemming the skirt); down the front of a blouse, pinafore, or apron bib; on sleeves, collars, pillow covers, and so on. You can stitch a row on each side of pintucks or fagoting to create a framing effect. Adding hand- or machine-stitched flowers, leaves, bows, and so forth, can create the look of expensive imported embroideries (see the photo above).

Fabric: Sheer wovens that have body or that can be spray starched (or stiffened with another product) to give body. Swiss organdy is ideal.

Thread: Machine-embroidery cotton. The size should be appropriate for the fabric, usually 50/2 or 60/2. A darker color on the bobbin will create more shadow.

Needle: Twin needles 2.5mm apart have enough space between them for the shadow, yet are narrow enough to be used with a stitch with width. Experiment also with twin needles having other spacing, but remember that as the needles get farther apart, the stitch width must get narrower. Test carefully. Also, needles spaced farther apart usually have larger needles. To have space for the shadow, you may have to use a needle one size larger than ideal for that fabric. For example, the 2.5mm twin needles are size 80 needles but may still be used for shadow work on most fine fabric where a size 70 would be ideal.

Foot: Basic zigzag or satin-stitch foot.

Stitch: Open, running-type stitches with a shape, such as tracery scallop (or arch), bracket, or serpentine (or multi-zigzag).

Experiment with other stitches. (Dense satin-type stitches can produce some interesting effects when stitched with twin needles, but they will not create a shadow-work effect.)

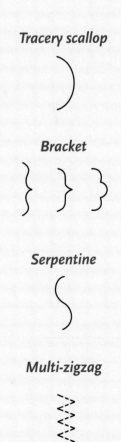

On sheer fabrics, the bobbin thread of twin-needle stitching can create a shadow-work effect, as seen here with a serpentine stitch (upper sample) and tracery scallop (lower sample). Adding machine-stitched flowers gives the look of expensive imported embroideries.

Tracery scallop

Bracket

Serpentine

Multi-zigzag

Width: As wide as possible without having one of the needles hit the foot or needle plate (see the photo at right). Start with a width of about 2mm, then increase width carefully, testing all the way to the right and left through the stitch pattern, as explained on pp. 66-67.

Length: Varies with the stitch used but must be relatively short for enough coverage on the underside.

Upper tension: Loosen (adjust to a lower number). (Loosening bobbin tension also creates "shadow" and can be done instead, if you prefer.)

Stabilizer: Spray-starch and press. For softer fabrics, do several applications of spray starching and pressing, or use

Twin-needle stitching can add texture, especially if the stitching is corded, as on this velveteen.

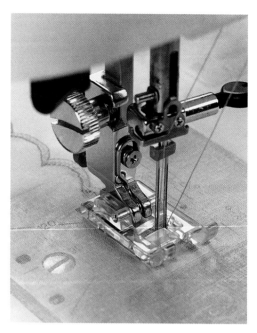

A stitch width that is as wide as possible without hitting the presser foot usually gives the best look. Test the stitch width carefully. Here a tracery scallop stitch is used.

another spray-on or paint-on stiffening product. (A regular tearaway stabilizer should not used because it would be caught in the stitching and show through the sheer fabric.)

Some of the stitches for twin-needle shadow work can be corded with pearl cotton to create more shadow when using a longer stitch length. Thread the cord through the hole in the needle plate (Bernina, Pfaff) or wind pearl cotton on the bobbin and use the bobbin-tension bypass hole (Elna) for the best results. On other machines, experiment. The shape of the stitch determines the ease of cording—more rounded stitches are easier to cord than stitches with sharp points.

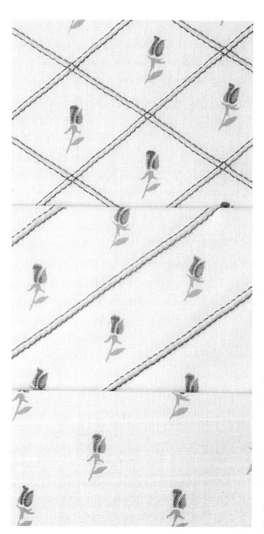

Twin-needle stitching can create unique companion fabrics to coordinate with the original fabric. In these examples, corded twin-needle stitching creates a diagonal pattern (center sample) and a diamond grid (upper sample) on a printed fabric.

Other twin-needle work

On many fabrics that are unsuitable for pintucks, you can use twin needles and a straight stitch to add texture and dimension, especially if the stitching is corded. The resulting ridges can totally change the surface appearance, often giving a quilted look. It's fun to experiment with twin-needle stitching on different solid-color fabrics (even velveteen), as well as on prints. You can create a unique companion fabric to coordinate with the original fabric and use it for bodices, yokes, sleeves, collars, pockets, and accessories. The bottom photo on the facing page shows an example.

You can use twin needles and a straight stitch to stitch two perfectly even rows of topstitching or to attach both sides of a narrow ribbon or trim at the same time (see the top photo at right). These applications are suitable for most fabrics.

You can also use twin needles with decorative stitches. The twin needles will create two rows of the stitch pattern that are either parallel to, adjoining, or over-lapping each other, depending on the space between the needles and the stitch chosen.

Hemming is one of my favorite uses for twin needles (for a detailed discussion, see p. 158). For knits, the zigzag on the underside provides the needed stretch. Pintucks or decorative twin-needle stitching can be used to hem many fabrics. Either technique is a particularly useful treatment for sheer fabrics (like organdy), where a traditional hem would show through unattractively. They can also disguise the crease line of the previous hem when you let down a hem.

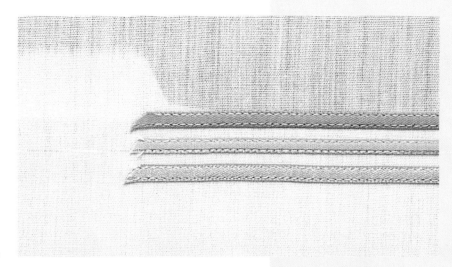

Twin needles and a straight stitch were used to attach both sides of narrow ribbon and at the same time re-hem the garment. (One of the three rows of ribbon covers the crease line from the original hem.) Loosened upper tension and a basic zigzag foot kept the ribbon flat.

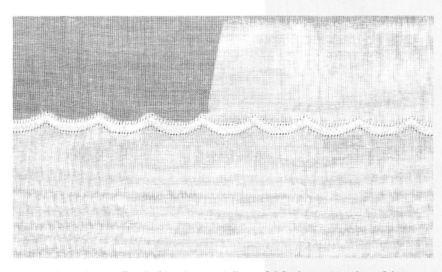

Decorative twin-needle stitching is especially useful for hemming sheer fabrics, such as organdy, where a traditional hem would show through. The hem is stitched from the right side, then excess fabric is trimmed up to the stitching on the underside.

To hem with twin needles:

1. Press the hem allowance to the wrong side.

2. Stitch from the right side so that the stitching is at least $1/4$ in. from the raw edge of the hem allowance.

3. Trim the excess fabric up to the zigzag on the underside, as shown in the bottom photo above.

Questions

How do you secure the beginning and end of twin-needle pintucks?

Ideally, twin-needle pintucks should be stitched on a piece of fabric larger than your pattern piece. After stitching the pintucks, block the fabric and staystitch just inside the cutting line to secure pintucks that run the full length or width of the pattern piece. Most of the time, the ends of the pintucks will be stitched again during construction, providing additional security.

Released pintucks are those that are not stitched the full length or width of the pattern piece; they are most often seen on the upper part of front bodices. Released pintucks need to be secured. Leave long thread tails where the pintucks end. Pull the two top threads to the underside, using a pin to help. Knot the two top threads together along with the bobbin thread at the end of the tuck. (If you cannot tie all of these threads, tying any two of the three should be secure enough.) For extra neatness, thread all three threads into the eye of a hand needle, bury the thread tails in the underside of the pintuck for about 1/2 in., then cut off the excess thread.

I thought that for twin-needle work the two threads should be separated at the upper tension disc. Recently I heard instructions to put both threads on one side of the tension disc. Which is correct?

I recommend separating the two threads at the tension disc, then doing some test stitching with conditions the same as on the project. If the results are not satisfactory and you are certain that you are using the correct thread and a new needle of appropriate size, that your machine is clean, and so on, check that the upper threads are not twisted together. (On most machines, twisting would be obvious just above the needle bar.) If the threads are twisted, carefully rethread each thread separately: Take the thread from the right spool to the right side of the tension disc and to the right needle, then the thread from the left spool to the left side of the tension disc and to the left needle. Also make sure the two threads do not rub together near the spools; either turn one spool over or use spool pins that keep the threads apart. If the stitching on the sides of the twin-needle stitch or pintuck still looks uneven, then experiment with different ways to thread (see the answer to the next question), including possibly putting both threads on the same side of the tension disc. All the sewing-machine representatives I have consulted agree that, in situations like this, it's best to experiment and then do whatever works best.

My twin-needle stitching (especially on pintucks) looks fine on one side but loose and uneven on the other side. How can I get the stitching on both sides to be acceptable?

First, follow the tips in the previous answer, including making sure that the twin needles are the correct system for your machine. But before trying both threads on the same side of the tension disc, try tightening upper tension to the point that it improves the loose side without causing puckering. It may also be helpful to increase tension on the thread that appears loose (by putting that thread through an additional guide at the top of the machine or on the needle bar) and/or reduce tension on the side that looks tight (take that thread out of either of these additional guides). If nothing seems to help, consult your dealer to see if the upper tension on your machine needs cleaning or adjustment.

Must twin-needle pintucks always be stitched in the same direction?

In keeping with the principles of directional stitching, this is usually best. (Directional stitching refers to the practice of stitching in a consistent direction to avoid distortion of the fabric.) For example, to stitch groups of pintucks on a blouse front, I usually stitch those in the center group first, then work out to the sides, using the grooves of a pintuck foot for perfect spacing, always stitching top to bottom.

There are exceptions, however. Occasionally I have seen pintucks that were closer together when stitched in one direction than in the other. In this case, the grooves in the foot appeared equally spaced, so the needle bar may have been slightly off to one side. In cases like this, of course, you have to do what works best (at least until the machine is adjusted).

Stitching more than a few rows of pintucks distorts the shape of most fabrics, regardless of stitching direction. The pintucked fabric should be blocked before proceeding with cutting or other stitching.

The amount of fabric caught in my twin-needle pintucks is inconsistent. As I stitch, I have to fight the tendency of more fabric being pulled into the tuck. Any suggestions?

If your presser foot has a wide opening in front, as some pintuck feet do, fabric can easily be drawn up into this open space, creating the problem you describe. Usually this can be remedied by switching to a presser foot that holds the fabric more securely in the front. If your machine company has a more closed pintuck foot, try it. (Pintuck feet with more grooves are generally more closed than those with fewer grooves.) If such a foot is not available for your machine, a foot designed for another brand may work. (An adaptor and/or a different shank may be needed.) Another option is to substitute a traditional buttonhole foot and change the needle position to align with one of the two grooves. (Check that the needles will not hit the foot.)

How do you press twin-needle pintucks?

Twin-needle pintucks are not usually pressed to the side as are traditional folded (single-needle) pintucks. I do not press the twin-needle pintucks themselves but rather the fabric next to them. (If the pintucks within a group are stitched very close together, then just press the fabric between each group of pintucks.) First spray-starch and press the fabric up to the first pintuck. Lay the fabric over the edge of the ironing board so that the first tuck is just off the edge. Now you can press up to the next tuck. Continue in this way until done.

Your pintucks should not be puckered, but if they are, you may need to block them. Put straight pins through the ends of the tucks and into the ironing board to hold them straight and taut. Spray-starch, and let dry. Then, if necessary, press the fabric next to the tucks.

Hemstitching

5

The beautiful look of hemstitching, once attainable only by hand or with the use of one of the very scarce hemstitching machines, can now be created on most sewing machines. Hemstitching has a classic appeal that never goes out of style. You can see it on antique garments and linens, as well as on current designer blouses, dresses, nightgowns, and table and bed linens. Hemstitching is an excellent option if you want an heirloom look without the frills of delicate laces, ruffles, and puffing.

Hemstitching by hand entails withdrawing threads from the fabric and bundling the remaining parallel threads with a needle and thread to form an open design. It is often used as a decorative finish at a hem. Although it is possible to copy this look using the machine by first withdrawing threads by hand, then machine stitching the sides of the area (see the bottom photo on p. 84), in fact machine hemstitching has a much broader meaning.

Tone-on-tone detailing added to this purchased linen blouse accents its simple lines. Corded adjoining rows of hemstitching with a double wing needle embellish the front and the sleeves. Before hemstitching the front, several threads were withdrawn to make the needle holes more distinct. A decorative stitch completes the details.

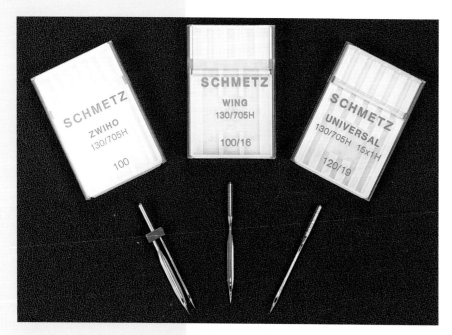

Needles used for hemstitching include (from left to right) the double wing needle, the wing needle, and the large Universal needle (size 120/19).

The term "hemstitching on the sewing machine" applies to sewing-machine versions of any of the following looks:

✘ the hand pin stitch (point de Paris), as used to attach lace (see the upper three collars in the bottom photo on p. 105), to hem, and for Madeira appliqué;

✘ hemstitching as produced on hemstitching machines from the 1920s and 1930s;

✘ entredeux, a ladder-looking trim used in heirloom sewing to attach laces, fabrics, and embroideries (see the photo on p. 112);

✘ other stitching in which the open look or "holes" are the main decorative focus, as on the blouse shown in the photo on the facing page.

The following specifications apply to all hemstitching on the sewing machine:

Fabric: Wovens with a high percentage of linen or cotton and little or no polyester give the best results. Always stitch test samples. Sometimes unlikely fabric content or texture gives surprisingly excellent results. For example, some faille moiré (51 percent acetate, 49 percent cotton), chambray, and some cotton piqués hemstitch very well.

Fabrics with body—for example, organdy—or those that can be spray-starched and pressed or stabilized to add body and crispness give better results than very soft fabrics. Loosely woven fabrics are easier to hemstitch than tightly woven ones.

Thread: Fine machine-embroidery cotton gives excellent results. Rayon, silk, and other fine decorative threads can also be used. The thread must be very fine. Good choices in cotton are: Madeira 80/2, YLI Heirloom 100/2 or 70/2, Zwicky 70/2, Mettler 60/2, and DMC 50/2.

Thread color should usually match fabric. A contrasting thread color is pleasing with some hemstitching techniques and stitches, such as the Parisian hemstitch, but unattractive with others. As always, testing is important.

Needle: Wing needles, double wing needles, or large Universal needles to help create the desired openings in the fabric. (Details on using the various needles are included with each hemstitching method.) Wing needles have metal extensions on each side that create very prominent holes. Use these with care— they can damage fine fabrics and laces.

Always test any wing or large Universal needles in your machine at a slow speed with a straight stitch first (see p. 65). Increase width carefully, if you want a wider stitch. If there is a clicking sound, the needle may be hitting something; do not use it until you check with your dealer.

Universal 120/19 needles have a larger than normal shank and can be difficult to get into the needle bar on some machines. Try several of these needles before giving up—they vary slightly, and sometimes out of a box of five, three will fit and two will not. If necessary, use the next smaller size (110).

Upper tension: Usually normal, but on heavier or stiffer fabrics, increase tension to create enough pull to open the holes; on very lightweight or soft fabrics, loosen tension slightly to prevent puckering.

Stabilizer: To avoid the puckering inherent in the use of such large needles, spray-starch and press the fabric several times until it is relatively stiff. Each time, spray a medium application of spray starch, then if possible, wait 15 sec. to 30 sec. before pressing, in order for the fibers to absorb the starch. (Saturating the fabric with spray starch can cause scorching.) Other spray-on or paint-on stiffeners can be used, but test them first.

The Turkish hemstitch adds a tailored finish to the outer edge of the collar of a classic linen blouse. The same detailing, repeated on the upper edges of the pocket flap and cuffs, gives an easy and elegant finish to this purchased garment.

With any of the following hemstitching conditions, a lightweight tearaway stabilizer may be needed under the fabric:

✗ stitching parallel to the lengthwise grain;

✗ hemstitching a long length;

✗ using more complicated hemstitches (those that have more steps in the pattern). For example, the Venetian hemstitch is more likely to need stabilizing than the Parisian;

✗ stitching multiple rows;

✗ stitching on corners, sharp curves, or multiple fabric layers, such as areas where cuffs, bands, or collars are attached;

✗ using a very soft or lightweight fabric that could not be adequately stiffened.

In addition to stabilizing, other ways to compensate for hemstitching's tendency to pucker include holding the fabric taut as you sew, loosening upper tension, shortening the stitch length, decreasing stitch width, using a metal presser foot rather than a lightweight plastic one, and using a smaller needle size (slightly less pronounced holes are better than puckered fabric).

Always test your stitching first on a fabric scrap, duplicating the conditions of the project.

Methods

There are three basic ways to achieve a hemstitched look on a sewing machine: double wing-needle adjoining rows, single wing-needle adjoining rows, and built-in hemstitches. When the fabric and application are appropriate, any of these three methods can be combined

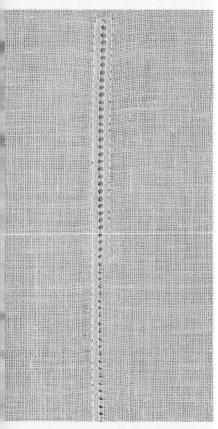

This hemstitching effect was created with a double wing needle and two passes of straight stitching. The lower part of the sample shows how the stitching appears after the first pass; the upper part shows the stitching completed.

with withdrawing threads from the fabric to create a hand-hemstitched look.

DOUBLE WING-NEEDLE ADJOINING ROWS

A double wing needle can be used on most sewing machines with twin-needle capability to create a beautiful hemstitched effect. Use it on fabrics appropriate for hemstitching, either as a decorative topstitch on a single or double layer (for example, through both the garment fabric and the facing) or to hem two layers (in this case, the excess fabric is trimmed up to the zigzag stitching on the underside), as on the blouse collar shown in the photo on p. 94.

Needle: Double wing needle (also called twin wing or double hemstitch needle). This variation of a twin needle actually has one regular Universal needle and one wing needle, not two wing needles, as its name implies.

Foot: Use a foot that provides visibility, such as an open-toe satin-stitch foot; a foot with a transparent plastic front; or one with a large opening, such as Bernina's buttonhole foot #3.

Stitch: Straight. (Other stitches can be used also, but a simple straight stitch gives excellent results.)

Length: 2mm to 2.5mm.

1. Holding the fabric taut, straight-stitch the desired distance.

2. With the needles and presser foot up, turn the fabric 180 degrees.

3. Lower the needles into the fabric so that the wing needle falls precisely in the last hole it made. (The other needle will go into unstitched fabric.) Lower the presser foot.

4. Stitch the second row slowly and carefully, making sure the wing needle continues to hit the holes it made on the first row. Sew with one hand on the fabric behind the needle and one in front. Pull slightly to the back or front when slight adjustments are necessary.

As long as you hit the previous holes precisely most of the time, it is unlikely that occasional misses will be noticeable on the finished project. After the second pass is complete, there may be stray threads down the middle of the row of enlarged holes; these occur when the wing needle stitching on the second pass does not quite overlap the first row. These threads can be carefully clipped

For hemstitching using double wing needles, the second pass is stitched in the opposite direction of the first, with the wing needle hitting exactly in the holes it made on the first pass. An open-toe foot provides the necessary visibility.

at the ends and picked out with a needle or pin.

Options To give more definition and, on sheer fabrics, to add color, you can cord double wing-needle stitching just as for twin-needle stitching (see pp. 69-70). It's easiest to thread cord between double wing needles with a dental-floss threader if you lower the needles just until the points pierce the fabric.

If it's practical, you can withdraw one or more threads from the fabric before pressing and stitching (see the photo on p. 76 for an example). Doing so will make the holes even more distinct and easier to hit on the second pass, and it also reduces the likelihood of puckering. Stitch on each side of the drawn threads so that the wing needle goes into the area where the threads have been withdrawn and the regular needle goes into the undisturbed fabric.

SINGLE WING-NEEDLE ADJOINING ROWS

In order for the holes in machine hemstitching to stay open, there must be stitching holding or pulling the holes open from several directions: either from front and back, as well as the side, or from multiple diagonal directions. In double wing-needle hemstitching (explained in the previous section), the bobbin thread zigzagging on the back of the overlapping stitching pulls the holes open. With single wing needles, partially overlapping zigzag stitching can create the desired effect.

Because this method relies on a simple zigzag stitch, even the most basic zigzag machine can produce an elegant hemstitched effect. As with the double wing-needle method, two passes are required.

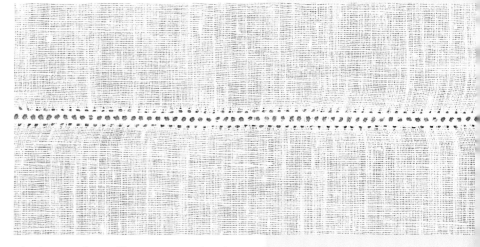

This hemstitching effect was created with a single wing needle and a simple zigzag stitch.

Needle: Size 100 wing needle or large Universal needle, usually size 120/19. For more delicate fabrics, Universal size 110/18 or smaller. (Size 120 wing needles should be used only on very loosely woven, sturdy fabrics, like those used for some table linens.)

Foot: Use a foot that provides visibility, such as an open-toe satin-stitch foot, a foot with a transparent plastic front, or one with a large opening, such as Bernina's buttonhole foot #3.

Stitch: Zigzag.

Width: 1.75mm to 2mm.

Length: 1mm to 1.25mm.

1. Stitch a row of zigzag stitching the length needed. Stop with the needle down on the left side.

2. Raise the presser foot. Turn the fabric 180 degrees, so that the line of stitching is now in front of the machine. Lower the presser foot.

3. Stitch a second row of zigzag stitching, guiding carefully so that each time the needle goes to the left, it hits exactly in the holes of

Hemstitching with zigzag stitch

Stitched with a wing needle, a simple zigzag stitch becomes a decorative hemstitch. (Arrows indicate stitching direction.)

1. Stitch first pass. At end, stop on left side with needle down.

2. Turn fabric 180 degrees.

3. Continue stitching. Left side of stitch enters holes on right side of previous stitching.

what is now the right side of the previous row, as shown in the drawing at left and the photo below. Use a slow speed, and hold the fabric taut with one hand on the fabric behind the needle and one in front, to adjust as necessary.

Options When practical, before you press and stitch the fabric, you can withdraw one or more threads from the area where the two rows will overlap. Doing so will make the holes more distinct.

You can also use other stitches. One that gives excellent results with this method is the picot (or "E") stitch (width 2mm, length 2mm to 2.5mm). This stitch resembles the Parisian hemstitch, but since the holes are not pulled open by repeated steps in its pattern, pivoting and overlapping part of the stitch creates a more distinct and finished hemstitched effect, as shown in the top drawing on the facing page and the photo on the facing page.

BUILT-IN HEMSTITCHES

The third method for achieving the look of hemstitching using the sewing machine is with built-in hemstitches. Many machines have stitches that automatically stitch in and out of the same holes as required for hemstitching. With them the need for multiple passes over the line of stitches is eliminated. When I began teaching fine-machine-sewing techniques in 1982, only a few sewing machines had any really usable hemstitches. Today there are more than 40 machines available that have the two most popular and useful of the hemstitches: the Parisian stitch (resembling the pin stitch made by hand) and the Venetian stitch (resembling entredeux).

Needle: Most often, Universal size 120/19. Use smaller Universal needles (110/18, 100/16, 90/14, etc.) on more delicate fabrics, especially when replicating the hand version of pin stitching, where the holes should be only slightly enlarged. Size 100 wing needles may be used for more prominent holes on sturdy, loosely woven fabrics, like most linens. Wing needles can damage the fibers of fine fabrics and laces. Test first.

Foot: When possible, use a foot that holds the fabric securely, such as the basic metal presser foot, to help reduce puckering. Stitches where thread builds up, like the Venetian stitch, may require

Hemstitching can be done using a single wing needle and side-by-side passes of zigzag stitching. On the second pass, each stitch to the left hits a hole on the right side of the previous stitching. If you do not have an open-toe foot, use a foot with a large opening, like this Bernina buttonhole foot #3.

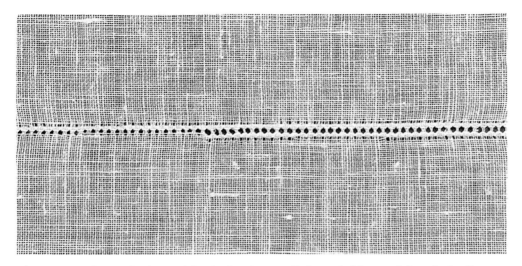

The picot stitch can also be used for single wing-needle hemstitching. At left, only the first pass has been completed; at right, the second pass has been stitched as well.

a satin-stitch foot (preferably metal and not open toe) to allow the stitching to feed easily without getting crushed. On many Elnas, the multi-cord sole (used with or without cord) works well as a metal satin-stitch foot.

Stitch: Consult your sewing-machine manual for any information on stitches for hemstitching. Usually the hemstitches are grouped together. Even if there are no stitches specified in the manual, look for and try stitches that have forward and reverse as well as sideways stitching in their pattern and that repeatedly stitch in and out of the same holes. The most common built-in hemstitches are:

✘ *Parisian (also called pin stitch, point de Paris)* The stitch pattern resembles the letter "L" (or a reversed "L"), repeating the vertical stitches and, on some machines, also the horizontal stitches.

✘ *Venetian* The stitch pattern goes repeatedly around a diamond shape, as well as vertically from the top to the bottom of the diamond; it can resemble entredeux, especially when corded.

✘ *Turkish* The Turkish stitch resembles the double overlock except each step in the pattern is repeated.

✘ *Four-sided* The stitch pattern goes repeatedly around a square or rectangular shape.

✘ *Rhodes* The Rhodes stitch resembles the honeycomb stitch, except each step in the pattern is repeated.

Other stitches that can produce a hemstitched look are:

✘ *Picot* Similar to the Parisian stitch, but no part of the stitch is repeated.

✘ *Daisy* or *star* Stitches in and out of center on each pattern repeat.

✘ *Cross stitch* A cross stitch can resemble the Venetian stitch if the needle goes into rather than across the center intersection.

Width and length: Vary with stitch. (Settings for some machines are listed in Appendix B on p. 195-197.) The most common settings for the two most-used stitches are:

Parisian

Rhodes

Venetian

Picot

Turkish

Daisy

Four-sided

Cross stitch

✗ *Parisian* width 2mm, length 2mm to 2.5mm.

✗ *Venetian* width 3mm to 4mm, length 2.5mm (except 1.3mm with the long-stitch button on Bernina 1130, 1230, and 1260).

Note that on most machines the automatic settings for hemstitches are generally too wide and long and should be narrowed and shortened.

Stitching a test sample with conditions exactly the same as the project—including the same fabric, number of layers, stabilizer, thread, needle, stitch length and width, presser foot, and even grain direction—is most important for hemstitching. If the enlarged holes are not clean and distinct or if threads cross them, the stitch alignment probably needs balancing.

COMBINING HAND- AND MACHINE-HEMSTITCHING TECHNIQUES

Withdrawing a few threads before any on-grain hemstitching will make the holes more open. But you can copy the look of hand hemstitching by withdrawing threads from the fabric either before or after stitching two parallel rows about $^{1}/_{4}$ in. to $^{1}/_{2}$ in. apart.

When threads are withdrawn before stitching, you can stitch hemstitches or other machine stitches (especially overlock stitches) along each side of the open area, as was done on the blouse pocket in the photos at left. (You can use a smaller needle for this than when hemstitching without withdrawing threads.) Stitch on each side of the withdrawn threads so that the vertical steps in the stitch pattern that enlarge the holes are just on the area where the threads have been withdrawn and the rest of the stitch is on the undis-

*(ABOVE AND BELOW)**The Parisian hemstitch adds wonderful detail to this pur-chased linen blouse. Threads were withdrawn from the pocket, and the remain-ing threads were outlined with the hemstitch: the forward and reverse stitches on the threads, the side stitches catching the fabric edge. An additional row of hem-stitching adds a topstitched look to the pocket hem. The simple edging on the collar and cuffs is sewn so the stitch to the side just clears the edge of the fabric.*

Balancing alignment

For beautiful hemstitching, it is critical that the needle hit precisely in the same hole or holes as it repeats parts of the stitch pattern. Thankfully, the stitches often align perfectly, and no adjustment is needed. But if they are misaligned at all, the holes will not be distinct or there will be stray threads across them, as you can see in the photo below. Since stitch alignment can be affected by the type of fabric, number of fabric layers, grain direction, stabilizer, and so on, many machines have a balancing feature to adjust the stitch.

Consult the machine manual for instructions on balancing, adjusting, or fine-tuning stitches. Stitch at a slow speed and watch the forward and reverse parts of the stitch. If the needle comes forward too far and overshoots a hole it should hit, shorten the forward stitches by adjusting toward minus (-). If the needle goes back too far for the hole it should hit, adjust toward plus (+). (On Pfaffs, the stitches are adjusted the reverse: If the needle comes too far forward, adjust toward plus [+] to compress the stitch; if the needle goes too far back, adjust toward minus [-] to spread the stitch.)

When you get the stitch aligned perfectly, make notes on your sample. Sketch the adjusted position of the fine-tuner or note the number of times you pressed (+) or (-). Save your samples and notes in your notebook. The next time you have a similar fabric combination, the adjustment will likely be the same or very close.

It will take some practice to be comfortable with balancing stitches, but it is worth the effort to learn to fine-tune stitching. It will allow you to perfect hemstitching, as well as other stitching where alignment is critical, such as the double overlock stitch, decorative stitches like the daisy or star, letters and numbers, and (on many machines) buttonholes.

If your machine does not have a fine-tuning feature and the stitches are not perfectly aligned, try additional stabilizing, either by applying more spray starching and pressing or by using a tearaway stabilizer underneath. Also experiment with stitch length and with mirror imaging, since these may also slightly affect the alignment.

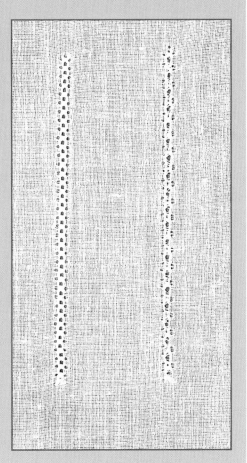

If a stitch is not balanced properly, the holes will not be distinct (stitching at right). After balancing (stitching at left), the look is clean and open.

TIP You do not have to have a twin needle in the machine to use the twin-needle option to reduce the stitch width. Engaging this feature on many machines permits a narrower stitch width than the preset parameters allow. Experiment. For example, the narrowest stitch width for the Parisian hemstitch on many Pfaff models is 2mm. For applications where a narrower stitch width would look more like a handsewn pin stitch, set the width at 3.5mm and engage the twin-needle width limit for a width of 1.5mm to 1.75mm (depending on the model).

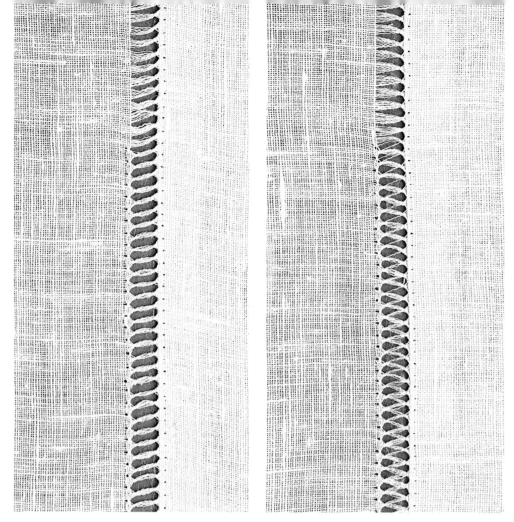

On both of these samples, the Parisian hemstitch was stitched along each side of an area where threads had been withdrawn by hand. On the hem side, the forward and reverse stitches are just into the drawn threads and the stitch to the side catches the hem. On the sample at left, the stitches on the other side hit the separated areas between thread groupings for parallel bars of threads in the open area. On the sample at right, the forward and reverse stitches on the second side hit the threads between the separated areas, creating zigzag bars of thread.

TIP ✳ Choose fabrics from which thread withdrawal is not difficult.

✳ If you like this look but do not want to withdraw long lengths of threads, small areas near the face, like blouse pockets or short sleeve hems, are good choices.

✳ Using a slightly longer stitch length (about 3mm) makes this technique easier. The width is still narrow—wide enough to go just into the open area and into the fabric just enough to be secure (about 2mm).

✳ To make hitting the space between thread groupings easier, make the openings more distinct by spreading the threads with a large needle or similar tool before stitching the second side. Also remember the option of hitting within the thread groups on the second row for zigzag bars. This is much easier because it does not have to be exact.

✳ A magnifier, such as MagEyes or one mounted on your machine, will make the threads and spaces more visible.

turbed fabric. For example, with the Parisian hemstitch, the forward and reverse stitches are just into the drawn threads and the stitch to the side catches the fabric.

Experiment with the second row of stitching: If the stitches on the second side are directly opposite those on the first, you will create parallel bars of threads in the open area (as in the photo above left); if the stitches on the second side are offset, you will create zigzag bars of thread (as in the photo above right).

Though this technique can embellish a single layer of fabric, it is especially effective for replicating the look of hand hemstitching on the hems of pockets, short sleeves, skirts, table or bed linens, and so on. (Of course, these areas must be straight on grain.)

To withdraw threads, hemstitch the open area, and hem at the same time:

1. Fold up about 1/2 in. (or desired hem seam allowance) along the hem. For accuracy, fold along a pulled thread.

2. Withdraw a thread double the desired hem depth from this fold. (For example, for pockets and short sleeves, withdraw a thread about 2 in. from the fold for a 1-in. hem.) Withdraw threads for about $\frac{1}{4}$ in. to $\frac{1}{2}$ in. above this, depending how wide you want the open area to be.

3. Fold the hem up to the lower edge of the withdrawn threads. Spray-starch, press, and pin or temporarily adhere the hem in place (with fabric glue stick or temporary adhesive).

4. Stitch the hem side with the Parisian hemstitch, so that the forward and reverse stitches are just into the withdrawn threads and the stitch to the side catches the hem.

5. Turn the fabric around and stitch along the other edge of the withdrawn threads, so that the forward and reverse stitches hit the separated areas of the withdrawn threads to create parallel bars of threads in the open area or hit within the grouped threads for zigzag bars of thread. An open-toe foot is helpful for visibility on this side.

An optional topstitched effect can be created on the hem by substituting the four-sided or Turkish hemstitch for the Parisian. The forward and reverse stitches of one side of the stitch pattern are just into the drawn threads and the rest of the stitch is on the fabric. For the same effect with the Parisian, turn the fabric 180 degrees and repeat the Parisian on the hem side, but this time with the forward and reverse stitches on the hem and the swing to the side into the open area. The stitches mirror-image those made on the first pass. (See the close-up

Before stitching the second row, you may want to make the space between the thread groupings more distinct by spreading the openings with a needle or similar tool.

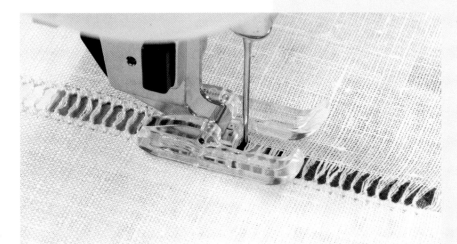

An open-toe foot provides visibility for hitting the separated areas of the withdrawn threads. The forward and reverse Parisian stitches enter the separated areas and bundle the threads into parallel bars. The stitch to the side goes into the fabric.

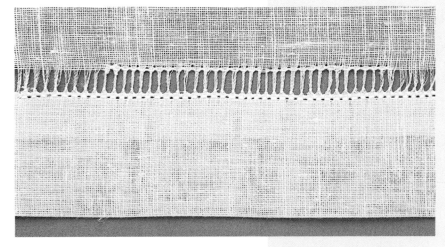

An optional topstitched effect can be created on the hem by substituting the four-sided or Turkish hemstitch for the Parisian stitch on that side. The Parisian hemstitch was still used to bundle the threads and catch the single layer of fabric on the other side of the open area.

The Venetian hemstitch sewn over blue cord highlights the collar and the edges of a bow on a classic white piqué blouse. The same detailing is repeated on the hem of the sleeves.

Withdrawing threads gives an exquisite effect, but it requires on-grain hemstitching—no curves or angles—and some time. An option that has many more application possibilities is a technique adapted from the hand-appliqué-cord technique.

Corded hemstitching

The description of appliqué cord in Margaret Pierce's *Heirloom Sewing II* (see Resources on p. 199) inspired me to adapt this hand-sewing technique to the sewing machine. For appliqué cord by hand, the pin stitch is used to couch cord on two facing adjoining rows. It creates the look of delicate entredeux inserted into the fabric. The machine technique is similar to an option shown for hemstitching with the single wing needle, where adjoining rows are stitched with the picot stitch (see pp. 82-83). To replicate appliqué cord, the side stitches on both passes couch cord. The machine version can look remarkably like appliqué cord by hand.

Experimenting with cording these and other hemstitches, both single and adjoining rows, and with different sizes and colors of cord, opened a world of creative options for the hemstitching capabilities of sewing machines. Hemstitching over cord is much more visible and looks more finished, and it permits the use of more color than hemstitching without cord. Cording also adds strength and stability. The look can be delicate or bold (see the photos on p. 92), depending on the cords used. There are so many possible variations for cording machine hemstitches that I am still finding new ones after 14 years of experimenting!

TIP Sudden changes in speed can affect the alignment of built-in hemstitches. Stitch with a smooth, even sewing rhythm at a medium speed.

Test and balance the stitch without cord first, then add the cord and make additional adjustments, if necessary.

of the pocket on the green linen blouse on p. 84.)

Do not use the four-sided or Turkish stitch (or the second row of Parisian) on the unhemmed side or on any single fabric layer, unless it is very stable. The additional stitching distorts the fabric unless it is medium- to heavyweight, loosely woven, and well starched or stabilized.

The other way to combine hand and machine hemstitching is to hemstitch two rows on grain and then withdraw the parallel threads between them afterward. Space the rows as desired, and experiment with different stitches. You can then leave the remaining threads as they are or group them by hand or by machine (stitching down the center of the withdrawn threads).

Cord: Multiple strands of thread or floss for a delicate look; for more visibility, size 5, 8, or 12 pearl cotton (the higher the number, the finer the cord), buttonhole twist/topstitching thread, or any similar cord that is colorfast and shrink resistant. Some of the wider hemstitches, like the Turkish and four-sided stitches, can also be stitched over very narrow (1/16-in.- to 1/8-in.-wide) ribbon. Cord color should usually match thread color for the Venetian hemstitch. (If an exact match is not possible, choose thread a shade lighter than the cord.) With other hemstitches, experiment with cord color that matches or contrasts with the thread and fabric.

Foot: Feet with holes or grooves to guide the cord(s) are very helpful. (A dental-floss threader makes it easier to thread cord through holes in a presser foot.) A foot to guide only one cord is needed with the Parisian, picot, four-sided, and Turkish hemstitches. For the Venetian hemstitch, which stitches over

TIP Besides cording a hemstitch as you stitch it, try weaving cord in and out of the enlarged openings with a hand needle after stitching—experiment with weaving through every hole, every other hole, or groups of holes.

The benefit of contrasting cording is especially apparent on dark-colored fabrics where the hemstitched openings (holes) do not show unless there is light coming from behind or a light-colored fabric underneath. Stitching over a contrasting cord or weaving cord through the holes afterward, as I did on the navy blouse in the photos at left and below, not only adds visibility but can create dramatic effects.

(ABOVE) The Parisian hemstitch was stitched along the folded edge of the front facings of this purchased linen/rayon blouse. (RIGHT) The effect of the stitching was not visible on this dark color until two strands of contrasting silk buttonhole twist were woven through the hemstitched holes next to the facings.

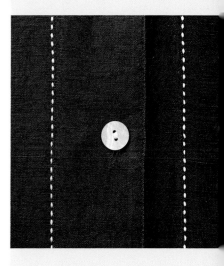

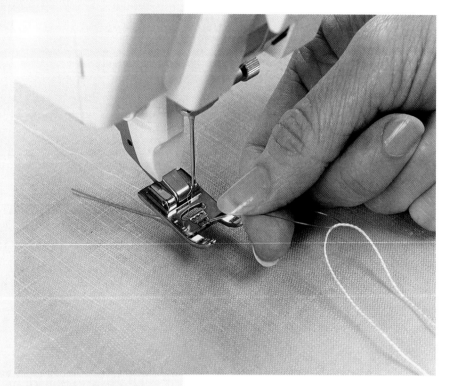

A dental-floss threader is helpful for threading cord through holes in a foot. Fabric under the foot keeps the threader from going down into needle-plate openings.

two slightly separated cords at the same time, use a foot that guides cords just left and right of center. The Rhodes hemstitch couches three cords: center and just left and right of center.

Try the cording or multiple-cord foot (those with five, seven, or nine holes will likely work for cording all these stitches), buttonhole foot with two grooves, pintuck foot, and braiding foot. Experiment with others. Feel the underside of presser feet. The underside of Pfaff's "fancy-stitch" foot #1A has two grooves that work well for guiding cord. If necessary, use a satin-stitch foot and guide the cords manually. When stitching adjoining rows, a foot that also provides some visibility in front is ideal.

Keep in mind that if the needle position on your machine can be changed when doing hemstitches, you can move the stitch to align with holes or grooves on feet, if necessary.

Stabilizer: Same as for hemstitching without cord, except that at the beginning and end of the corded hemstitching, a lightweight tearaway stabilizer under the fabric may also be needed.

PARISIAN OR PICOT STITCH OVER CORD

Both the Parisian hemstitch (also called the pin stitch or point de Paris) and the picot stitch are attractive when stitched over cord (see the photos below and top left on the facing page). Their forward and reverse stitches should be right next to the cord, and the stitches to the side should go just over the cord. With the Parisian stitch the holes will be more prominent because of the repeated stitches.

If your machine does not have the Venetian hemstitch (which allows you to

The Parisian or the picot stitch is effective when stitched over cord, whether as a single row (bottom) or as two adjoining rows (top).

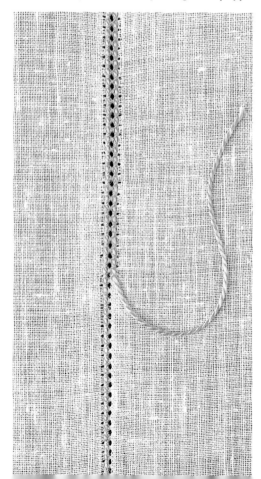

Two adjoining rows of the Parisian or picot stitch over cord replicate the hand-appliqué-cord technique. The forward and reverse stitches on the second pass hit the holes created on the first pass. The stitch to the outside couches cord on both passes.

stitch over both cords at the same time), you can replicate the hand-appliqué-cord technique with the Parisian hemstitch or the picot stitch on two adjoining rows.

1. Stitch a row of the Parisian hemstitch or picot stitch so that the stitch to the side goes over the cord to couch it. Experiment with different feet, and note which one is most helpful for guiding the cord; for this application, the foot ideally allows some visibility for hitting the same holes on the reverse pass.

2. At the end of the row, pivot and stitch a second row, partially overlapping the first, as shown in the photo above. (Pivot, with the needle down, immediately before or after the stitch to the side. For machines that take two stitches to the

side, pivot after the first one.) The cord goes around the needle when you pivot. The forward and reverse stitches on the second side must hit exactly the same holes as the forward and reverse stitches made on the first pass. The stitch to the side goes over the cord, as before.

CORDED VENETIAN HEMSTITCH

If your machine has the Venetian hemstitch, you do not need to pivot and stitch a second row. You can stitch one row of the Venetian hemstitch over two cords simultaneously, as shown in the photo below, and create the same look as that of adjoining rows of the Parisian hemstitch. Each side of the Venetian hemstitch couches a cord; the enlarged holes are down the center between the two cords. Look for a foot to guide the cords just left and right of center, such as the multiple-cord foot or a buttonhole foot with two grooves.

The photos on p. 92 show examples of corded Venetian hemstitching. With size 8 pearl cotton or buttonhole twist/topstitching thread, the corded Venetian hemstitch resembles entredeux. The corded Venetian hemstitch is also very effective for fagoting (see pp. 146-148).

TIP When cord must be cut before it's applied to the fabric, make it extra long. For example, in order to have two lengths of cord for the Venetian stitch, you have to cut off enough for one side of the stitching, unless you have two balls of cord. Because the cord slightly conforms to the shape of the stitches, more is used than you would think. Wasting some cord (which is relatively inexpensive) is much better than running out a few inches short of the end of a row of stitching!

With the Venetian hemstitch, you can stitch over two cords at the same time. A multiple-cord foot makes it easy to guide the cords just left and right of center.

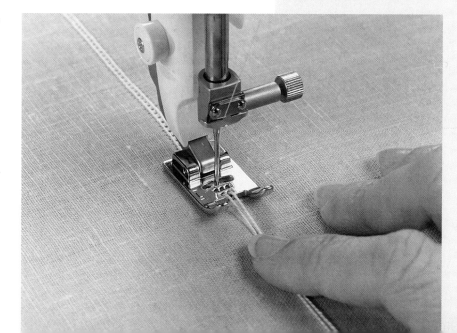

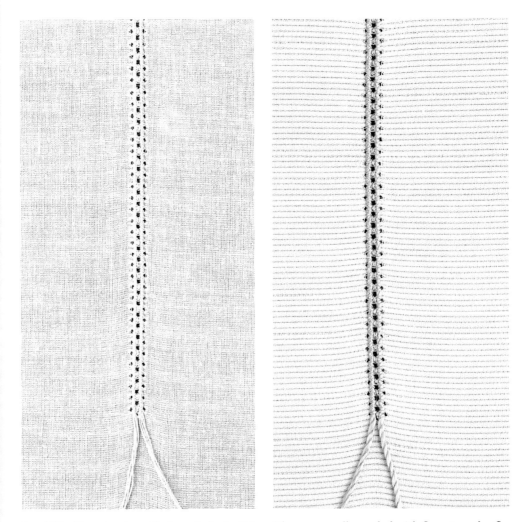

(LEFT) The Venetian hemstitch on Swiss batiste with a 110 needle corded with four strands of thread has a delicate look. (RIGHT) On cotton piqué with size 5 pearl cotton and a wing needle, it has a bolder look.

FOUR-SIDED OR TURKISH HEMSTITCHES OVER CORD OR RIBBON

Four-sided and Turkish hemstitches create an interesting decorative effect when stitched over cord or ribbon (see the top photo on the facing page). Over ribbon, they can create the look of beading. Adjust the stitch width so it just clears the cord or ribbon.

CORDED RHODES HEMSTITCH

If your machine has the Rhodes (triple honeycomb) hemstitch, try cording it with three cords for a look similar to adjoining corded Venetian hemstitch rows

(stitched on the collar of the blue linen blouse on p. 95) without having to stitch and align overlapping rows. Use a foot with multiple holes to guide one cord in the center, one just left of center, and one just right of center. Adjust stitch width and cord spacing so that the stitches are just clearing each of the cords (see the center left photo on the facing page).

STARTING AND ENDING CORDED HEMSTITCHING

The beginning and the end of corded hemstitching are often hidden in a seam. In situations where they will show, leave long tails of cord at each end. Thread

The Turkish hemstitch over matching size 5 pearl cotton (left) and the four-sided hemstitch over contrasting ¹/₁₆-in. ribbon (right) both create interesting decorative variations.

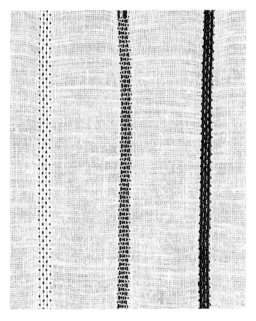

Totally different looks can be created by matching or contrasting the color of the thread and cord (size 8 pearl cotton) with the Rhodes hemstitch.

The Rhodes (triple honeycomb) hemstitch couching three cords can resemble adjoining corded rows of the Venetian hemstitch.

each cord tail into the large eye of a hand needle with a tapestry needle threader. Take it to the back of the fabric, and weave it into the stitches for about ³/₈ in., as shown in the photo at right. Then trim the excess cord.

An option with the Venetian hemstitch is to start stitching with a loop of cord pulled taut around the needle.

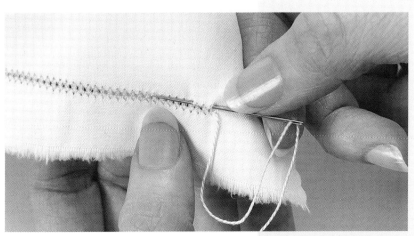

To hide the end of a cord, weave it in the stitches on the wrong side of the fabric for about ³/₈ in.

Hemstitching at corners

Many hemstitching applications necessitate turning corners. For example, when hemming or attaching lace around a square collar or using hemstitching to appliqué any shapes with points, you need to be able to turn corners neatly.

The double wing-needle hemstitching method is effective and attractive for hemming (see the photo below). To turn the corner of the outer row of stitching when using this method (as would be required on a square collar), "walk" the outside needle (the Universal needle) around the corner for one or two stitches, with the wing needle hitting the same corner hole each time. (To "walk," lift the presser foot enough to move the fabric, lower it, then manually turn the flywheel toward you for each stitch.) On the inner row of stitching, the wing needle must again hit the same corner hole while you walk the Universal needle to turn the corner, so the inner stitches must overlap for a stitch or two. With such fine thread, these stitches will not be noticeable.

TIP Never hemstitch directly on a raw edge because the stitching would not be secure. Instead either hemstitch at least ¼ in. from the raw edge and trim up to it or hemstitch over a folded edge.

The crisp white collar of a middy blouse is hemstitched with adjoining rows of straight stitching using a double wing needle. Excess fabric is trimmed up to the stitching on the underside of the single-fold hem.

To stitch corners with adjoining rows of corded Venetian hemstitching, as on this blouse collar, make a sharp turn for the inner row. Turn the outer row in two steps, stitching one complete pattern diagonally, before completing the turn.

In general, with any of the built-in hemstitches, turn the corner at the end of the stitch pattern. Since these stitches are formed differently on different machines, it is best to practice cornering with the hemstitches on your machine and make careful notes.

Machines that have the option of stopping automatically at the end of the stitch pattern usually stop at the correct point for pivoting and turning. Simply engage this feature along with the needle-down option during the last stitch before the turn. When the machine stops, raise the presser foot, turn the fabric, lower the foot, and continue. If the machine does not stop at the right place to turn the corner, I usually use this feature anyway,

then tap the foot pedal as many times as necessary to get to the best pivot point. For example, the Elna 7000, 9000, and Diva stop at the left point of the diamond pattern on the Venetian hemstitch. Tap the foot pedal twice to get to the low point of the diamond, then pivot to turn.

Unless a sharp corner is absolutely needed, with the Venetian hemstitch I like to turn the corner in two steps, stitching a short diagonal across the point as shown in the drawing at right. Stop at the end of the stitch pattern just before the corner, turn the corner halfway (45 degrees), stitch one or two complete stitch patterns, then turn another 45 degrees to complete the corner.

Use a lightweight tearaway stabilizer under the fabric whenever turning corners with cord. When turning a corner with corded Venetian hemstitching where both sides of the stitch are being corded at the same time (see the top photo on p. 3), the outside cord covers more distance than the inside cord; to compensate, give a slight tug on the inside cord to take up the slack. With most of the other hemstitches, keep the cord to the outside of the needle when pivoting.

With sharp curves, you may have to stop repeatedly and pivot at the end of the stitch pattern. This may not be necessary with more gradual curves. Test by stitching a similar curve on a scrap before stitching the project.

Applications

Hemstitching is one of my favorite embellishments because of its classic look and because of the unbelievable number of decorative as well as practical ways it can be used. With all the different hemstitching methods and variations, includ-

Turning a corner with the Venetian hemstitch

The Venetian hemstitch can be cornered in one or two steps.

One-step method

Stop at end of stitch pattern. Turn fabric 90 degrees; continue stitching.

Two-step method

Stop before corner.

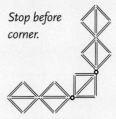

Turn fabric 45 degrees. Stitch one (or two) patterns. Stop and turn fabric 45 degrees. Continue stitching.

The corded Venetian hemstitch traces the collar, cuffs (see p. 3), and placket of a purchased linen blouse. For added definition, silk buttonhole twist is woven into the holes of the hemstitching.

TIP Keep on the look-
out for suitable garments
and linens to embellish.
I get most of mine from
stores and by mail order.
(Some stores will find a
garment in a particular
size and color if it is available at any of their loca-
tions or from their catalog
warehouse.) Many people
have told me that they
have found high-quality
garments at resale shops.

$40. Of course, I buy the basic blouse and hemstitch it myself. You can hemstitch the collar, pocket(s), cuffs, placket, hem (including short-sleeve hems), folded tucks, or around the neck and armbands, or any appropriate combination of these. On purchased garments, first test the stitching on an area that will not show, such as a seam allowance or the lower part of a blouse that will be tucked in. You can also hemstitch purchased linens to give them a designer heirloom look.

To free the upper part of a pocket for decorative stitching (as seen on the blouses on p. 84 and p. 99), unstitch the sides about halfway or as far as necessary. Embellish. Restitch the sides using a fine thread and needle and a short straight stitch. For a clean and secure finish, take the thread tails to the back, knot the two together close to the fabric, bury the tails into the fabric along the pocket seam allowance for about $1/2$ in., then trim the excess thread. Since the pocket was not completely removed, there is no concern about getting it back in the right spot.

In general, almost any hemstitch can be used to decorate a single or double layer of fabric, such as for topstitching or for a single-fold hem. The Parisian hemstitch is usually the best choice to hemstitch a folded or finished edge, such as a double-fold hem, or to appliqué ribbon.

Almost any application stitched from the right side of the fabric may also be corded to add visibility, color, strength, stability, or a more finished appearance. (With the four-sided or Turkish hemstitches, an alternative is to stitch them over a narrow ribbon or trim.) An additional option is to weave cord, floss, or very narrow ribbon through the stitches or the holes after stitching (see the photo above).

ing cording, the range of creative possibilities is almost endless.

Suitable patterns are easy to find. The main criterion is that they be designed for fabrics appropriate for hemstitching.

The time I can devote to sewing is limited, as it is for so many sewers, so I look for ready-to-wear garments of acceptable fabric, quality, and price to individualize with hemstitching and other embellishments. More than once I have seen hemstitched designer blouses for $150 or so and the same, or very similar, blouse without hemstitching on sale for $35 or

TOPSTITCHING AND OTHER ROWS OF DECORATIVE STITCHING

You can embellish collars, yokes, bodices, blouse fronts, pockets, cuffs, sleeves, the lower edges of skirts, and so on, with one or more separate rows of hemstitching. For example, the Turkish hemstitch was used as a decorative topstitch on the collar, cuffs, and pocket flaps of the purchased red blouse shown in the photo on p. 79.

FACINGS AND PLACKETS

One practical as well as decorative use for hemstitching is to embellish a garment and finish its facings at the same time—for example, around a jewel neck opening or on a placket. To hemstitch a garment and its unfinished facing, stitch from the right side through both layers, staying at least $^1/_4$ in. to $^1/_2$ in. from the raw edge of the facing underneath. Then trim the excess facing fabric up to the stitching on the underside.

A facing whose outer edge has been folded under is especially easy to hemstitch with the Parisian hemstitch or picot stitch, as was done on the front facings of the dress shown at right and on the contents page. Position the fabric so that the forward and reverse stitches are on the single layer of fabric next to the facing and the stitch to the side catches the facing. (This can usually be stitched from the wrong side so that the facing is visible during stitching.) An interesting variation is to make the facings a design element, putting them on the outside of the garment, like neck and arm bands. They can match or contrast with the garment color.

Other stitches may be used with folded facings, but they will be easier to guide if they are on the single layer of fabric right next to the folded edge (as on the gray blouse in the top photo on p. 98) rather than actually catching it.

ADJOINING ROWS

Multiple adjoining rows of hemstitching can create some wonderful effects, including a very attractive machine version of a hand pulled-thread technique called fil tiré (see the photos on p. 99). To avoid puckering and fabric distortion, and be-

A purchased linen dress gets an easy and elegant detail: a Parisian hemstitch sewn down both sides of the front facings. The lower edge of the dress is narrow hemmed and Parisian hemstitched in one step.

To hemstitch a facing from the right side (for any application that will be corded as it is stitched or for stitches that look better from the right side): Before hemstitching, stitch facings in place with a straight stitch (length 2mm), very fine thread that matches the fabric color, a fine needle, and a slightly loosened upper tension. (To prevent shifting, you may adhere the facing in place with fabric glue stick first.) Straight-stitch along the folded edge, sewing wrong side up so that the facing is visible. Then switch to the hemstitching needle, and hemstitch from the right side using the straight stitching as a guide. Stitch from the top to the lower edge for both the straight- and hemstitching.

I have never had to remove the straight stitching. It is almost invisible even if you do not stitch directly over it.

The four-sided hemstitch over a contrasting narrow ribbon adds a classy touch next to the front facings and on the cuffs of this purchased linen/rayon blouse.

cause it is difficult to form a shape other than a rectangle while stitching the rows, it is best to stitch more than two or three adjoining rows on a separate piece of well-stabilized fabric. The desired shape is then cut out and appliquéd onto the background fabric. The fabric under the appliqué may be trimmed away.

Parisian and picot adjoining rows

With the Parisian and picot hemstitches, you can stitch the adjoining rows so that the stitches to the side go to the outside and the forward and reverse stitches overlap (resembling Venetian hemstitching, as in the single wing-needle adjoining rows). You can also stitch them in the opposite direction, so that the stitches to

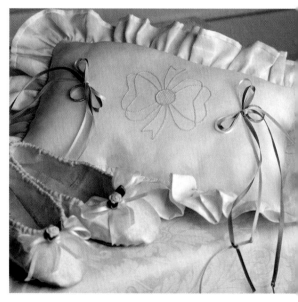

For this ring bearer's pillow, the Parisian hemstitch over cord traces the bow with fil-tiré center on organdy.

the side overlap in the center creating a square or rectangle, just like the four-sided stitch. Both methods, shown in the drawing below, create attractive effects.

Venetian adjoining rows Two adjoining rows of corded Venetian hemstitching can resemble double entredeux. (Double entredeux looks like two side-by-side rows of entredeux.) I used this technique on the collar of the blue linen blouse shown on p. 95 to make the hemstitching more visible.

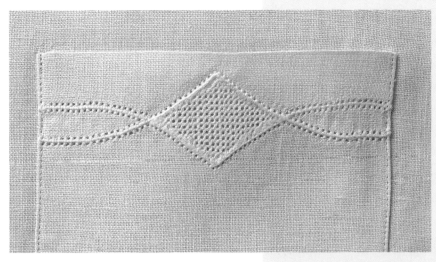

The blouse pocket was unstitched about halfway. A diamond shape was cut from adjoining rows of the four-sided stitch on white linen, then appliquéd onto the upper pocket with a corded satin stitch and the Parisian hemstitch. Additional corded hemstitiching frames the design. The upper pocket was restitched with a fine needle and straight stitch.

These folded blouses show simple yet elegant embellishments that look handsewn. The pocket and sleeve hems of the purchased linen blouse on top were decorated with an appliquéd fil-tiré design (see pocket detail above right) and corded Parisian hemstitching.

Parisian and picot adjoining rows

Either side of the Parisian and picot stitches can adjoin.

The forward and reverse stitches can overlap (left) or the stitches to the side can overlap (right).

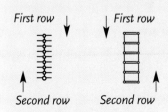

First row   First row

Second row   Second row

Arrows indicate direction of stitching.

Two adjoining rows of the corded Venetian hemstitch can resemble double entredeux. The first row is stitched over two cords as usual. For the second row, only one additional cord is needed.

Stitch the first row as usual over two cords so that the large holes are between the cords (see p. 91).

Stitch the second row so that it overlaps one side of the first row. The stitches to one side of the second row go over one cord and into the large holes of the first

row of stitching. Therefore, you need to cord only the outside edge of the second row, as shown in the photo at left. You can stitch additional rows the same way.

Turkish, Rhodes, and four-sided adjoining rows Multiple adjoining rows of the Turkish, Rhodes, or four-sided stitches create an effective machine version of a hand pulled-thread effect called fil tiré. Usually the multiple rows are stitched on a separate piece of well-starched or stabilized fabric, then cut out and appliquéd onto background fabric.

Additional specifications for the machine version of fil tiré:

Fabric: Suitable for hemstitching, such as natural woven fabrics with body, like most linens and cottons. When stitching multiple rows on delicate fabrics (such as imported batiste or organdy), experiment with using two layers. Always test on scraps.

Needle: Large size Universal needles—size 120/19, 110/18, 100/16, etc.—or wing size 100, as appropriate for the fabric (i.e., a finer needle for a finer fabric).

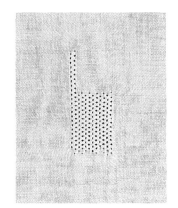 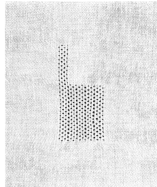 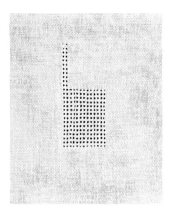

Adjoining rows of the Turkish (LEFT), Rhodes (CENTER), or four-sided hemstitches (RIGHT) can be used to create a pulled-thread effect called fil tiré.

Stitch: Four-sided, Rhodes, Turkish, Parisian.

A simple zigzag may be used if tension is increased to open the holes. The Venetian hemstitch is rarely used for fil tiré because any more than a few rows may become dense and distorted.

Width and length: Vary with stitch and fabric. The automatic settings on most machines are generally much too wide and long. To look most like hand fil tiré, the holes should be more prominent than the stitches between them, especially on more delicate fabrics.

Most common width and length settings for both the four-sided and zigzag stitches are 1.5mm to 2mm.

For appliquéing with the Parisian hemstitch—stitch length 2mm to 3mm, width just wide enough to clear the cord (or 1.5mm to 2mm).

Foot: An open-toe foot is very helpful both for stitching the adjoining rows and for appliquéing because of the visibility it allows. Otherwise, experiment with any foot that is transparent in front or has a large needle-hole opening for as much visibility as possible.

Stabilizer: To avoid puckering and for the best results, stabilizing is very important when stitching multiple rows. Spray-starch and press the fabric several times until relatively stiff. Putting the starched fabric in a hoop is helpful. Otherwise, one or more layers of an additional lightweight tearaway stabilizer (such as Sulky Tear-Easy) is often needed.

One of my favorite fil tiré projects was one I designed for a class. It combines fil tiré with both corded satin stitch and Parisian hemstitch appliqué techniques and was used on both the pillow on p. 98 and the pocket on p. 99.

1. Trace the desired design shape onto a very-well-starched piece of linen (or other appropriate fabric). It is best to keep the design small (no larger than about 1½ in. by 1½ in.) and simple, like an oval or a diamond shape. Most fabrics should also be stabilized in a hoop or with a piece of lightweight tearaway underneath.

2. Stitch multiple adjoining rows of the four-sided, Rhodes, or Turkish hemstitch with a 120 Universal needle to cover the traced design plus about ¼ in. extra all around (see the bottom left photo on p. 102).

3. Remove the markings. Spray-starch and press to block. Trace the design onto the stitched area again.

4. Staystitch over the traced line with a short straight stitch (length about 1.5mm) and a regular needle (70 Universal), then cut out the design.

Problem solving As always, stitch a test sample first. If the holes do not look clean, try more spray starching and pressing, hooping or additional stabilizer, adjusting (balancing) the alignment of the stitch, slight changes in stitch length/width, or a different stitch.

Fabric has more give crossgrain than lengthwise, so try to stitch crossgrain (i.e., selvage to selvage). Experimenting with stitching on the bias is another option.

TIP Suzanne Sawko has digitized the fil-tiré design so that machines with hooped embroidery can stitch a block of fil tiré automatically. (No pivoting and manually aligning each row of stitches required!) It was digitized for a Pfaff 7570 but can be converted to most other formats. It is offered as a free download at Sherry DeRosia's Pfabulous and Pfree Pfaff page (www.sewdesigns.com/derosia/Sawko/Sawko.htm). If the stitching is not clean, Suzanne recommends stitching it at a slow speed and on the bias. From this block of fil tiré, you can cut out your design and appliqué it.

Now appliqué the fil-tiré design onto a larger piece of linen, as follows:

1. Stitch the design in place using a corded satin stitch with a lightweight tearaway stabilizer underneath (stitch width about 2mm, length about 0.6mm, over size 5 or 8 pearl cotton, with fine cotton thread, and size 70 Universal needle). Guide the cord manually. It should be just onto the fil-tiré design.

2. If you wish, trim the fabric (and the tearaway stabilizer) from behind just the appliqué. A loosely woven fabric will be more secure if left untrimmed.

3. Stitch another pass, this time with the Parisian hemstitch (stitch width about 2mm, length about 2.5mm, 120 Universal needle, open-toe or satin-stitch foot). The forward and reverse stitches are just outside the satin stitch. The stitch to the side goes over the cord and onto the fil tiré.

FOLDED TUCKS

Folded tucks, from narrow ones to wide pleat-like ones, can be attractively hemstitched with the Parisian hemstitch or the picot stitch, as was done on the blouse in the left photo on the facing page.

1. Fold and stitch the tuck as usual. Use fine thread, a regular needle, and a normal straight stitch.

2. Press the tuck in the desired direction.

For the machine version of an appliquéd fil-tiré design:
1. *Stitch multiple adjoining rows (such as the four-sided stitch shown here) with a size 120 Universal needle to cover the traced design. On each row, the stitches should hit exactly into the outermost holes of the previous row.*
2. *After staystitching and cutting out the design, appliqué it onto the background fabric. Use a size 70 needle and small zigzag, manually guiding the cord to be just onto the fil-tiré design.*
3. *For a pin-stitched look, stitch another pass, this time with the Parisian hemstitch and a 120 Universal needle. The forward and reverse stitches are just outside the satin stitch, and the stitch to the side goes over the cord onto the fil tiré.*

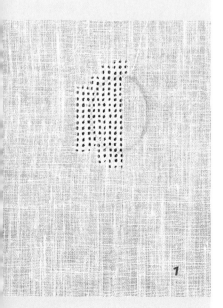

1

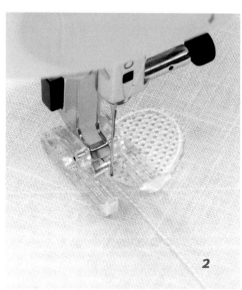

2

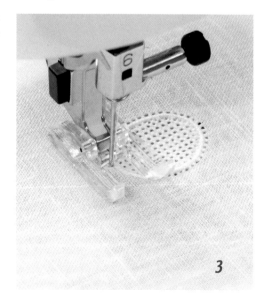

3

3. Parisian hemstitch (most often with a 120 Universal needle) over the stitched line. The forward and reverse stitches are on the single layer of fabric next to the tuck, and the stitch to the side goes just onto the tuck itself, as shown in the top photo at right. The original straight stitching should not show enough to have to be removed.

APPLIQUÉING FOLDED OR FINISHED EDGES

The Parisian hemstitch (or the picot stitch) can be used to appliqué folded or finished edges to resemble hand pin stitching, as shown in the bottom photo at right. Use it to appliqué ribbon, trims, and embroideries, including shaped embroidered medallions. If the trim or medallion is sheer, you can trim away the fabric under it for a more open effect. (A loosely woven fabric will be more secure if left untrimmed.) Use the Parisian hemstitch on the folded edges of delicate ap-

Folded tucks are attractive with Parisian hemstitching. The hemstitching is done after the tuck has been stitched and pressed.

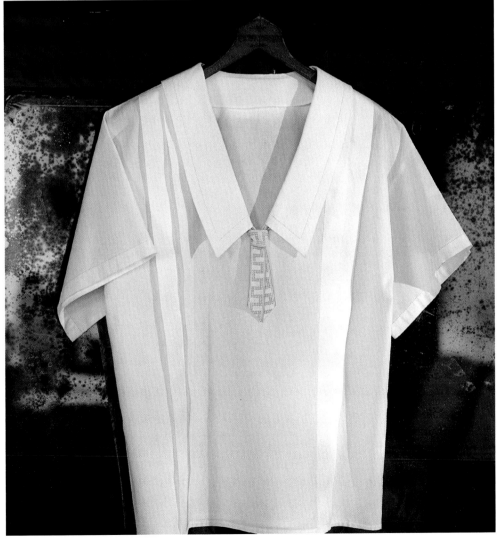

Topstitching with the Parisian hemstitch adds a subtle accent to the collar and tucks on a simple white cotton blouse. The double-fold sleeve hems are hemmed and hemstitched in one step using the same stitch.

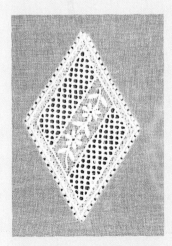

When the Parisian hemstitch is used for appliquéing, the effect is of hand pin stitching. The fabric under sheer appliqués may be trimmed away for a more open effect.

TIP When mixing different fabrics on a project, always prewash them. Otherwise you risk unsightly puckering if one fabric shrinks more than another on the finished project.

pliqué pieces to resemble Madeira appliqué. Hemstitch from the right side, so that the stitch to the side catches the appliqué and the forward and reverse stitches creating the large holes are alongside the appliqué.

SHADOW APPLIQUÉ

The elegance of hemstitching can easily be combined with the beauty of shadow appliqué. Because of its sheerness and body, imported organdy is ideal for this technique. You can also use other sheer fabrics, such as Swiss batiste, if they are sufficiently spray-starched and pressed or put in a hoop; also use a smaller needle. Both layers of fabric can be the same color, or you can use a darker fabric under a lighter one. I usually use the same fabric for both layers, but a nonsheer fabric could be used for the underlayer.

1. Trace the design onto the top piece of fabric.

2. Lay this over the other fabric, and pin in place.

3. Hemstitch from the top side following the design as shown in the photo above. You can use almost any hemstitch, but if the shape of the design is small, a narrow hemstitch like the Parisian or Venetian gives better results than a wide stitch.

4. Carefully trim away the fabric around the design from the back. (For a variation, you can trim the fabric from inside the design instead, leaving the double layer of fabric surrounding the design.)

ATTACHING LACE TO FABRIC

When you use sewing-machine hemstitching to attach lace to fabric, the

stitching can resemble hand pin stitching, entredeux, hemstitching from old hemstitching machines, or just a pretty, embroidered open effect (see the collars and pinafore-style bib shown in the bottom photo on the facing page). Hemstitching the lace can be a real problem solver, especially when you are attaching lace in shapes, such as loops, teardrops, and so on—applications where attaching lace with entredeux and traditional machine-heirloom techniques is difficult.

In most cases, either of two very practical and easy methods can be used to attach lace to fabric with hemstitching. With the first method, the lace is positioned in place, the lace headings are hemstitched to the fabric, and the fabric behind the lace is trimmed. This method is ideal for attaching shaped lace (with curved edges, loops, and so on). Most of the hemstitching techniques and stitches can be used with this method, but the Parisian and Venetian stitches are especially appropriate since they resemble hand pin stitching and entredeux, respectively. Cording the stitches is also an option.

The second method involves hemstitching, usually with the Parisian (or picot) stitch, over a folded fabric edge next to the lace. This method is much more secure, a factor that is a consideration when you are attaching lace to stress areas on a garment or if hard wearing and washing are likely.

There is a third method. Briefly, this method involves hemstitching about $1/2$ in. from the fabric edge, trimming the fabric, then zigzagging the lace to the hemstitching right sides up. One side of the zigzag stitch goes into a hole of the hemstitching; the other side goes just across the lace heading. I rarely use this method because it involves extra steps and because the thread from the zigzag stitching often shows. Only the first two methods will be covered in more detail with reference to the applications that follow.

Needle: Most often, Universal size 120/19. Use smaller Universal needles (110/18, 100/16, 90/14, etc.) on more delicate fabrics, especially for the look of hand pin stitching. Wing needles can damage laces; test carefully.

Lace: For best results, use laces with a high percentage of cotton. For a less frilly look, choose more tailored or heavier laces, such as Cluny lace or tatting. Any lace that will not be gathered should be spray-starched and pressed carefully without stretching. If it will be applied straight, press it as straight as possible. If it will be attached to a curve, shape it into a similar curve, press, let cool, and handle with care to maintain the shape. (Spray starching and pressing also preshrink the lace, which is especially important with tatting and Cluny laces.)

Insertion laces Insertion laces are straight on both edges and are "inserted" within the garment rather than along an edge. They are applied straight or in shapes almost anywhere on a garment—yokes, sleeves, skirts, and so on.

With either the first or second method, first stitch the lace onto the fabric in the desired position with a straight stitch (length 2mm) along both headings. Use a regular needle (size 60 or 70), a basic zigzag presser foot, and the same fine thread you will use for hemstitching. Then switch to the desired hemstitch needle.

To use the first method of attaching lace to fabric, hemstitch along each edge of the lace so that one side of the stitch goes just over the lace heading and the rest of the stitch is on the fabric. The large holes of the stitch should be on the

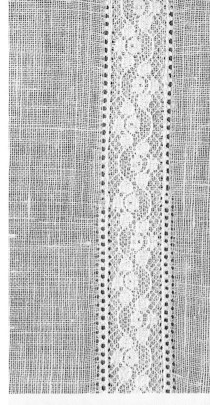

Hemstitching is a practical and attractive way to attach lace to fabric. With the first method the lace is positioned, then the headings are hemstitched to the fabric. Two suitable stitches are the Parisian stitch (left) and the Venetian stitch (right).

The pinafore-style bib (left) is embellished with Venetian-hemstitched lace insertion and gathered edging, as well as with corded pintucks. The square collar (upper right) has tatted edging attached with the Venetian hemstitch, ribbon appliquéd with the Parisian hemstitch, and rows of Turkish hemstitching. On the spoke collar (center), lace insertion and edgings were attached with the Parisian hemstitch. The batiste collar (lower right) features rows of lace joined with fagoting.

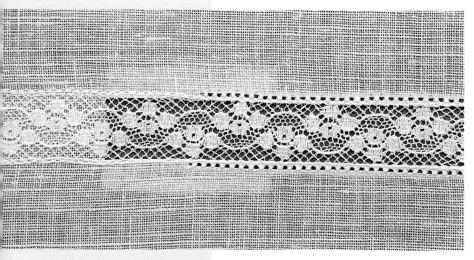

The sample above shows the stages of hemstitching insertion laces using the second method. From left to right:
1. The lace is straight-stitched in place.
2. The fabric behind the lace is cut (photo at right) and pressed to the sides.
3. Parisian hemstitching is worked along the folded edges.
4. Excess fabric on the back is trimmed away.

fabric right next to the lace heading (see the top photo on p. 105). If you wish, carefully trim the fabric from behind the lace, as I did on the blouse on p. 62. Always stitch a test sample and adjust settings.

With the second method, after you have straight-stitched the lace in place (the photos above illustrate the process):

1. Carefully cut down the center of the fabric behind the lace.

2. Press each side back toward the fabric along the stitching line. For shaped lace, like curves or loops, clip into the seam allowance where necessary so that it can be pressed flat.

3. Parisian hemstitch so that the forward and reverse stitches are on the fabric close to the fold and the stitch to the side goes just over the fold and into the lace.

4. Trim the excess fabric from the back.

Edging laces Edging laces have one straight side (the heading) and one scalloped side. They are applied, either flat or gathered, on an outside edge—for example, on collar edges or on any ruffled edges.

To attach edging laces using the first method:

1. With right sides up, straight-stitch (length 2mm) the lace heading to the fabric about $1/2$ in. from the fabric edge. Use a regular needle and basic sewing foot.

2. Switch to the desired hemstitch needle. Hemstitch so that the large holes in the fabric are next to the lace heading and one side of the stitch is just over the heading.

TIP ✶ Laces whose headings (straight edges) are narrow give better results for hemstitching, especially since with some hemstitching techniques, the headings remain showing.

✶ Many "cotton" laces today have up to 10 percent synthetic fibers. To avoid damage when pressing, use a medium (not high) setting on the iron.

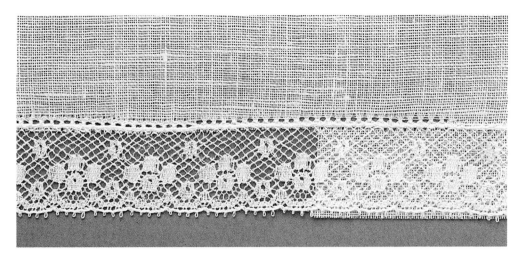

For hemstitching edging laces using the first method, the lace is straight-stitched in place, then hemstitched. This sample shows Parisian hemstitching (right) and Venetian hemstitching (left). The fabric behind the lace is trimmed away afterward, as at left.

3. Carefully trim the excess fabric from behind the lace. (A sample is shown in the photo above.)

Most good-quality laces have threads in the heading that can be pulled for gathering. If the lace does not have a pull thread, stitch one or two rows of slightly lengthened straight stitching (length about 3mm) along the heading. Do not starch lace that is to be gathered.

To attach gathered lace, the first method is usually best:

1. Pull one or two gathering threads in the heading to gather the first few inches of the lace. Do not gather lace too fully except where it is to be attached to sharp curves or corners.

2. Stitch the gathered lace onto the fabric in the desired position with a straight stitch (length 2mm) or tiny zigzag stitch (width 1mm, length 1.5mm) along the heading, gathering the lace as you go. Use a regular needle (size 70) and basic sewing foot. (If the gathered heading is bulky, use a satin-stitch foot.)

3. Switch to the desired hemstitch needle, and hemstitch with one side of the hemstitch on the fabric and the other side over the lace heading. Both the Parisian and Venetian stitches work well (a sample is shown in the photo below). The large holes will be in the fabric right next to the lace heading. Always stitch a test sample and adjust settings.

4. Carefully trim the fabric from behind the lace.

TIP On collars and pinafore-style bibs that are to be lined, the seam attaching the garment to the lining may be eliminated by hemstitching the gathered lace to both layers, as was done on the bib in the bottom photo on p. 105. Cording the hemstitching will add stability and strength, but this technique is not recommended for loosely woven fabrics.

Gathered lace is first stitched in place, then hemstitched along the heading. This sample shows Parisian hemstitching (right) and Venetian hemstitching (left). The fabric has been trimmed behind the portion at left.

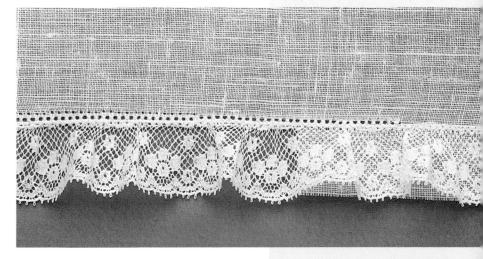

For hemstitching edging laces with the second method, the lace heading is straight-stitched about ½ in. from the fabric edge (right sides together) with the scallops away from the fabric edge (right). Then the seam allowance is pressed toward the wrong side of the fabric with the lace extending (left).

To attach edging laces using the second method:

1. Position the lace and fabric right sides together, so that the scalloped edge of the lace faces away from the fabric edge and the heading is about $^1/2$ in. from the fabric edge. Straight-stitch the lace heading to the fabric using a regular needle and basic sewing foot.

2. Press the seam allowance (the $^1/2$ in. of fabric along the edge) toward the wrong side of the fabric along the seam line so that the scalloped edge of the lace extends from the fabric, as shown in the photo above.

3. Switch to a hemstitch needle, and with right side up, Parisian hemstitch so that the large holes are in the fabric near the folded edge and the stitch to the side goes just over the folded edge and into the lace. Trim the excess fabric from the back. (A sample is shown in the top photo on the facing page.)

Side-by-side adjoining laces Use the technique described here for attaching two side-by-side lace insertions (as seen on the front of the pinafore-style bib in the bottom photo on p. 105) or an insertion and an adjoining edging to fabric.

Arrange the laces so that their designs meet in a pleasing way.

1. Spray-starch, and press the laces as straight as possible, without stretching.

2. Stitch one lace insertion onto the fabric in the desired position with a straight stitch (length 2mm) or tiny zigzag (width 1mm, length 1.5mm) along both headings. Use a regular needle (size 70) and basic sewing foot. Do not straight-stitch the other lace in place in case you need to adjust the spacing between the laces.

3. Switch to the desired hemstitch needle and, if necessary, a satin-stitch foot. Stitch the Venetian hem-stitch between the two lace head-ings so that one side of the stitch goes over one heading and the other side goes over the other heading, stitching it in place (see the photo below). Always stitch a test sample to determine exactly how far apart the headings should be.

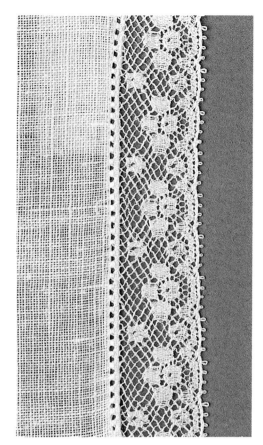

In this sample of the second method of attaching edging laces, Parisian hem-stitching was worked over the lace heading and the folded edge of fabric. The excess fabric has been trimmed from the back.

Two side-by side adjoining laces can be hemstitched using the Venetian stitch. In the left section of the sample the stitch is corded.

TIP If the lace heading itself is cordlike, it is not necessary to cord the side of the stitch that goes over it. For example, to Venetian-hemstitch such a lace to fabric, cord would be needed only on the side of the stitch that goes into the fabric (see the photo at right). To Venetian-hemstitch two insertions with cordlike headings side by side, additional cord may not be needed at all. Likewise, the gathered heading of laces may be thick enough to have the same raised effect as cord.

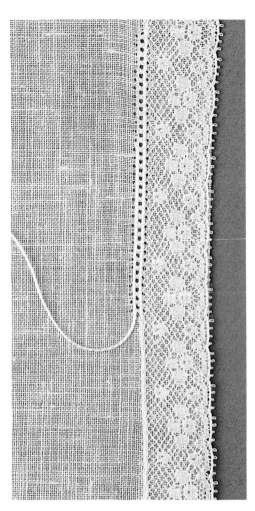

Cording the hemstitches for attaching lace to fabric (center of sample) adds stability and a finished appearance.

If you don't have the Venetian hemstitch, use the Parisian hemstitch between the laces, with the stitch to the side catching the heading of one lace. Then pivot the fabric and stitch the second pass, hitting the same holes between the laces and letting the stitch to the side catch the other heading.

If you wish, carefully trim the fabric from behind the lace.

Attaching lace with corded hemstitches Hemstitches attaching lace can also be corded. The cord creates a more raised and finished appearance and also adds stability. In general, the cord(s) should be directly over the lace heading(s). A presser foot with holes or grooves to guide the cord is ideal. (Cords, presser feet, and cording different stitches are discussed on pp. 88-92.) With Venetian hemstitch, you can stitch over two cords and lace headings at one time, creating the look of lace joined with entredeux.

HEMMING

Besides replicating the open look of hand hemstitching by withdrawing threads at a hem (described on pp. 84-88), you can use hemstitching to put in a hem or to topstitch over a skirt, sleeve, pocket, or square-collar hem. There are two basic methods to hem with hemstitching. One involves hemstitching through the garment and a single-fold hem. The other involves Parisian hemstitching the traditional double-fold hem. Either method works well to hide a crease line when you are letting a hem down.

Single-fold hemstitched hem For the single-fold hem, any of the hemstitching methods and stitches, as well as cording, can be used. It is a great way to hem sheer fabrics where a traditional hem would be unattractive (see the photo on p. 94). Shaped hems, where the lower hem edge is straight and the stitched edge of the hem is shaped—for example, in large scallops or zigzags—are especially easy to do with this method. (In this instance, the seam allowance of the shaped edge is not turned underneath.)

1. Press the hem with the raw edge to the wrong side.

2. Hemstitch from the right side, so that the stitching is at least 1/4 in. from the raw edge of the hem allowance underneath.

3. Trim the excess hem-allowance fabric to the hemstitching, as shown in the photo at right.

Double-fold hemstitched hem For the traditional double-fold hem, the Parisian hemstitch is preferred, although other hemstitches can be used. The Parisian hemstitch is easy to do and gives the look of an elegant hand pin-stitched hem.

1. Press the raw edge of the hem allowance under about $^3/_8$ in., then pin the hem in place.

2. Since the Parisian hemstitch often looks the same from either side, you can usually stitch this hem wrong side up, as shown in the photo below. Stitch a sample to test. The forward and reverse stitches should be on the single layer of the garment close to the hem. The stitch to the side should be just wide enough to catch the hem. An

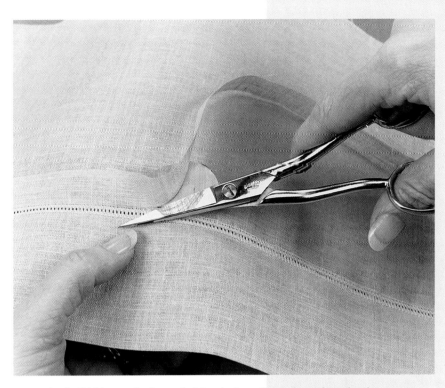

On a single-fold hem, the hemstitching is done from the right side, then excess fabric is trimmed from the wrong side. This method is good for sheer fabrics.

adjustable blind-hem, edging, or similar foot will help with guiding. (Changing the needle position may be necessary to align this stitch with the guide on some feet.) If necessary, use a basic zigzag foot. Guide the fold just left of center, in most cases.

If you wish to cord the stitch or if the stitch looks better from the right side:

1. Straight-stitch the hem in place from the wrong side close to the turned-under edge. Use fine thread, a fine needle (usually 70 Universal), and normal stitch length (about 2mm).

2. Hemstitch (over cord, if you wish) from the right side, so that the stitch to the side goes into the hem and the forward and reverse stitches creating the large holes are in the single layer of fabric next to

The Parisian hemstitch is a good choice for hemstitching a double-fold hem. It can usually be stitched from the wrong side. The forward and reverse stitches are right next to the hem, and the stitch to the side catches the hem.

TIP Shaped turned-edge hems and borders (like the scalloped hems covered in chapter 8 and pictured on both the white-and-yellow linen dress hem and collar on p. 160 and the cream-and-royal pillowcase on p. 168) are hemstitched like double-fold hems. Align the forward and reverse Parisian hemstitches on the single layer of the garment close to the hem. The stitch to the side should be just wide enough to catch the hem. An open-toe foot will give the visibility necessary to follow the hem shape.

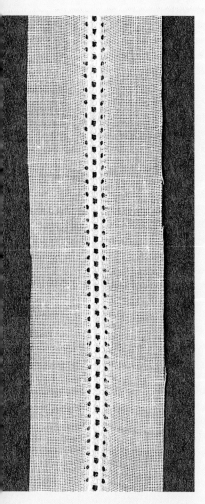

the hem. (Use a 120 Universal or other large needle for hemstitching.) The line of straight stitches acts as a guide and usually will be covered by the cord or disguised by the stitching so that removal is not necessary. However, if the straight stitching shows too much on your test sample, stitch it a little farther from the turned-under edge, using a stitch length of about 3mm and slightly loosened upper tension. Use the stitching as a guide, then remove it.

Additional applications for hemstitching include stitching a narrow hem and hemstitching at the same time (see pp. 190-191) and cording the Venetian hemstitch to create fagoting that resembles entredeux (see pp. 146-148).

Questions

I want to purchase a sewing machine with the Parisian hemstitch (pin stitch) and the Venetian hemstitch. Is there a moderately priced machine with these stitches?

These stitches are most often included on the mid-range to top-of-the-line machines. Check the chart on pp. 195-197 for machines with these stitches. If the current models are out of your price range (remember to inquire about sales), ask the dealer about good used machines.

Is it possible to make entredeux on the sewing machine?

The corded Venetian hemstitch can look remarkably like entredeux (see the photo at left). But why make entredeux on a strip of fabric, only to have to trim it and zigzag it to lace or fabric, when you can do it all in one step? Cord the Venetian hemstitch when using it for any of the applications described in this chapter, and you will have the look of entredeux without the additional steps and seam allowances.

In the rare event that you do need to make the entredeux separately (for example, if the garment fabric is not appropriate for hemstitching), follow the instructions for corded Venetian hemstitch on p. 91. Use fine machine-embroidery cotton thread, such as Madeira size 80 or Mettler size 60/2. Use size 8 pearl cotton or topstitching thread/buttonhole twist for the cord.

Good-quality purchased entredeux comes on a strip of Swiss batiste. But since all, or at least most, of the fabric is trimmed after it is applied, you can substitute a similar fabric such as a pima cotton batiste. Stitching crossgrain (selvage to selvage) is always easiest. If you need a longer length than the fabric width allows, remove the selvages and overlap the fabric by about 1/4 in. Another option is to piece stitched lengths together, overlapping one or two holes when applying it, the same way entredeux is pieced.

Put a lightweight tearaway stabilizer under the fabric. Tear it away gently after stitching. A size 100 wing needle will create good-sized holes but is hard on the fabric. For a more delicate look, like that of baby entredeux, try a 120/19 Universal needle. The automatic stitch settings on most machines are too wide and long. Narrow and shorten them to approximate the size of entredeux.

I have not been able to get good results using a wing needle to hemstitch lace onto polyester/cotton batiste dresses for my daughter. My attempts at hemstitching down the front of a polyester/cotton (65 percent polyester, 35 percent cotton) broadcloth blouse for myself look terrible. Help!

It is the polyester in both these fabrics that makes your hemstitching problematic. It is very difficult to hemstitch polyester/cotton broadcloth, especially lengthwise (parallel to the selvage), without getting unsightly puckering. Try the following recommendations for hemstitching any difficult fabric:

✘ Avoid hemstitching long lengthwise rows. Consider using just touches of crossgrain hemstitching instead. For example, on a girl's batiste dress, hemstitch lace to the edge of smocked or gathered sleeves and possibly to the collar. On your blouse, hemstitch the collar and possibly the pocket or, if it is short sleeved, hem the sleeves with hemstitching.

✘ Prewash broadcloth or other fabrics where sizing on the surface could be a factor. Stabilize the fabric. First, try multiple applications of spray starching and pressing. If the test samples still pucker, use a lightweight tearaway stabilizer under the fabric. After stitching, tear it away very gently.

✘ Use a new, good-quality Universal needle. A wing needle usually causes puckering on fabrics other than loosely woven cottons and linens. Use the smallest size that will give the desired effect. (Remember that for the stitching to resemble hand pin stitching, the holes should be only slightly enlarged.)

✘ Use fine machine-embroidery cotton thread, such as Madeira size 80 or Mettler size 60/2.

✘ Use a simpler hemstitch, such as the Parisian hemstitch, with fewer stitches in its pattern.

✘ Use a short stitch length and a narrow width.

✘ Try a basic metal zigzag presser foot to hold the fabric more securely. If a satin-stitch foot is needed, a metal one will hold better than a plastic one.

✘ Stitch at a smooth, even, slow to medium speed.

✘ Try cording the hemstitching. It adds stability.

✘ If there is puckering, loosen upper tension (i.e., adjust to a lower number). If the stitches are too loose, tighten upper tension only as much as absolutely necessary.

Always stitch a test sample with conditions the same as on the garment, including grain direction and stabilizer. If you try all these tips and there is still unsightly puckering, the best solution may be to change either the embellishment or the fabric. Because of its tight weave, 100 percent cotton (pima or pinpoint cotton) broadcloth is not as easy to hemstitch as linen, but it is much easier than polyester/cotton broadcloth. Chambray (the one used for the blouse on p. 103 is 80 percent cotton/20 percent polyester and comes in white and pastel colors), Swiss cotton piqué, and, of course, other fabrics with a high percentage of linen or cotton are all good choices.

Replicating Vintage Lace and Entredeux Techniques

An elegant yet simple, imported-cotton lawn nightgown features twin-needle pintucks and joined entredeux, beading, and laces.
(Pattern adapted from Margaret Pierce's Ladies Gowns.)

$\mathcal{F}$ortunately, there has been a return of appreciation for all things classic, vintage, and heirloom, including the handsewn look on garments and linens. I started teaching machine heirloom sewing in 1981 and started writing about it shortly afterward. Since then, its popularity has grown far beyond the world of smockers and heirloom sewers (who were among the first to revive this art), as evidenced by the appeal of *Victoria* magazine.

We can easily replicate the techniques and materials used on the fine handsewn garments of the late 1800s to early 1900s. Although done elsewhere, this handwork was most often associated with that done in convents by French nuns, so it is often referred to as "French hand sewing." Machine heirloom sewing refers to machine methods of achieving a French handsewn look. We can now create these beautiful things in a fraction of the time that it took by hand, and they are much stronger than those entirely handsewn. Of course, you can combine

Lace insertion, ribbon woven through an entredeux-edged beading, and softly gathered lace edging grace the hemline of a luxurious silk charmeuse petticoat. The laces and beading were dyed in coffee to match the ivory-colored silk.

hand and machine techniques, too. For example, you can do smocking or embroidery by hand but attach lace and construct the garment by machine. Ideally from the right side (without using a magnifying glass), the garment should still appear to be handsewn.

Typical heirloom items include baby garments (especially christening gowns), little girls' and doll dresses, collars, pinafore-style bibs, pinafores, dressy aprons, bonnets, and slips. For older girls and ladies, there are: blouses, skirts, collars, jabots, nightgowns, camisoles, slips, and petticoats. Table and bed linens,

handkerchiefs, and pillows are other possibilities.

Do you feel machine heirloom sewing is too frilly for your taste? It can be tailored, especially when combined with pintucks, shadow work, hemstitching, or fagoting. For example, a linen blouse with pintucks and tatting down the center front and sleeves, like the one on p. 62, can be simple yet elegant. Vintage garments show wonderful examples of such combinations.

Do you live in a colder region and think you and your children would freeze in anything with machine heirloom sewing? Put an heirloom jabot, collar, or bib (like the ones shown on p. 105 and p. 140), or a pinafore/apron (like the one on p. 67) over a heavier fabric, like velveteen or wool challis. The collars are also very pretty with dressy sweaters.

Look in fine stores, magazines, and ads for ideas and inspiration. *Creative Needle* and *Sew Beautiful* magazines, in particular, feature heirloom sewing. (See Resources on p. 199.)

Use only good-quality materials. You will be disappointed in the results if you don't. Yes, these materials can be expensive, but there are easy ways to keep the cost down. If you are on a budget, use good quality but less quantity. For example, make a beautiful detachable collar, bib, or pinafore similar to those on p. 67 and p. 105. These take little yardage, will not be outgrown for years, and are beautiful over different dresses for different seasons and looks. Also use fewer rows of a fine lace rather than many rows of a cheap, nylon lace. Use more pintucks and

Doll clothes and linens embellished with fine trims and decorative stitching are fun to sew. They also provide a great way to use leftover bits of trim and fabric. This doll dress with folded tucks, beading, and embroidered edging was stitched by Carol Clements.

Miniature bed linens for a special doll or full-sized linens for a gift or for yourself are perfect projects for experimenting with all fine machine-sewing techniques. This sheet and the pillowcases were finished with entredeux and a wide embroidered edging. The tiny sham on the center pillow showcases twin-needle pintucks and scallops with entredeux along the edge, and the bolster pillow cover has a "no-trim-around" scalloped edging.

✖ White entredeux and cotton laces may be dyed ecru in 1 cup of coffee or tea with 2 tablespoons white vinegar added (see the photo on p. 116). Remove the trims from the solution when they are lighter in color than you want. Rinse, pat with a towel, and dry flat. You can always repeat the process to make them darker. (Additional tip: We dyed white satin ballet slippers the same way for the flower girls in my daughter's wedding. See the photos on p. 66.)

✖ Be careful not to stretch fabric, laces, or trims when pressing, stitching, or handling. If they are stretched—for example, during pressing—and stitched to the project that way, they will shrink when washed, causing puckering.

hemstitching. These add greatly to the look without adding to the expense. These classic looks never really go out of style.

Though much faster than handsewing, this is not the kind of sewing you do in a rush. You are creating heirlooms. Working with these fine materials and creating something special for yourself or someone you love can truly be a joy.

Fabric: Traditionally, fine, all-natural fabrics are used, and these will give the prettiest results. Swiss cotton batiste, handkerchief linen, and Swiss organdy are the classic choices, followed by pima cotton, wool challis, and lightweight silk. Your fabric pieces should be "on grain." To straighten or cut, clip through the selvage. Then pick up a thread, and gently pull it. When it breaks, cut to that point, then pick up another thread and continue. This gets easier with practice and is worth the effort for the difference it makes in how your garment hangs. Good-quality, lightweight polyester/cotton blends may be used, but prewash them.

Entredeux: A trim typical of the French handsewn look, entredeux literally means "between two." It looks like a row of tiny squares (with holes in the middle of each square) stitched down the middle of a narrow strip of batiste. Entredeux is decorative and adds strength. It may be used between two laces, two fabrics, or between fabric and lace. If entredeux will be applied to a curve, clip into the batiste enough to allow shaping into a similar curve, press, let cool, and handle with care to maintain the shape. The right side of the entredeux is more rounded and smoother than the wrong side.

Trims for heirloom sewing include entredeux, fine laces, and embroideries: (top to bottom) entredeux, entredeux beading, lace beading, lace insertion, lace edging, eyelet insertion with entredeux, eyelet edging, eyelet edging with entredeux.

Lace: For the best results, use laces with a high percentage of cotton. Any lace that will not be gathered should be spray-starched and pressed carefully without stretching. (Spray starching and pressing also preshrink the lace, which is especially important with tatting and Cluny laces.) Most "cotton" laces today have up to 10 percent synthetic fibers for strength. To avoid damage when press-

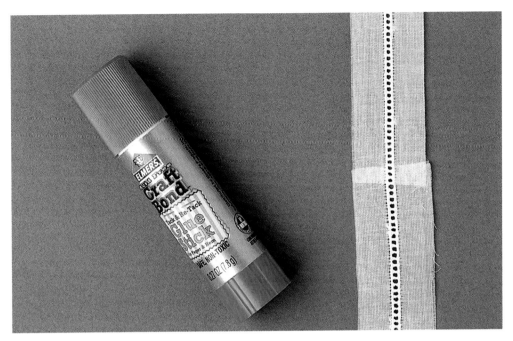

Entredeux may be pieced by overlapping a couple of the squares so that the holes align. To prevent shifting, use fabric glue stick to hold the overlapping batiste edges in place. Let the glue dry, then use as if one piece.

ing, use a medium (not high) setting on the iron.

Insertion laces are straight on both edges and are "inserted" within the garment rather than along an outside edge. They are applied straight or in shapes almost anywhere on a garment—yokes, sleeves, skirts, and so on. Beading is a trim (most often lace insertion) with openings through which ribbon may be woven.

Edging laces have one straight edge and one scalloped edge. Use on the edges of sleeves, ruffles, collars, and so on.

Embroidery: Embroidered strips of fabric, both insertions and edgings, are often used in heirloom sewing. The better ones are called "handlooms." Pretty white-on-white embroideries are readily available. These often already have entredeux on the edge, which saves money and time.

Consider making your own embroidery with your decorative stitches. Be sure they look delicate to go with the fine fabrics and laces.

Thread: Most often fine machine-embroidery cotton—Madeira size 80/2, YLI Heirloom 70/2, Mettler 60/2, or DMC 50. Finer thread (indicated by a higher size number) will show less and look more like handsewn, but do not use it for construction on projects where strength is a concern. For example, the size 80/2 or 70/2 thread may be used throughout the project for a doll's dress, pillow, or collar, but for an active toddler's outfit, after using fine cotton thread to attach laces, entredeux, etc., I would switch to Coats Dual Duty Plus Extra-Fine Cotton-Covered Polyester for Lightweight Fabrics for seaming. It is fine, but its polyester core makes it strong.

White thread may be used on pale pastel fabrics.

TIP ✹ The straight edge(s) with heavier threads on laces are called headings.

✹ For most techniques, laces whose headings are narrow give pleasing results more easily than those with wide, thick headings.

✹ Wide headings may look bulky in applications where the heading remains visible or where the lace is gathered. When choosing laces for these applications, I look for those with narrower headings first. If, however, I fall in love with a lace with a wider heading, I check to see if a few of the heavier threads in the heading may be removed to make it less bulky. Test to see if some of the threads can be removed without too much effort and without damaging the lace. (Leave at least two or three in place for gathering.) Removing these threads may take some time, so I usually choose to do it on smaller lace projects.

✹ If the right and wrong side of a lace are different, choose the side you like for the right side, and be consistent in using it. If the right and wrong side of a lace are not obvious, do no worry about it.

Needle: Use the smallest size appropriate for the fabric and thread being used—most often 60-70 Universal with fine cotton thread, and 70 Universal with Coats Dual Duty Plus Extra-Fine for Lightweight Fabrics.

Foot: Use a presser foot that holds the fabric and laces as securely as possible. For most straight stitching and flat zigzagging (for example, to attach flat lace to flat lace), use a basic metal zigzag foot. An edging foot with a center guide is helpful for many of the joining techniques.

Straight-stitch feet (including patchwork, quilter's, and ¼-in. feet) will help prevent puckering when seaming lightweight fabrics. Patchwork, quilter's, and ¼-in. feet have guides for the accurate narrow seams essential to this kind of sewing.

The most common way to finish fabric edges in machine heirloom sewing is the machine version of a hand technique called rolling and whipping. For this finish, a zigzag over the fabric edge curls the edge inward and encloses it in a smooth, narrow roll. A foot that is indented underneath allows the fabric to roll. A satin-stitch foot, traditional buttonhole foot (with two grooves underneath), and even a pintuck foot should be tested to see which works best for this technique on your machine. If none of these gives good results, try the basic metal zigzag foot.

Upper tension: Slightly loosened to prevent puckering.

Pattern: The shops listed in Resources (on p. 199) have beautiful heirloom sewing patterns, but what is great about this kind of sewing is that you can truly design your own unique garment. Don't be scared. It's fun!

All you need are basic, simple patterns in classic styles. With a basic blouse pattern that buttons down the back, you can stitch pintucks, insert lace, and do anything else you like down the front and sleeves. With a girl's basic dress pattern, do any machine heirloom work you want on the bodice/yoke and around the skirt. (With patterns not designed for heirloom sewing, consider adding to the gathered skirt width for more fullness.)

Creating a block of fabric

In most cases, attach your laces, entredeux, and fabric, and do pintucks or any other embellishment work to create a

TIP Do not cut your laces, embroideries, entredeux, etc., into pieces ahead of time. Attach as needed, then cut.

How much to buy

Shops specializing in English smocking usually carry heirloom sewing supplies. They can be a great help with designing these garments and for figuring the supplies you will need.

Here are some guidelines for estimating how much entredeux, lace, embroidery, etc., to buy:

✗ For embellishing skirts with bands of trim, you will need the width of the skirt, plus about 2 in., times the number of times you want to go around the skirt. Example: For two rows of lace insertion around a 70-in. skirt width, purchase (70 in. + 2 in.) x 2 = 144 in. or 4 yd.

✗ Yoke, bodice, or collar: length (if rows will be vertical) or width (if rows will be horizontal) of pattern piece, plus about 1 in., times the number of rows. Example: For 2 rows of entredeux across the front of a 12-in. wide square collar, you need (12 in. + 1 in.) x 2 = 26 in.

✗ Gathered edging: usually use 2 to 2½ times the finished edge. Example: For gathered lace for sleeves 8½ in. wide, you need 8½ in. x 2 = 17 in. x 2 sleeves = 34 in.

✗ Lace will have to be gathered more fully around curves or corners, so allow more for those.

✗ Get more of any fabric or trim that has a design to match.

✗ Always get a little extra.

Create a block of fabric from which to cut the pattern piece by joining the laces, entredeux, and fabric.

block of fabric a little longer and wider than your pattern piece. That way, you are assured of accuracy when cutting out the pattern piece without having to be concerned with the amount of fabric taken up by decorative work. For example, for a yoke, you might start with an embroidered insertion to go down the center. (It should be the length of the yoke plus a little extra.) Then you might attach entredeux to each side of it. Attach lace insertion to the entredeux on each side. Then attach entredeux to the other side of the lace and attach fabric to the entredeux. When all the decorative work is done, lay the pattern piece over the fabric/lace block you have created (see photo above).

1. Sparingly mark the cutting line with a fabric marker.

2. Stitch (length about 1.5mm) just inside this line for stability.

3. Cut out the pattern piece.

If you are only doing heirloom work on the edges of the sleeves, cut them out of the fabric as usual. (Shorten sleeve-ruffle length if adding a wide edging, however.) If you are doing work on the sleeve itself (for example, pintucks and lace down the sleeves), create blocks and then cut the sleeves from them. Gathered skirts usually have no shape to cut out. Therefore, you only need to know the required width and length to make.

Techniques

As you create your block, usually you will start by sewing a strip of laces, entredeux, etc., together. Then you will sew this strip to the larger fabric piece. For each of these steps, you will be using one or more of the following techniques. There are many variations for most of these techniques. These are the ones that I find easiest and use the most.

ATTACHING LACE TO LACE

1. Align laces right side up, with headings just touching. If the headings are wide, you may slightly overlap them. Some laces have designs on them that are more pleas-

TIP ✼ Some fabric markers may leave markings that are difficult to remove from natural fabrics. Test the marker on a scrap. To be safe, mark no more than necessary. Remove markings before pressing, following the instructions on the marker package.

✼ Whenever possible, start with your pieces securely under the presser foot rather than trying to start stitching right at the edge. You will waste about 3/8 in. at the beginning of each row, but it is worth it. It takes much more time and effort to try to line up the pieces to start perfectly at the edge. Usually the edges are cut off when you cut out your pattern anyway.

✼ Gently pulling your top and bobbin thread tails may make it easier to start stitching at the beginning of a row.

ing if they are matched on adjoining laces. This is more important on
laces with large designs—like relatively big roses, for example—than
on those with small designs.

2. With the basic metal zigzag foot or
an edging foot with a center guide,
zigzag (width about 2.5mm, length
1mm), with one side of the zigzag
going into or just over one heading
and the other side of the zigzag going into or just over the other heading. The zigzag will pull the two
headings together. The stitch width

will vary slightly with the width
of the headings and how much of
the heading is caught in the stitch.
Test, because what looks best will
vary with the lace. Avoid stitching
into the lace beyond the heading or
making the joining wide or bulky.

ATTACHING LACE TO ENTREDEUX

1. Trim the batiste from one side of
the entredeux.

2. With right sides up, have the
trimmed side of the entredeux and

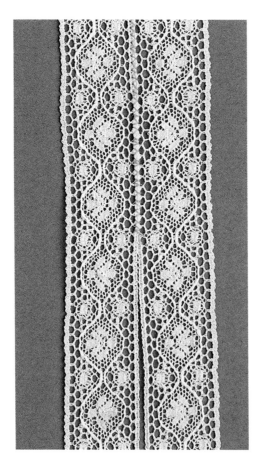

*To join laces, lay them side by side, right
sides up. Align the designs on the laces if
they look more pleasing that way. With a
fine zigzag, zig into or just over one heading,
and zag into or just over the other heading.
The zigzag will pull the two headings
together.*

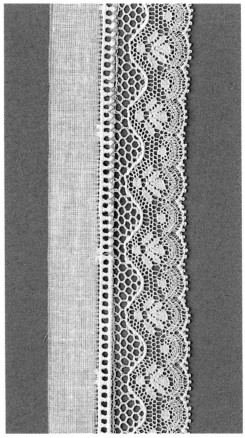

*To join lace to entredeux, align the trimmed
side of the entredeux and the lace heading
side by side, right sides up. With a fine
zigzag, zig into a hole of the entredeux, and
zag into or just over the lace heading. (In all
samples, contrasting thread was used to
make the stitching more visible.)*

the lace heading just touching. (If the lace heading is very wide, it may be just barely under the trimmed side of the entredeux.)

3. Zigzag (width about 2mm, length about 1mm), with one side of the zigzag going just over the lace heading and the other side going into the holes of the entredeux. It is ideal if the stitch goes into each hole of entredeux, so change the stitch length and make occasional adjustments as you stitch, if necessary. But if you keep the width narrow and never go across the holes of entredeux, you really do not have to worry about that.

ATTACHING LACE TO FABRIC

This method attaches lace to fabric and creates a rolled and whipped fabric edge.

1. Put the lace and fabric right sides together with the lace heading $^1\!/_8$ in. from the edge of the fabric.

2. Straight-stitch (length 2mm) along the heading.

3. Roll and whip the fabric edge with a zigzag (width about 4mm, length 1mm). Let the right side of the zigzag go completely over the edge of the fabric. The left side will go just into the lace heading. The fabric will roll toward the lace heading.

4. Open flat and press the roll toward the fabric.

5. Optional topstitch to keep the roll toward the fabric and to add strength: With the right side up, stitch a very tiny zigzag (width 1mm, length 1mm), with one side of the zigzag going just onto the

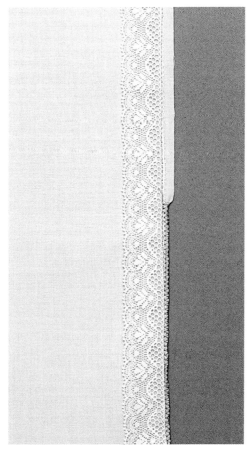

The steps for joining lace to fabric are:
1. Put the lace and fabric right sides together so that the lace heading is $^1\!/_8$ in. from the edge of the fabric. Straight-stitch along the heading (upper part of sample).

2. Roll and whip the fabric edge with a zigzag. Zig just into the lace heading, and zag completely over the fabric edge to roll it toward the lace (lower part of sample).

An optional topstitch will keep the roll toward the fabric. With the right side up and the roll pressed toward the fabric, stitch a very tiny zigzag with the zig just onto the fabric and the zag just onto the lace so that it is barely visible (lower part of sample).

lace and the other side going just onto the fabric. This zigzag must be so tiny that it is barely visible.

Lace may also be appliquéd onto the fabric—an ideal alternative for attaching lace to fabric in shapes (loops, diamonds, and so on). The two ways to appliqué lace to fabric are identical to the ways lace was hemstitched to fabric on pp. 104-108, except that a fine zigzag is substituted for the hemstitch on the final stitch-

TIP Accurate and con-
sistent stitching is critical
but easy to achieve, if you
find a line or an edge on a
presser foot or some other
guide to use. You may have
to watch where the needle
hits at the beginning of the
stitching, but after that,
use a guide rather than
watching the needle. (In
addition, your eyes will not
tire as quickly!)

Lace may also be appliquéd onto fabric. The two methods used are variations of the ways lace is hemstitched to fabric. (TOP) In the first, the lace is positioned in place, and the headings are stitched with a fine zigzag. The fabric behind the lace may be trimmed away. (BOTTOM) In the second, the lace is straight-stitched to the fabric (left), and the fabric is folded under along that stitching (center). A fine zigzag is then stitched over the fold and just into the lace (right). The excess fabric is trimmed away. This method is more secure and gives a more finished appearance.

ing. This is an excellent option for fabrics that are not appropriate for hemstitching and for machines without built-in hemstitches.

With the first method, the lace is positioned in place and the headings are stitched with a fine zigzag. The fabric behind the lace may be trimmed away if the fabric is tightly woven and the area will not get stress. (Lace or embroidered motifs may be appliquéd to fabric the same way, except substitute an open-toe foot so that the edge of the motif will be visible for stitching.)

In the second and more secure method, the lace heading(s) is straight-stitched to the fabric, then the fabric is folded under along that stitching. (For insertion laces, the fabric is cut down the center behind the lace, then each side is folded back and pressed. See the photo at right on p. 106. For edging laces, the seam allowance is pressed toward the wrong side of the fabric with the lace extending, as in the photo on p. 108.) From the right side, a zigzag is stitched over the fold and just into the lace. The excess fabric is then trimmed from the back.

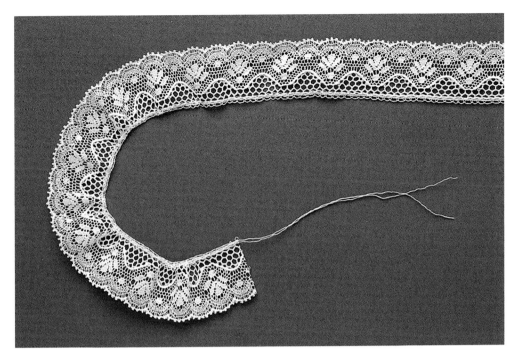

To gather lace, pick up and pull one or two of the threads in the lace heading with a pin or needle. If the topmost thread of the heading is loopy (as can be seen on the ungathered section above), try to pull it to eliminate the loops and create a neater heading to stitch (as seen on the gathered section below). Test first.

For all of these, use a very fine zigzag that is secure but barely visible. Start with a width of 1.5mm and a length of 1mm, then adjust according to the fabric and lace. Zig on the fabric next to the lace. Zag over the lace heading or fabric fold and just into the lace.

GATHERING LACE

1. Quality laces usually have pull threads in the heading to use for gathering. For a lace with no pull thread, create one by stitching a gathering thread (straight stitch length 3, loosened upper tension) on the heading.

2. Fold the lace in half, then in fourths, and then eighths if necessary for a long piece, and finger-crease. Mark these crease points on the heading. Do the same with the fabric or entredeux you will sew

the gathered lace onto. For evenly distributed gathers, these marks on the lace should be matched to the corresponding marks on the fabric or entredeux.

3. Use the point of a pin or needle to pick up one or two pull threads in the lace heading near the end where you will start sewing.

4. Gently gather the lace along the pull thread(s) for several inches. Do not gather the entire length ahead on a long project or the lace will twist and tangle.

5. The lace design will show more if a lace is not gathered too fully (especially on a narrow lace). But you should gather it more fully at corners and on curves or it will flip up.

TIP ✱ The presser foot will tend to flatten the lace, so gather the lace slightly more fully than desired as you guide it into the presser foot.

✱ A small wooden skewer, cuticle stick, or a similar tool to hold the gathered lace heading to the entredeux is helpful, especially with narrower laces.

✱ Wider gathered lace may be held with your fingers close to the right side of the presser foot. The side of your index finger moves along the side of the presser foot with the lace.

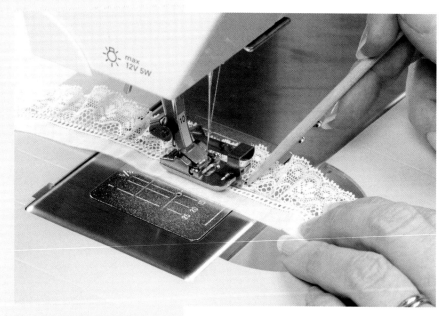

To attach gathered lace to entredeux, align the trimmed edge of the entredeux next to the gathered lace heading, right sides up. Zig into the holes of the entredeux, and zag into or just over the lace heading. A cuticle stick will help hold the gathered lace heading to the entredeux for stitching.

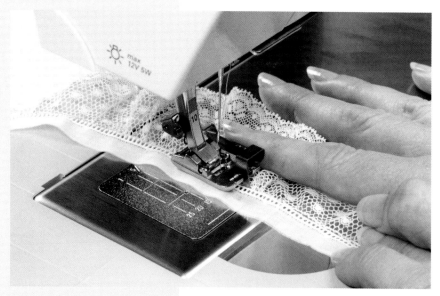

An alternative with wider laces is to hold the gathers with your fingers just to the right side of the presser foot.

ATTACHING GATHERED LACE TO ENTREDEUX

1. Trim batiste from one side of the entredeux.

2. Pull one or two heading threads to gather several inches of the lace.

3. Put the lace heading next to the trimmed edge of the entredeux, right sides up. (Flattening the gathers for about the first $1/2$ in. of the lace will make it easier to align the lace and entredeux at the beginning.)

4. Zigzag (width about 2.5mm, length 1mm), with one side going into the entredeux and the other side going into or just over the lace heading. Stop occasionally with the needle down in the entredeux, and lift the presser foot to adjust the gathers, as necessary.

5. Continue picking up a pull thread (when necessary), gathering, and stitching several inches at a time. Adjust fullness to match any markings, if necessary. Remember to gather more fully on corners and curves.

6. Trim hanging pull threads.

ATTACHING EXTREDEUX TO FLAT FABRIC

1. Do not trim the batiste from the entredeux. Put right sides together with the edge of the fabric even with the edge of the batiste on the entredeux. Straight "stitch in the ditch" as close to the entredeux as you can (length 2mm).

2. Trim both fabric edges (or seam allowances) to $1/8$ in. (If the fabric has tucks or other treatment that adds thickness, it will not roll easily. In this case, trim the entredeux batiste edge to just under $1/4$ in., and trim the thicker fabric edge to just under $1/8$ in.)

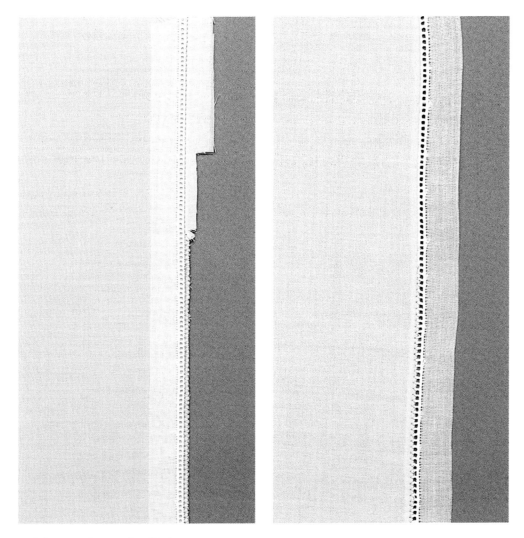

To join entredeux to flat fabric:

1. *(LEFT) Put the right sides of untrimmed entredeux and the fabric together with the edges even. Straight "stitch in the ditch" close to the entredeux (upper part of sample).*
2. *(LEFT) Trim both seam allowances to ⅛ in. (center). Zigzag to roll and whip the fabric edges. Zig right next to the entredeux, and zag over the edge of the fabrics (lower).*
3. *(RIGHT) An optional topstitch will keep the roll toward the fabric. With the right side up and the roll pressed toward the fabric (upper), stitch a very tiny zigzag, with the zig just barely onto the fabric and the zag onto the entredeux (lower).*

3. Roll and whip (width 3.5mm to 4mm, length 1mm), with one side of the zigzag going over the edge of the fabrics and the other side going right next to the entredeux. (With tucked or thick fabric, use a slightly wider and possibly slightly shorter stitch. The wider batiste next to the entredeux will roll over the narrower tucked fabric edge.)

4. Open flat, and press roll toward the fabric.

5. Optional topstitch to keep the roll toward the fabric: With right side up, stitch a very tiny zigzag (width 1mm, length 1mm), with one side of the stitch going onto the entredeux and the other side just barely onto the fabric. You don't have to

hit each hole of entredeux, just be sure you don't go across any part of the holes.

ATTACHING ENTREDEUX TO GATHERED FABRIC

1. Fold the fabric and the entredeux in half, then in fourths, etc., and mark these points.

2. Sew two rows of gathering threads (length 3mm to 3.5mm, upper tension loosened) $1/4$ in. and $5/8$ in. from the edge of the fabric. Use stronger thread (like polyester) for these gathering rows, if the strip to be gathered is long (like a ruffle around the bottom of a skirt).

3. Pin the fabric to the entredeux (right sides together) matching these marks for even gathers. Pull up the gathering threads, and adjust the gathers. The entredeux should be between the two gathering threads (see the top photo on the facing page).

4. Straight "stitch in the ditch" (length 2mm) as close to the entredeux as possible.

5. Pull out the gathering threads.

6. Trim the batiste entredeux seam allowance to just under $1/4$ in., and trim the gathered fabric edge to $1/8$ in.

7. Roll and whip the seam allowances (width 4mm to 5mm, length 1mm or slightly shorter), with one side of the zigzag going over the edge of the batiste and the other side going right next to the entredeux. The wider batiste next to the entredeux will roll over the narrower gathered-fabric edge.

8. Open flat, and press roll toward the fabric. (I usually omit the optional topstitch on the right side of gathered fabric because it can flatten the gathers.)

PUFFING

Puffing refers to a strip of fabric that is gathered on both sides and inserted into a garment for a decorative handsewn look.

Follow the same directions as for "Attaching entredeux to gathered fabric" on both sides of the fabric strip. Line up the halfway and quarter marks, etc., on the two sides so that the gathers will be even.

Construction

Heirloom projects are usually constructed with French seams (see p. 37). On batiste, organdy, and other lightweight fabrics, trim the first seam allowance to just under $1/8$ in. The final finished seam should be no wider than $1/8$ in. to $3/16$ in.

Classic closures are pearl buttons or tiny bar pins called beauty pins. I especially like to use beauty pins to close the back of detachable collars because they allow you to adjust the collar neck size for different garments. If ribbon is used, it should be double-faced because both sides show when it is tied.

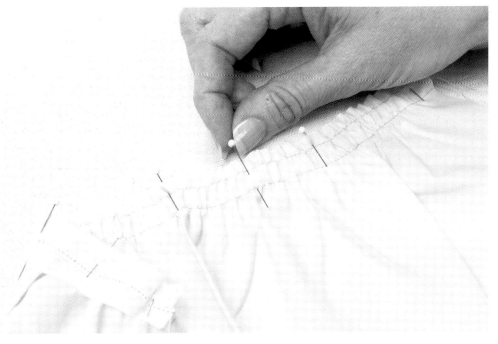

To join entredeux to gathered fabric:

1. Fold the fabric and the entredeux in half, then in fourths, etc., and mark these points. Straight-stitch gathering threads ¼ in. and ⅝ in. from the edge of the fabric. Pin the fabric to the entredeux (right sides together) matching these marks for even gathers. The entredeux should be between the two gathering threads. Adjust the gathers.

2. Straight stitch as close to the entredeux as possible.

3. Trim the batiste entredeux seam allowance to just under ¼ in., and trim the gathered fabric edge to ⅛ in. Roll and whip the seam allowances, with one side of the zigzag going right next to the entredeux and the other side just over the edge of the batiste. The wider batiste will roll over the narrower gathered-fabric edge.

Care and storage of heirloom garments

Generally, these garments should be washed in cool water by hand. (Ivory Liquid works well.) Rinse thoroughly several times. Absorb excess water with towels and lay flat to dry. Spray-starch, iron, and hang the garment, only if it will be worn within a few months. If there is embroidery on the garment, iron it with the right side down on a towel to avoid crushing the embroidery. Otherwise, these garments generally may be ironed from either the right or wrong side.

Store textile heirlooms clean, but not starched or pressed, in a new box lined with acid-free tissue (available at shops carrying machine-heirloom supplies), washed cotton muslin, or a clean cotton sheet. Do not store them in plastic. Use a cedar chest only for wool. Cushion folds and stuff sleeves with crumpled pieces of acid-free paper. About once a year, check the garment, and lay it on a bed to air out overnight.

Fold lines tend to weaken, so fold differently each time the garment is repacked.

I hope this introduction to heirloom techniques will encourage you to try it. Just a touch of lace or entredeux can transform a project from ordinary to vintage-looking. The shops listed in the Resources on p. 199 will gladly recommend books and patterns for additional information and inspiration.

Questions

Do you recommend preshrinking lace and entredeux?

It's really a judgment call. After several years of heirloom sewing, I noticed that, after some projects were washed, puckering showed up on areas where lace, entredeux, and embroideries were joined. It was obvious that a trim, most often the lace, had shrunk more than the trims and fabrics around it.

I now know that much of this problem occurs if any of the pieces being joined are inadvertently stretched. If stretched—for example, during pressing or stitching—a trim or fabric will shrink at least back to its original size when washed, causing puckering.

In testing many trims by measuring before and after preshrinking, I have found that some did indeed shrink quite a bit (in particular, heavier Cluny laces), while there was no measurable shrinkage in others.

On a very special project, it is always safest to take a little time and effort to test shrink a piece of each trim. Measure it, soak it in warm water for 5 minutes or so, pat gently with a towel, let dry flat, then remeasure. If there is more than slight shrinkage, then you will know to preshrink the entire piece.

Careful spray starching and pressing (with a medium heat setting), taking care not to stretch, seems to adequately preshrink most trims. Trims that will be gathered do not need starching and pressing, because there is ease in the gathers and starched lace is more difficult to gather.

I avoid preshrinking laces in water unless absolutely necessary, because it makes them limp and it takes quite a bit of effort to spray-starch and press them afterward. Shrinkage on entredeux and embroidered trims varies. Unlike lace, entredeux that has been preshrunk in water is still easy to handle. Of course, any entredeux or lace that has been dyed in coffee or tea has been preshrunk in the process.

If a large quantity of a trim is to be dyed or preshrunk in water, wrap it very loosely around a clean plastic lace bolt (ask if your heirloom shop has one to spare), a rectangular plastic storage-container lid, or anything similar. (For dyeing, avoid overlapping many layers, so that the dye can reach all the layers quickly and evenly.) This will keep the trim from twisting and tangling during the process. After it is dry, spray-starch the outer layers, unwrap, and press them. Continue, being careful to avoid any stretching, until the entire piece is pressed. My friend Janice Ferguson wraps trim around a piece of cardboard, ties the wraps together loosely on one side with ribbon, and slides it off the cardboard to wash, soak, or dye. Since the loops are tied, they do not tangle. After drying, most of the trim can be spray-starched at once, then unwrapped for pressing.

Do you recommend prewashing Swiss batiste or handkerchief linen before making a garment?

I rarely prewash either of these fabrics because I like to take advantage of the body they have before washing to make stitching easier. However, prewashing should be considered in situations where shrinkage or color bleeding could be a problem.

Most of the garments we make from batiste and handkerchief linen fit loosely, but for a more fitted garment, I would recommend prewashing a scrap of the fabric to check for shrinkage. (Measure the scrap before and after washing.) If there is more than slight shrinkage, it would be worth the precaution to prewash the fabric. Most of the body can be restored with spray starching and pressing.

Another possible reason to prewash would be to remove excess dye. For example, before doing white decorative stitching or adding a white trim to a dark-colored linen such as navy, black, or red, I would suggest prewashing the linen (or at least a test scrap). If any color bleeds into the water, keep rinsing until the water is clear.

Fagoting

$\mathcal{M}$any of the stitches on your sewing machine may be used for fagoting, a decorative technique used to join fabric or lace. With fagoting, space for decorative stitching is purposely left between the two pieces being joined. You can use fagoting to join two pieces of folded or finished fabric, or to join fabric to lace or lace to lace to create a look amazingly like handstitched fagoting (and without all the latter's basting and marking!). It is a beautiful effect that gives a classic, handsewn look to blouse fronts, yokes, sleeves, collars, lingerie, pinafore-style bibs or aprons, and table or bed linens. And it is also a decorative way to lengthen a dress or skirt. The sidebar on pp. 134-135 suggests ways to use this technique to embellish your garments.

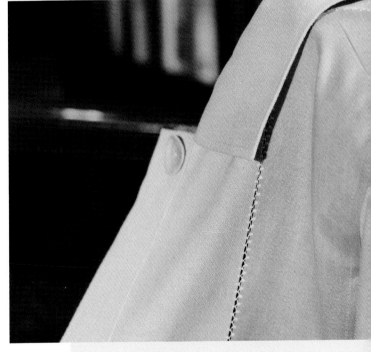

Fagoting can look tailored! Each fagoted panel on this tone-on-tone linen jacket is actually a wide turned tube of fabric, so there are no raw edges inside. (Because of the weight of the fabric, the seams are centered on the back of each panel, rather than pressed to the edge as they are on lightweight fabrics.) (Fagoting stitched by Carol Ahles, constructed by Nancy Snell.)

Fagoting fabric to fabric

The specifications for machine fagoting to join two fabrics are as follows:

Fabric: Usually light- to medium-weight wovens, but almost any fabric with body or fabric that can be spray-starched and pressed to give it body. Always test on scraps first.

Thread: Cotton or, for more shine, rayon. Experiment with other decorative threads. Thread size is determined by the look desired. For more visibility, thread two threads through the needle, or wind

Using fagoting on a garment

Fagoting and other decorative work should be done before the pattern piece is cut out. The garment must be planned to include a way to finish the raw edge under each fold. Since fagoting is often used on garments with a handsewn look, the fabric may be sheer. With sheer fabrics, simply overcasting the pressed-under edges is often unacceptable because this would show through the fabric.

Here are some creative but easy ways to finish the raw edges under the folds. (Keep in mind that, unless the fabric is very loosely woven, you can safely trim up to a medium to wide zigzag stitch and its variations.)

✗ Hemstitch through both layers an attractive distance from the fold, then trim away the excess fabric on the underside up to the hemstitching.

✗ Stitch a dense decorative stitch, such as a scallop (other than the tracery scallop, which is not dense), through both layers, then trim, as was done on the front of the blouse in the photo on p. 26.

✗ Use twin needles and a decorative stitch, such as a tracery scallop, to stitch through both layers, then trim (see the photo at right). The bobbin thread zigzags with twin-needle stitching, so that the excess fabric may be trimmed up to the stitching on the underside. The decorative stitch can "frame" the fagoting for the effect of embroidered insertion.

✗ Use twin needles with a straight stitch, catch both layers in pintucks, then trim.

✗ Plan the garment so that both layers extend to the outer edge of the project. The edges will be caught in the seams or attached to the edging. This method in effect gives the piece a lining and is suitable for small pieces such as a pinafore-style bib, yoke, or square collar.

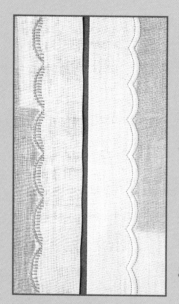

Scallops (a dense decorative scallop on the left and twin-needle tracery scallops at right) are attractive ways to finish the raw edges under each fold prior to fagoting. In either case, the excess fabric on the underside can be trimmed to the stitching.

✗ Zigzag over cord along the folded edges (see "Fagoting corded edges" on p. 138). Use a pintuck foot for fagoting, then trim away the fabric up to the stitching on the underside.

✗ Hide the raw edge in a folded tuck (see the photos at left on the facing page). This was done on the sleeves of the blouse on p. 26.

✗ Stitch the fagoting on narrow or rolled hem edges (as long as the stitching or bulk of the hem does not detract from the fagoting).

✗ Use turned tubes of fabric to provide finished folded edges for fagoting projects, like the neck-roll pillow covers (see the bottom right photo on the facing page) and the baby bibs (see the top photo on p. 143). See also the tip on p. 144.

heavier thread or cord onto the bobbin and sew with the right side of the fabric down. Thread color may match or contrast with the fabric color.

Needle: Appropriate for fabric and thread being used, most often 80 Universal.

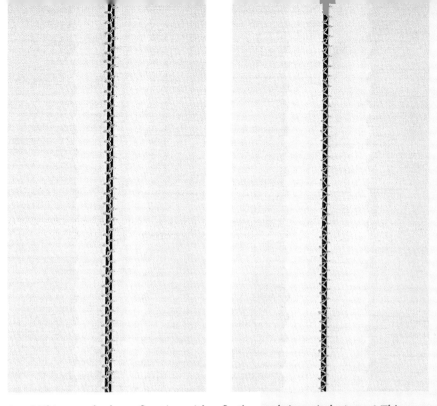

(*LEFT*) *This sample shows fagoting with a feather, or briar, stitch.* (*RIGHT*) *This sample is a honeycomb stitch (which looks very different stitched across space than it does on fabric).*

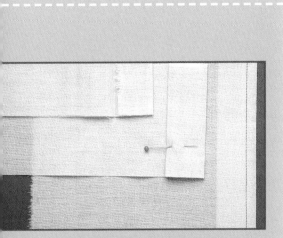

A folded tuck is a practical way to conceal the raw edge under the fold for fagoting.

1. *The raw edge is pressed under (1 in. in this sample).*
2. *The folded edge is turned and pressed again.*
3. *The tuck is stitched 1/4 in. from the second fold.*
4. *If the tucks are to frame the fagoting, they should then be opened and pressed away from the edge to be fagoted.*

These elegant fagoted neck-roll pillow covers reflect the renewed appreciation for luxurious bed linens. Tubes of fine imported cotton were first joined with handsewn-looking fagoting. These joined bands were feather-stitched (blue) and Parisian hemstitched (white) onto rectangles of the fabric cut to fit a standard bolster pillow form. The rectangles were seamed and ribbon casings on the sides created with a 6mm narrow hemmer.

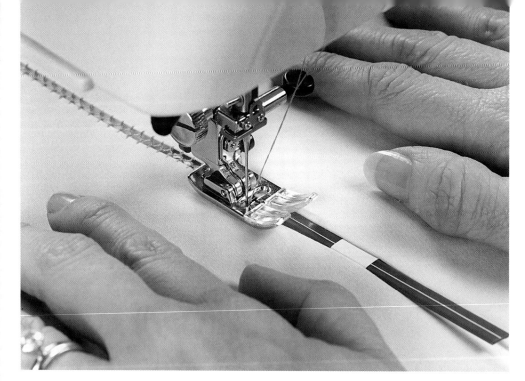

A flat coffee stirrer taped in front of the presser foot makes an effective long guide for fagoting straight strips of fabric or trim. The folded edges of the fabric are guided along each side of the stirrer.

TIP For machines that stitch only up to 4mm or 5mm wide, you can trim a plastic coffee stirrer to make it narrower, if necessary.

TIP ✖ It is easier to hold larger pieces of fabric. If you need smaller or narrower pieces, stitch larger ones and trim them afterward.

✖ If the fabric is rippling, try additional applications of spray starch and pressing before stitching. Be sure to keep the fabrics flat and parallel, and avoid doing a lot of adjusting.

✖ If the two pieces are being pulled together and the space between them is closing, try loosening upper tension a little more. Be sure the presser foot and your hands are holding the fabrics securely.

Foot: For the best results, the presser foot should hold the pieces being joined securely over the feed dogs and have a wide opening for the needle in order to accommodate a wide stitch—most often a basic metal zigzag foot. A pintuck or other foot can be substituted if it has grooves or markings that would be helpful for guiding the fabric edges, as long as it holds the fabric well. An open-toe foot may be advantageous for the visibility it allows, but it may be necessary to hold the project taut with your hands to compensate for the area in front not being held by the foot.

Stitch: Many stitches can be used for machine fagoting, including:

✖ feather and briar variations

✖ honeycomb

✖ cross stitch and herringbone variations

✖ overcasting or multiple zigzag

✖ block capital letter "I"

✖ Venetian hemstitch

Experiment with other stitches. With cord on the bobbin, choose less dense stitches, such as the multiple zigzag.

Width: 4mm to 6mm (or wider). Note: Stitch numbers and settings for some machines are listed on pp. 195-197.

Length: Varies with stitch used and look desired; most common range is 1.5mm to 2.5mm.

Tension: Significantly loosened upper tension (most often to about 2); normal bobbin tension usually. Do not put the bobbin thread through the hole in the finger of the bobbin case, if your machine has one. (With cord on bobbin: upper tension normal to tightened; bobbin tension loosened or bypassed.)

Accessories: Flat coffee stirrer or frame spacer (see "Guiding aids" on the facing page). For Elnas and Pfaffs, a fagoting plate. Slide-on sewing table for larger work surface, if your machine has one.

Always stitch practice samples first. Fold under about 1 in. to 1½ in. on the

136

two pieces of fabric. (For metric conversion, see the chart on p. 30.) Spray-starch and press several times; giving the fabric body helps prevent puckering and rippling. Hold the two folded edges parallel about 1/8 in. to 3/16 in. apart, and begin to stitch. The stitch should go into one folded edge, then "in the air" (across the space between the two fabrics), and into the other folded edge.

Adjust the space between the fabrics on your practice piece according to the stitch width. The stitches should look the same on both fabrics. If only one stitch is being taken on one fold and three stitches are being taken on the other fold, adjust your guiding so that the same number of stitches will be taken on each side. (In most cases, this will be one stitch.) Stitch slowly, with an even rhythm.

GUIDING AIDS

You can guide the two edges along markings on a presser foot or the needle plate on some machines. (For example, the two red lines on Pfaff foot #0A and the inner cutout on Viking foot #A are perfect fagoting guides with the settings on p. 197.)

Elna and Pfaff have wide and narrow fagoting plates that snap onto the needle plate of many of their models to help maintain an even distance between the two pieces. (On models with wider stitch-width capability, I prefer the wide fagoting plate.)

A flat coffee stirrer taped directly in front of the presser foot (or in front of the fagoting plate) makes a useful long guide for fagoting straight strips of fabric or trim. Simply guide the edges to be fagoted along each side of the stirrer. Since not all stitches are exactly centered, test to find the best placement for the stirrer. Stirrers come in slightly different widths for greater or less distance between the pieces. Look for suitable ones when you get coffee to go!

A similar guiding aid, recommended by my friend Kerry Reynold, is a short piece of a picture-framing spacer. These are clear plastic strips sold by the inch at framing shops. (About a 3-in. length of the 1/8-in.-wide spacer works well.) Remove the paper strip covering the adhesive to adhere the spacer in front of the presser foot. When no longer needed, lift the strip from your machine and reattach the paper strip.

About a 3-in. length of a 1/8-in.-wide framing spacer also makes a helpful fagoting guide. Remove the paper tape from the sticky side of the spacer and temporarily adhere in front of the presser foot.

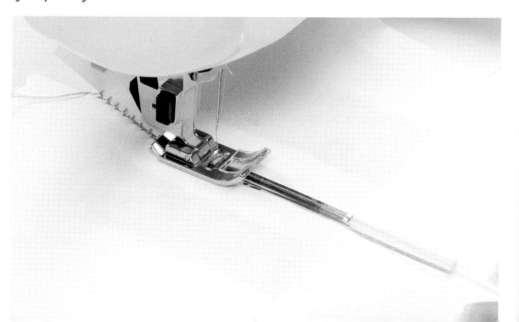

Feather and briar variations

Honeycomb

Cross stitch and herringbone variations

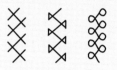

Overcasting or multiple zigzag

Block capital letter "I"

Venetian hemstitch

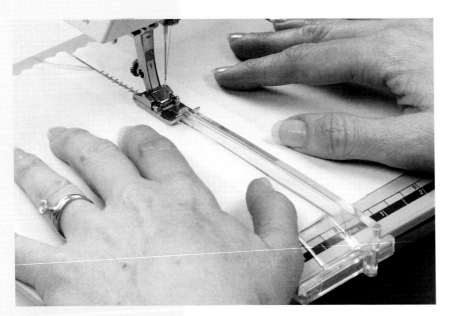

Create a fagoting guide on Bernina models with a clear-plastic seam guide (that slides along the front of the sewing table) by purchasing an extra guide and cutting it to fit into the open cutout space in the front of foot #1.

An excellent alternative on newer Bernina models with a clear-plastic seam guide (that slides along the front of the sewing table) is to buy an extra guide and trim the tip. Cut off just enough for the guide to fit into the open cutout space in the front of foot #1.

FAGOTING CORDED EDGES

If you find guiding tedious even with the guiding aids, try fagoting corded edges. First, cord each folded fabric edge by zigzagging over cord (see pp. 44-45). The cord and thread color may match or contrast with the fabric. The cord size should be appropriate for the fabric and the look desired. (For example, use relatively small size 8 pearl cotton for a delicate look on lightweight fabrics.) Since a five- or seven-groove pintuck foot is needed for the next step anyway, experiment with it for cording also. Guide the cord into the center groove, and align the fabric fold just to the left of it. Stitch so that the "zig" is into the fabric and the "zag" is just over the cord. Lifting, but

not pulling, the cord in front will help to keep it in the groove. Make the zigzag just wide enough for the stitch to "bite" securely into the folded fabric (a stitch width of about 2mm to 2.5mm); the length should be a little longer than a satin stitch (about 0.8mm). Adjust guiding and/or stitch width, if necessary.

For fagoting, position the corded edges under a five- or seven-groove pintuck foot so that the cord rides in the grooves right and left of center. This will make guiding much easier. Adjust the stitch width so the stitches go just into the fabric on each side. Unless the fabric is loosely woven, it may be trimmed away up to the stitching on the underside.

ALTERNATIVE METHODS

The method described above produces fagoting that looks the most like hand-stitched, but there are other ways to achieve the look of fagoted fabric to fabric on your sewing machine. Some of these involve stitching two flat pieces of

Guiding for fagoting is much easier when the fabric edges have been corded first. With a five- or seven-groove pintuck foot, you can guide the corded edges into grooves right and left of center.

fabric right sides together with a very loose stitch; the fabrics are then folded back along the stitching and pressed. The loose stitch (usually a zigzag stitched over a looping, fringe, or tailor-tack foot) allows space to be left between the two folded edges. The threads between the two sides may be bundled by hand with a needle and thread. Viking has a hem-stitch fork that goes between the two fabrics. The fabrics are stitched with a loose, long straight stitch between the prongs of the fork; the fork creates distance between the two fabrics so that when the fabrics are pressed open, the loose straight stitches become ladder-like fagoting.

A navy linen blouse gets a classic finish. The pocket and sleeves of this purchased garment were cut; the edges were folded and finished with a corded edge, then joined with briar-stitch fagoting. The pintuck foot makes easy work of guiding the corded edges for the fagoting.

TIP ✖ Ideally the cord is right along the folded edge. If it tends to roll to the top or underneath, try a different presser foot. If this still happens, it is acceptable as long as the cord is near the fold and consistent, i.e., not on top for part and underneath for part. If the cord consistently rolls under, consider stitching the corded edge with the fabric right side down so that the cord will be on top for fagoting.

✖ The corded edge may be used to finish a double layer of lightweight fabric. This was done on the upper pocket and lower sleeve pieces on the blouse at left rather than hemming these areas. To finish a double layer of fabric, straight-stitch the two layers together along the fold line before pressing the fold and stitching the corded edge. This step ensures that the two layers will not separate.

For this vintage-looking jabot, the tatted insertion was attached to the linen with the corded Venetian hemstitch. The tatted edging was then fagoted to the insertion with a handsewn-looking feather stitch.

Fagoting lace

The following are specifications for fagoting lace:

Lace: Best with mostly cotton laces that have narrow headings. (A heading is the straight edge on one side of a lace edging and on both sides of a lace insertion.) Very straight laces at least $^5/_8$ in. to $^3/_4$ in. wide are easiest to handle, but narrower laces may be used. (Embroideries with entredeux attached and some other trims also work well for fagoting.) The laces should be spray-starched and pressed several times, keeping them as straight as possible for straight applications and shaping for curved applications. Use medium heat, and take care not to stretch the laces.

Stabilizer: Tearaway or water-soluble stabilizer. With water-soluble stabilizer, press two layers together (between pressing cloths, with medium heat and little or no steam) to give more body, or use a heavier water-soluble stabilizer, like

TIP Take advantage of laces with a cordlike heading, like the tatting on the jabot by positioning the headings under the grooves just right and left of center on a five- or seven-groove pintuck foot. Similar to "Fagoting corded edges" on p. 138, consistent stitching will be easier.

Before fagoting, the tatted edging was spray-starched and pressed into a curved shape and fused to water-soluble stabilizer. Then the feather stitch and a seven-groove pintuck foot were used for fagoting the tatted edging to the insertion.

Super Solvy. To fuse fabric and/or lace temporarily in the desired position, lightly spray-starch the wrong side of the fabric or lace, lay it in place over the stabilizer, and press (again with a dry iron and press cloth). After stitching, tear or cut away excess stabilizer; the rest will dissolve with water.

There are two basic problems to deal with when fagoting lace. The first is that because lace is usually so soft and open, it easily gets distorted and pulled. The second is that holding the lace securely is difficult. Both conditions can cause the lace to be pulled out of shape and toward the piece to which it is being joined, closing the desired gap.

Compensate for lace's softness by carefully spray starching and pressing the lace several times until it is stiff. It is important not to stretch the lace. If it is stretched, then spray-starched, pressed, and stitched, it will relax with the first washing, causing ripples in your beautiful project.

The easiest way to compensate for the problem of holding the lace securely is to choose wider laces. I find that I can adequately hold the outside edge of a lace that is at least $3/4$ in. wide by using my entire index finger (not just the fingertip) as it passes under the presser foot. For a narrower lace or any lace that is difficult to hold, attach the lace to stabilizer so that you then have something that is easier to hold. Baste the lace (by machine with loosened upper tension) over a strip of tearaway stabilizer that is about 3 in. wide. Leave about $1/4$ in. of the lace (the heading plus a little extra) extending beyond the stabilizer so that the stabilizer will not be caught in the fagoting stitches. The loosened tension makes the basting stitches easy to remove when the stabilizer is no longer needed.

If the outermost thread along the lace heading is loopy (as on the left), pull it just taut enough to make the edge straight (as on the right). Test a small area first. This step ensures more attractive and secure fagoting and also works well for many other heirloom-sewing techniques using flat lace.

Another option is to fuse the lace temporarily to water-soluble stabilizer. Press two layers of stabilizer together, as explained previously, or use a heavier water-soluble stabilizer, like Super Solvy. Lightly spray-starch the back of the lace, lay it in place over the stabilizer, and press (with a dry iron and press cloth) to fuse.

Although you can stitch fagoting through water-soluble stabilizer, in most cases I prefer the look of fagoting stitched "in the air," so whenever practical I let

TIP If you want straight rows of fagoting, look for very straight laces.

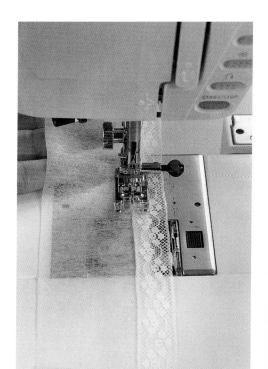

Basting a narrow lace to tearaway stabilizer makes it easier to hold the lace for fagoting. The edge to be fagoted should extend beyond the stabilizer about $1/4$ in.

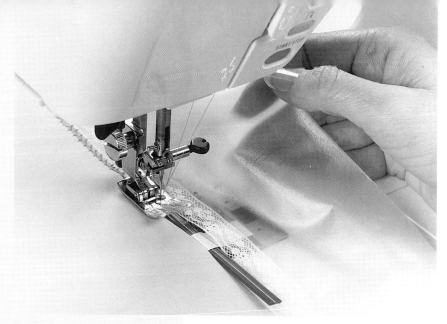

When fagoting lace to fabric, the fabric fold and the lace heading should be parallel and ⅛ in. to 3/16 in. apart. Here the lace has been temporarily fused to water-soluble stabilizer (two layers fused together) to make holding the lace easier. A coffee stirrer aids guiding.

the lace heading extend as described for tearaway stabilizer. (The exceptions to this are "Fagoting curved bias strips" on pp. 143-146 and "Fagoting with appliqué cord and the Venetian hemstitch," discussed on pp. 146-148.) The water-soluble stabilizer can usually be pulled gently from the lace after stitching and can even be reused. If your lace was very damp when it was fused, it will not pull away easily; so trim off the excess stabilizer, and dissolve the rest in water.

FAGOTING LACE TO FABRIC

Always stitch practice samples before working on your project. Spray-starch and press the folded fabric and the lace several times. Finish the fabric edge, using one of the suggestions in the sidebar on pp. 134-135 or any finish you prefer. A corded edge, done with a fine cord that matches the fabric, makes an attractive simple finish for fabric being fagoted to lace (see the lower collar in the bottom photo on p. 105). Unless the lace is wide enough to be held securely, baste it to tearaway stabilizer or temporarily fuse it to a water-soluble stabilizer.

Hold the fabric fold and the lace heading parallel about ⅛ in. to 3/16 in. apart, and stitch. The stitch should go into the

fabric fold, across the space, and then just over the lace heading, catching the heading only. Adjust the space and the guiding, if necessary. If the two edges are being pulled together, loosen upper tension a little more.

FAGOTING LACE TO LACE

As always, stitch practice samples first. Spray-starch and press the laces several times. If your project requires the other heading of one or both laces to be attached to fabric, this step is best done before the fagoting so that you will not have to attach the lace to stabilizer. Otherwise, baste the lace to tearaway stabilizer or temporarily fuse it to a water-soluble stabilizer.

Hold the two lace headings parallel about ⅛ in. to 3/16 in. apart, and stitch. The stitch should go just over one lace heading, across the space between the laces, and then just over the other lace heading. Catch only the headings with the stitches. Adjust the spacing, guiding, and tension, if necessary.

You may also want to test stitching through water-soluble stabilizer to see which method you prefer. If so, fuse one lace near the center of the water-soluble stabilizer. Lay the other lace about ⅛ in. to 3/16 in. from the fused one. Do not fuse this lace in place, because you would then have no way to adjust the spacing. Stitch as before. Instead of being "in the air," the stitching between the two laces will go into the stabilizer. After stitching, trim the excess stabilizer, then dissolve the rest in water. After the stabilizer has dissolved, notice on your test piece if the stitching between the laces has stretched, distorting the appearance of the stitch. Tightening tension slightly may help if the stretching is excessive.

Dressy baby bibs such as these can protect special garments until the last moment for a photo or can be added under the collar of a simple outfit to dress it up. This duo of bibs (one linen, one batiste) was inspired by some that were mine as a baby and used to protect the christening gown when my children were baptized. Fagoted narrow bias tubes on the edge and machine-pinstitched embroidered motifs from Capitol Imports add a touch of elegance.

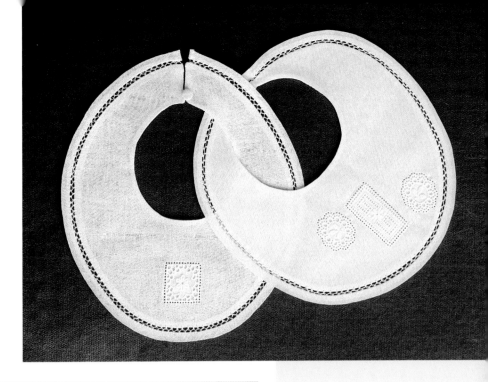

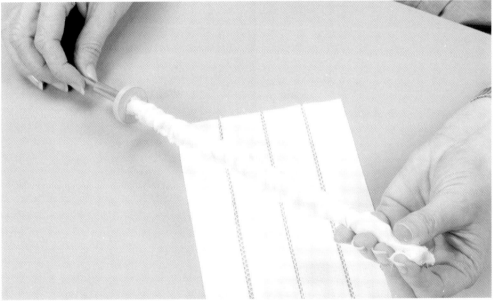

Turned tubes of fabric provide finished folded edges for fagoting. Fasturn cylinders make turning even very narrow fabric tubes easy.

TIP Before planning to stitch fagoting through any stabilizer, test on scraps first. Many factors, including the stitch density, affect ease of removal and the end result.

Fagoting curved bias strips

Narrow bias strips fagoted to curved collars, pockets, yokes, bibs, and so on, create an especially attractive handsewn-looking embellishment. Preparing the very narrow bias strips and stitching them to curved shapes with machine fagoting is a little more challenging than handling wider, straight strips. But a few tips and ever-emerging new products

make curved fagoting projects much easier than they used to be. Simple but elegant dressy bibs, like those shown above, are perfect for experimenting with these products and techniques.

As mentioned with fagoting lace, the major problem with fagoting very narrow pieces of fabric (or lace) is that they are difficult to hold securely for accurate guiding. And again, the solution is to adhere them to something, such as a stabi-

The decorative bands on the pillow with blue stitching (see the bottom right photo on p. 135) were made by joining three long turned tubes of fabric with feather and herringbone stitch variations for fagoting.

lizer, that is large enough to hold onto. When fagoting narrow strips to a curve, however, it is likely that you will need to stitch through the stabilizer. Therefore, it must be removable without disturbing any delicate stitching. One possible product that fills this bill is water-soluble stabilizer, as described above. Recently I have been experimenting with another product called Clear 'N Melt Stabilizer from America Sews (available from Viking dealers or by mail order from Clotilde). It also looks like clear plastic, but Clear 'N Melt disappears with low heat, which can be an advantage on projects that you do not want to wet after stitching. It also seems less likely to distort fagoting stitches than water solubles.

The following are specifications for preparing narrow bias tubes:

Fabric: Lightweight wovens, such as batiste and handkerchief linen.

Thread: For stitching narrow bias tubes, use a fine thread with the strength of a polyester core, such as Coats Dual Duty Plus Extra-Fine for Lightweight Fabrics (article #240). Avoid fine cotton thread, since it may break during turning.

Stitch: Seam very narrow bias tubes with a slight zigzag to allow some give for turning (length about 1.5mm, width about 0.5mm, upper tension slightly loosened to about 4).

PREPARING AND FAGOTING NARROW BIAS TUBES

1. Strips of fabric to be stitched to a curved shape should be cut on the bias. A rotary cutter, mat, and ruler will make cutting accurate bias strips quick and easy. Use the bias markings on the mat or purchase a large triangular ruler (available very inexpensively from office-supply stores).

2. Spray-starch and press the bias strip(s) carefully without stretching. This stabilizes and helps prevent the bias strip from stretching during handling.

3. Fold the strip lengthwise, meeting cut edges and seam by stitching slightly more than the desired finished tube width from the fold. For example, for tubes approximately $^3/_{16}$ in. wide using Fasturn cylinder #1, stitch just over $^1/_4$ in. from the fold. Stitch a test piece a couple of inches long, then try slipping the Fasturn cylinder inside. If the fit is tight, stitch slightly farther from the fold.

4. Trim tube seam allowances to $^1/_8$ in.

5. Slide the tube onto the Fasturn cylinder, and gently turn right side out with the Fasturn wire, or use the turning method you like. Avoid stretching.

6. After turning, slip the cylinder back into the now-turned tube to help smooth it.

7. Press the seam to the edge or just over. Shape the tube into a curve with the seam to the inside, again being careful not to stretch. Spray-starch and press.

8. Cut a piece of Clear 'N Melt at least 1 in. larger than the project.

9. Over a press cloth or paper, lightly spray KK 2000 temporary adhesive on the back of the piece to which the bias tube will be fagoted,

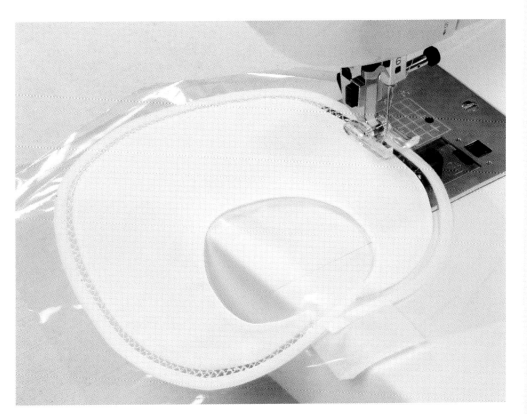

The finished bias tube is adhered to a piece of Clear 'N Melt about ⅛ in. to 3/16 in. from the outer edge of the bib. For fagoting, stitch into the edge of the bib, across the space, and then just into the bias tube. To help with feeding, a small piece of Stitch & Ditch paper stabilizer is placed under the Clear 'N Melt at the beginning and end of the stitching.

in this case the stitched-and-turned bib. Position the bib, right side up, in the center of the cut Clear 'N Melt. Then lightly spray KK 2000 on the back of the curved tube (again, over a press cloth), and position it approximately ⅛ in. to 3/16 in. away from the finished outside edge of the bib. Leave about 1 in. of extra tube at the beginning and end.

Another option is to temporarily fuse the bib and curved tube to water-soluble stabilizer. Press two stabilizer layers together or use Super Solvy. Lightly spray-starch the back of the bib, place over the stabilizer, and press using a press cloth and little or no steam. Then

do the same with the bias tube. (After stitching the fagoting, trim off the excess stabilizer, and dissolve the rest by soaking the project in water.)

10. The fagoting stitch should go just into the finished bib edge, across the space, and then just into the finished tube edge. Adjust the space and the guiding, if necessary.

If the two sides are being pulled together: loosen tension a little more, hold taut with your hands, experiment with different stitches (some are easier than others to guide), and/or use two layers of Clear 'N Melt under the entire project.

TIP For most seaming, you stitch a certain distance from the edge of the fabric, but for perfectly even, narrow tubes, it is equidistant space from the fold to the stitching line that is critical. Measure from the folded edge rather than from the cut edge when stitching very narrow tubes. (Being slightly off is not as noticeable on wider tubes.) See tips for precision sewing in chapter 2.

TIP The beginning and end of the fagoting may be difficult to stitch evenly because of the bulk of the corner of the bib. If necessary, slip a small additional piece of Clear 'N Melt or Stitch & Ditch stabilizer underneath these areas to give the feed dogs something to grab. Extend most of it beyond the ends so that it is only caught in a stitch or two.

11. When fagoting is complete, trim away excess Clear 'N Melt. Then touch remaining Clear 'N Melt with a dry iron on synthetic/silk setting. (A hotter setting makes melting more difficult, not easier.) The stabilizer disappears! Discard any small, bead-like residue that may roll off. It will not stick to the iron or board cover. Any remaining bits of stabilizer (Clear 'N Melt or Stitch & Ditch) may be easily removed with tweezers.

Fagoting with appliqué cord and the Venetian hemstitch

Combining appliqué-cord hemstitching with fagoting techniques creates a very finished and strong corded fagoting stitch that very closely resembles entredeux, a ladder-looking trim used in heirloom sewing as well as on designer ready-to-wear. As with fagoting without cord, you can join fabric to lace, lace to lace, or fabric to fabric using this technique.

Both lace and fabric should be prepared as for other fagoting techniques. The specifications that differ from those for other fagoting are as follows:

Thread: Extra-fine machine-embroidery cotton (Madeira 80/2, YLI Heirloom 70 or 100, Mettler 60/2, Zwicky 70/2, or DMC 50/2). Color should match cord color or be a shade lighter.

Cord: Topstitching thread, buttonhole twist, cordonnet, or pearl cotton (usually size 8). Cord color should match thread color or be a shade darker.

Needle: Large Universal—120/19, 110/18, 100/16, etc., depending on the fabric chosen and the look desired.

Foot: Ideally, foot with holes to guide the cord (such as Bernina's five-groove foot #25, either of Elna's multiple-cord soles, and Pfaff's 7/9 hole or Viking's seven-hole cording foot), or a foot with

In this sample, the corded Venetian hemstitch was used to fagot an insertion lace to fabric and an edging lace to the other heading of the insertion lace. (It's best to do any lace-to-fabric fagoting before doing the lace-to-lace work, as the fabric gives you something to hold onto.)

grooves immediately left and right of center (such as a traditional buttonhole foot or Pfaff's foot #1A). If your machine does not have such a foot, perhaps another brand's foot will work on it with the use of an adaptor and/or a different shank. A satin-stitch foot can be used, but guiding the cords will be harder.

Upper tension: Usually normal, but if the holes created between the cords are not distinct, slightly increase upper tension; if there is puckering, slightly decrease upper tension.

Stitch: Venetian hemstitch.

Width: Usually 3mm to 4.5mm. Test.

Length: Varies by machine, but usually the same as for hemstitching with this stitch. (See the chart on pp. 195-197.)

FAGOTING LACE TO FABRIC WITH APPLIQUÉ CORD

As always, test on scraps first.

1. Fuse the starched and folded edge of fabric in place over two fused sheets of water-soluble stabilizer or one sheet of Super Solvy.

2. Position the lace (without fusing) so that the heading is about $1/16$ in. to $1/8$ in. from the folded fabric edge.

3. Stitch with the Venetian hemstitch so that the left side of the stitch just catches the fabric, the right side goes just over the lace heading, and the prominent holes are centered between the lace and the fabric. Adjust the spacing between the fabric and lace, and balance the stitch, if necessary (see the sidebar on p. 85).

4. Stop with the needle down in the center, and raise the presser foot.

5. Lay the cords on each side of the needle or, if you are using a cording foot, use a dental-floss threader to thread the cord through the holes just left and right of center (see the top photo on p. 90).

6. Lower the presser foot, and stitch. The left cord should be just on the fabric fold; the left side of the stitch will now go over it. The right cord will be over the lace heading, and the right side of the stitch will now go over it. The large holes will be centered between the two cords. Slight additional balancing of the stitch may be necessary.

Note: The cord over the folded fabric edge is optional. Remove the left cord, and stitch a few inches on the test sample with just the right cord over the lace heading, to see which you prefer.

FAGOTING LACE TO LACE WITH APPLIQUÉ CORD

Prepare the laces in the usual way. Fuse one of the laces in the desired position over two fused sheets of water-soluble stabilizer or one sheet of Super Solvy. Lay the other lace heading in position about $1/16$ in. to $1/8$ in. from the fused lace heading.

Stitch with the Venetian hemstitch so that the left side of the stitch goes just over one lace heading, the right side goes just over the other lace heading, and the prominent holes are centered between the two laces. Adjust the spacing between the laces and balance the stitch if necessary. Stop with the needle down in the

Venetian hemstitch

center. Add cords, as instructed in steps 5 and 6 on p. 147, so that a cord is over each heading, and stitch.

FAGOTING FABRIC TO FABRIC WITH APPLIQUÉ CORD

The technique for fagoting fabric to fabric with appliqué cord is a little different from the technique for lace. There are two ways to do it; samples made with each method are shown in the photos on the facing page. With either method, a smaller needle than usual (such as an 80 Universal) will help reduce puckering.

With the first method, the first step is to finish the folded fabric edges with cord (see pp. 44-45). Then stitch the Venetian hemstitch so that the sides of the stitch go just over each corded edge. The spacing of the grooves on pintuck feet may not be helpful with this stitch. Instead, try a standard buttonhole or other foot with two grooves, or a satin-stitch foot plus a guiding aid such as a coffee stirrer. This method is usually easier than the second method and also

looks more finished. With it, you can trim up to the stitching on the underside.

The second method is more like fagoting lace with appliqué cord. If you are using a foot with grooves, lay a cord over each folded edge, and lower the presser foot to align the cords (and fabric edges) with grooves that keep them $1/16$ in. to $1/8$ in. apart. If you are using a cording foot, use a dental-floss threader to thread cord through holes just left and right of center. Lower the foot so that the left cord is just over the left fabric fold, and the right cord is just over the right fabric fold. Stitch so that the sides of the stitch catch each cord and the folded edge, and the large holes are down the center between the cords.

Questions

I have slightly loosened the upper tension, but the two pieces of fabric are still being pulled together by the fagoting stitches. What else can I do?

First, try loosening the upper tension more. Also check that there is nothing along the thread path putting extra resistance on the thread. If there are optional guides at the top of the machine or over the needle, try taking the thread out of them. Do not put the bobbin thread through the hole in the finger of the bobbin case, if your machine has one.

Be sure to use a stitch that takes multiple steps as it crosses from side to side, such as one of those suggested on p. 137. (A regular zigzag with one wide stitch from side to side pulls the fabrics together.) Use a presser foot that holds the fabric securely, such as the basic metal zigzag foot, and hold the fabrics firmly with your hands as you guide.

When fagoting lace to lace using appliqué cord, one lace should be fused to water-soluble stabilizer. The Venetian hemstitch stitches over both cords (and the stabilizer) at the same time. A presser foot with holes to guide the cord is helpful.

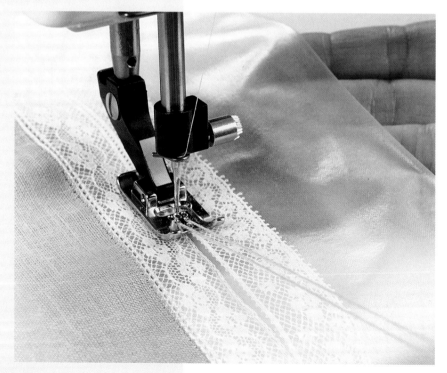

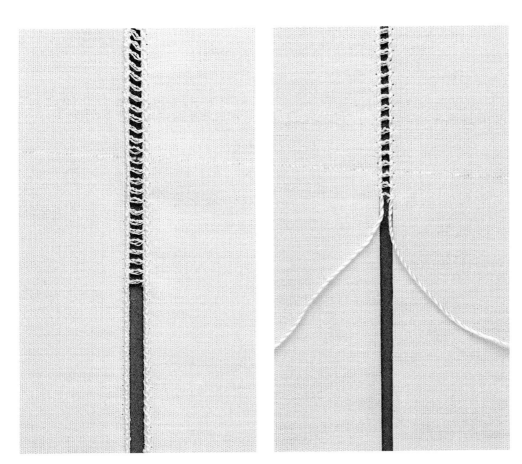

There are two methods for fagoting fabric to fabric using appliqué cord. Either cord both fabric edges first, then stitch the Venetian hemstitch to join them (LEFT) or cord them as you are stitching the Venetian hemstitch (RIGHT).

If the gap between the fabrics is still disappearing, perhaps your bobbin tension is too tight. Try bypassing or loosening bobbin tension. (If you have a separate bobbin case set for a looser tension for heavier threads, try it.)

Another option is to use a water-soluble stabilizer underneath. Fuse one fabric to the stabilizer. Leave the other unfused so you can adjust the space between them, if necessary. Test carefully, because the stitching sometimes stretches when the stabilizer dissolves.

I understand that lace can be attached to fabric using the fagoting-with-appliqué-cord technique (over water-soluble stabilizer) or using the hemstitching-appliqué-cord technique (over fabric). Both create the look of entredeux. Which is better?

Choosing between the two methods is mostly a matter of personal preference. Hemstitching over fabric is a little easier to do than fusing water-soluble stabilizer. However, you can use a smaller needle with fagoting, so this technique may work better on fabrics unsuitable for hemstitching with a large needle. I would suggest that you stitch a sample of each and see which you like better—for both the look and the process.

Hemming and Re-hemming, Plain or Fancy

8

Hemming is a part of almost every garment you sew. There are times when basic blind hemming is appropriate and times when a more creative treatment is called for. Creative hemming techniques can be used either for their decorative value alone or for solutions to problem-hemming situations, such as for hemming sheer fabrics when traditional blind hemming would show through unattractively or for disguising a crease line when lowering a hem.

The feather stitch delicately hems and decorates this little girl's smocked dress, which has a growth tuck hidden on the underside of the hem. The sleeve edges are highlighted with lace attached with the Parisian hemstitch. The ruffles of the blue sundress are finished with "no-trim-around" scalloped edging.

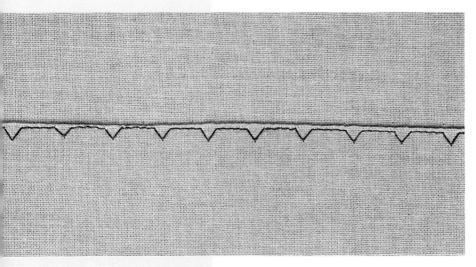

With the standard method of blind hemming (ABOVE), the stitching on the wrong side is less than ⅛ in. from the top edge of the hem. With the "in the air" method (BELOW), it is difficult to tell, even from the wrong side, that the hem was stitched by machine. (In both samples, contrasting thread was used to make the stitching more visible.)

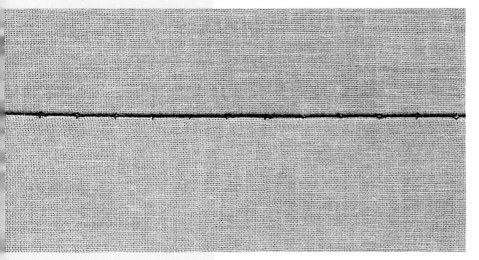

Blind hemming

With a few tips and a little practice, you can blind-hem by machine virtually any garment you would have blind-hemmed by hand, with equally nice results. No one should be able to tell from the right side of the garment that a blind hem was stitched by machine. Blind hemming by machine not only saves time but also makes the hems more secure than those stitched by hand.

Like most sewers, I was frustrated and disappointed with my first blind hems by machine. With practice and refinement (like using finer thread and loosening upper tension), my machine-stitched blind hems became not only acceptable but almost invisible. Yours can too.

There are two methods for blind hemming. The first is the standard method, where on the wrong side the stitching is less than ⅛ in. from the hem's top edge. The second method differs in that some of the stitching is "in the air." The result is that, even from the wrong side, it's hard to tell the hem was stitched by machine.

Fabric: Almost any fabric suitable for blind hemming by hand can be blind-hemmed by machine.

Thread: Fine thread is best because the stitches will show less (and thus look more like handsewn): Coats Dual Duty Plus Extra-Fine cotton-covered polyester for Lightweight Fabrics (article #240) or fine cotton machine-embroidery thread, such as Mettler 60/2, DMC 50, or Madeira 50. Because of its polyester core, the Coats Dual Duty Plus Extra-Fine is a good choice if strength is a concern, as long as the color you need is available. (An exact match is not essential for hemming with such fine thread. If there is not an exact match for a dark color, use a shade darker, but white is best on all light pastel fabrics.)

Needle: Use the smallest size appropriate for the fabric and thread being used, most often 70 Universal.

Foot: A blind-hem foot has a guide that helps keep the bite of the stitch into the garment consistent. If the guide is adjustable, start with the vertical guide just to the left of the center mark on the foot. (Note: Blind-hem feet may look very different, depending on the machine brand. See the bottom photo on p. 14.)

Stitch: Blind stitch (also called blind-hem stitch) for blind hemming woven fabrics.

Some machines also have a stretch blind stitch for hemming knits. The additional zigzags allow more stretch.

If your machine has only one of these stitches, use it for all blind hemming.

Width: Start with the automatic setting or 2mm to 3mm, then adjust.

Length: 2mm to 3mm. (On Vikings, 0.6mm to 0.7mm.)

Needle position: On some Bernina models, a needle position to the right is recommended. Consult the machine manual or start with the automatic needle-position setting, then adjust if necessary. With light- to medium-weight fabrics, a needle position of center to just right of center (rather than far right) will reduce the likelihood of tunneling on the hem extension.

Upper tension: Loosen (adjust to a lower number) slightly. (Putting more thread into each stitch helps eliminate puckering, dimpling, and tunneling.) With some blind-hem feet, the stitch to the side goes over a metal wire or finger; loosening tension is less likely to be needed with these but still may be required if there is puckering or tunneling. Do not put thread through the hole in the finger of the bobbon case if your machine has one.

HEM DEPTH AND CURVED HEMS

The depth of the hem will depend on the bulkiness of the fabric and the shape of the hem, as well as on personal taste. Bulky fabrics and curved hems require a shorter hem depth. The more curve there is, the shorter the hem must be to minimize the extra fullness in the turned-up hem. Circular skirts should be narrow-hemmed. (Narrow hemming is covered in chapter 9) I find that the majority of girls' garments in light- to medium-weight fabric and on straight grain looks nice with 5-in.- to 6-in.-deep hems. The weight of the hem is attractive, and there is enough hem for letting out as the child grows.

On all curved areas (sometimes only part of the hem, such as the sides, is curved), stitch a row of slightly longer

Blind stitch

Stretch blind stitch

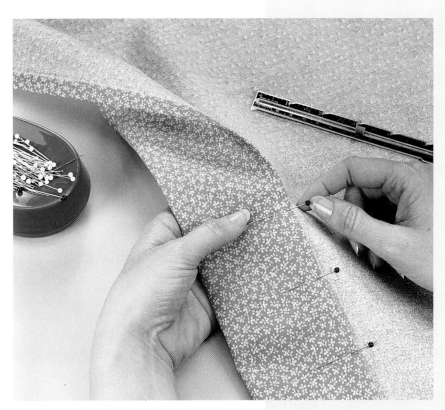

For blind hemming light- to medium-weight fabrics, press the lower edge of the garment under about 3/8 in., then measure and pin the hem the desired depth. Place the pins perpendicular to the hem edge with their heads pointing away from the hem, so they can easily be removed as you stitch.

straight stitches about $^1\!/_4$ in. from the edge of the hem for easing in the fullness. Leave long thread tails.

PREPARATION

Finish the lower edge of the garment to prevent raveling. On light- to medium-weight fabrics, press under about $^3\!/_8$ in. On heavier or thicker fabrics, turning under the edge would create too much bulk. Instead, overcast, serge, cover with seam tape, or enclose the edges in a nylon-tape product such as Seams Great. (When you use seam tape on a curved hem, attach the tape after you have eased in the fullness and pressed.)

MEASURING, PINNING, AND FOLDING

Next, measure and pin the hem the desired depth. Place the pins perpendicular to the hem edge with the heads away from the hem, as shown in the photo on p. 153, so that they are easy to remove as you stitch. Draw up the straight stitching as necessary to ease in the fullness of the curved areas. Steam-press the eased areas.

Now take the garment, wrong side out, to the sewing machine. Lay the garment on the machine so that the upper part of the garment is to the left, out of the way. Where you will begin hemming, fold the hem under along the pinned hem edge (specific folding instructions for each method follow). The pinheads will protrude to the right.

STANDARD BLIND HEMMING

When you fold the garment for standard blind hemming, the finished upper edge of the hem should extend approximately $^1\!/_8$ in. to $^1\!/_4$ in. to the right, as shown in

to the hem edge with the heads away from the hem, as shown in the photo on p. 153,

At the machine, the garment will be wrong side out, with the hem to the right. Fold the hem under to the right side of the garment along the pinned edge. For the standard blind hem, the top edge of the hem extends about $^1\!/_8$ in. to $^1\!/_4$ in.

With the guide on the blind-hem foot against the garment fold and the top edge of the hem extending to the right, stitch so that the straight stitches are on the hem extension and the zigzag stitches just catch the garment fold.

the photo on the facing page. Put this hem extension under the blind-hem foot with the garment fold against the guide on the foot (see the photo above).

Start stitching at a slow speed. Remove the pins as you reach them. The straight stitches will be on the hem extension. When the needle swings to the left to make the wide zigzag, it should barely catch the garment fold so that these stitches will be almost invisible from the right side. If too much of the garment is being caught, adjust by decreasing the stitch width (or with an adjustable foot, by moving the guide to the left). If the zigzag totally misses the garment, widen the stitch (or with an adjustable foot, move the guide to the right).

Once the settings are adjusted satisfactorily, use the guide on the foot to feed evenly.

"IN THE AIR" BLIND HEMMING

The standard method of blind hemming by machine is more secure and is usually easier to stitch than the "in the air" method. The advantage of "in the air" blind hemming is that, even on the wrong side, it is difficult to tell that the garment was hemmed by machine (see the bottom photo on p. 152).

With this method, the straight stitches are "in the air"—they do not go into fabric at all—and the left swing of the zigzag catches the garment fold and the hem at the same time.

Instructions for this method usually indicate that when the garment is folded for hemming, the hem edge and the fold

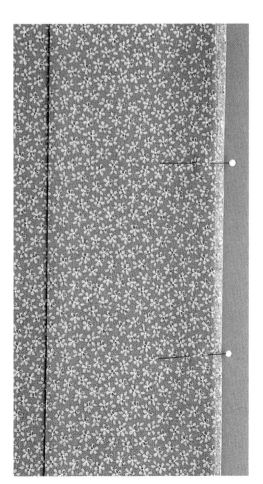

No! A common mistake is to put the hem on top. In this case, the entire pin shows, not just the head, letting you know immediately that the hem is not folded properly. Refold before stitching.

TIP When properly folded for blind hemming, only the upper part of the pins and pinheads are visible. A common mistake, especially on solid-colored fabric, is to have the hem on top, which looks very much the same, but will definitely not create a barely visible hem since you would be stitching a fold in the garment. In this case, the entire pin shows, not just the head, letting you know immediately that the hem is not folded properly and should be refolded before stitching.

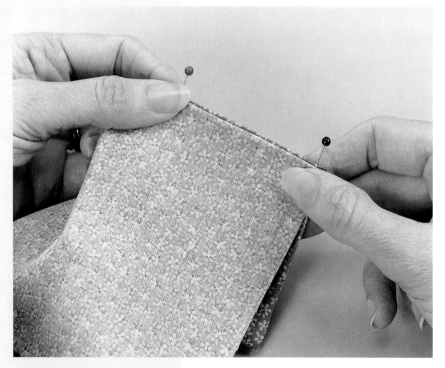

of the garment should be even. The problem with this arrangement is that, since the zigzag should barely catch the garment, it is too easy for the stitch to miss the hem entirely, creating gaps where the hem is not secured at all. To correct this potential problem, extend the hem edge just enough to be seen (much less than $1/16$ in.), as shown in the bottom left photo. This way, when the zigzag catches the garment, it cannot miss the hem.

Since the stitches are "in the air," there is a tendency for the stitching to draw up. Compensate by loosening upper tension a little more and holding the fabric taut in front of and behind the presser foot as you stitch.

Do not be concerned if you or your machine have trouble with the "in the air" method. Some machines do not like stitching "in the air." With either method,

if you can machine-stitch a hem that is almost invisible on the right side of the garment, you have a very usable skill.

Like most skills, blind hemming gets easier and better with practice; so make yourself use it. Start by hemming prints or other fabrics where the stitches will not show so much. Your skill will improve, and soon you will be able to blind-hem almost anything on your sewing machine and no one else will know it was not done by hand.

PRESSING

After you have stitched the hem, press it flat, taking care not to stretch the fabric at the hem as you press. If you may eventually let down the hem (as with garments for children), do not press the crease at the lower edge unless necessary—for example, to press in pleats.

TIP ✖ If possible, practice on a scrap before hemming the garment so that you can adjust width and tension. If there is puckering, loosen upper tension.

✖ Start hemming at the back of the garment so that any further adjusting will have been done by the time you get to the front.

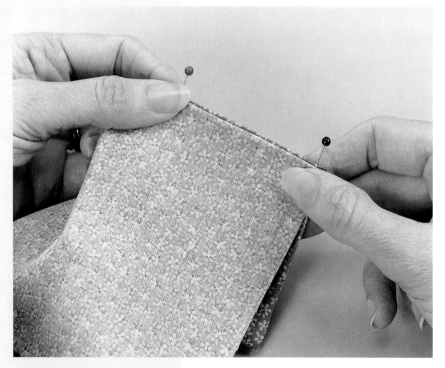

For "in-the-air" blind hemming, the hem edge should extend just enough to be seen (less than $1/16$ in., but exaggerated here and in the photo at right for clarity), so that when the zigzag catches the garment, it cannot miss the hem.

With the guide of the blind-hem foot against the garment fold, the straight stitches are "in the air," and the zigzag stitches catch both the garment fold and the hem at the same time. Taut sewing may be necessary.

Lengthening a hem

It often seems that no sooner do you get a child's garment hemmed, than the child hits a growth spurt and the garment is too short. Occasionally ladies' dresses and skirts also need lengthening to accommodate changes in style or taste. Simply lowering the hemline is often unacceptable because the original crease line would show too much. When this is the case, you can creatively hide or disguise the crease line. The method you choose must be appropriate for the garment and should look as though it was part of the original garment design, rather than an afterthought.

To prepare for re-hemming, first remove the original hem's stitching. Remove machine blind-hem stitching by pulling what was the bobbin thread (the thread visible on the wrong side of the garment). Flatten the crease left from the original hem by spray starching (if appropriate for the fabric) and pressing it. If the original hem edge was turned under $3/8$ in., leave the edge as is if you plan to lower the hem halfway, and re-hem the double-fold hem with either the blind stitch for an invisible hem or, for a more decorative hem, the Parisian hemstitch, the feather stitch, or another similar stitch. For most other decorative-hemming techniques, unfold and press the edge flat.

The original crease line is most easily concealed if the hem is lowered exactly halfway down. That way the folded (or finished) edge of the hem meets the crease line and helps camouflage it, and the new stitching line along the crease will further disguise it. The drawings on p. 158 show how. If the crease does not look worn or folded, you can restitch the hem with the traditional blind stitch, or you can use the Parisian hemstitch or the feather stitch to catch the folded hem. A crease line that looks worn can be concealed with fagoting or with decorative stitching over a single-fold hem. It can also be covered with a ribbon or trim or hidden in a folded tuck, as described below.

Decorative hemming and re-hemming

Hemming offers perfect opportunities to use decorative stitches and techniques. Many of the techniques featured throughout this book can be adapted for creative hemming. For other options, see the sidebar on p. 161.

The drawings on p. 158 show how. For other options, see the sidebar on p. 161.

TIP If the fabric is loosely woven, choose one of the techniques that does not require trimming up to the zigzag stitching on the underside of the hem.

To remove blind-hem stitching in preparation for re-hemming, pull the thread visible on the wrong side of the garment (the bobbin thread).

Letting down a hem

Letting down a hem exactly halfway helps conceal the crease line of the original hem.

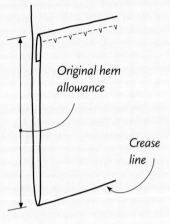

Original hem allowance

Crease line

To re-hem with a double-fold hem, leave the hem edge turned under.

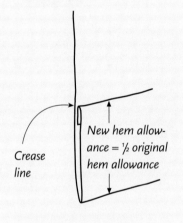

Crease line

New hem allowance = ½ original hem allowance

To re-hem with a decorative technique stitched from the right side through both fabric layers, press open the turned-under edge.

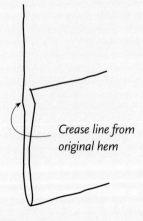

Crease line from original hem

HEMSTITCHING

If the fabric is appropriate (i.e., mostly cotton or linen), hemstitching is an attractive way to hem or re-hem a garment. You can either hemstitch from the right side through both the garment and single-fold hem and then trim the excess fabric, or you can Parisian hemstitch from the wrong side over a folded hem edge. In the latter case, the large holes are on the single layer of the garment and the stitch to the side catches the folded edge of the hem. (For more information on hemming with hemstitching, see pp. 110-112.) When you are re-hemming a garment, let the hem down halfway and hemstitch over the crease line using either hemstitching method.

TWIN-NEEDLE PINTUCKS

You can hem or re-hem with several rows of twin-needle pintucks stitched from the right side through both layers of fabric (garment and hem). The photo on p. 64 shows an example. If you are re-hemming, let down the hem approximately halfway, and stitch one of the rows directly over the original crease. Increase upper tension for a more raised effect. Cording the pintucks will also create more of a ridge; if the fabric is sheer, the cord can be used to show a shadow of color. On the underside, trim away the excess fabric above the stitching (see pp. 68-71).

TWIN-NEEDLE DECORATIVE STITCHING

Decorative stitches have a new look when stitched with twin needles. Experiment with twin needles and the stitches

on your machine to find effects you like. For hemming or re-hemming, the stitch chosen must be appropriate for the garment or it will make the garment look homemade. Stitch from the right side of the garment through both layers (over the crease line if you are re-hemming). To avoid breaking expensive twin needles, test the stitch width very carefully. Slightly loosen upper tension. A lightweight tearaway stabilizer under the fabrics will reduce tunneling. On sheer fabrics, you can create a shadow-work effect with the stitching. Before stitching, give soft sheers body by spray starching and pressing; several applications may be necessary. Trim excess fabric from above the stitching (see pp. 70-73).

ATTACHING NARROW RIBBON WITH TWIN NEEDLES

Another decorative hemming technique is to attach a narrow ribbon using twin needles, stitching from the right side through both layers of the fabric to hem and attach the ribbon at the same time. The top photo on p. 73 shows an example. When re-hemming, position the ribbon over the crease. Decrease upper tension to keep the ribbon flat. (A lightweight tearaway stabilizer under the fabric may also be needed.) Trim excess fabric after stitching. You can stitch single or multiple rows of ribbon; multiple rows of ribbon could be different colors.

Ribbon widths vary, but usually 2.0/70 or 80 or 2.5/80 twin needles will stitch both sides of ⅛-in. ribbon simultaneously. Hold the points of the needles over the ribbon to decide which size to buy. Twin needles that are farther

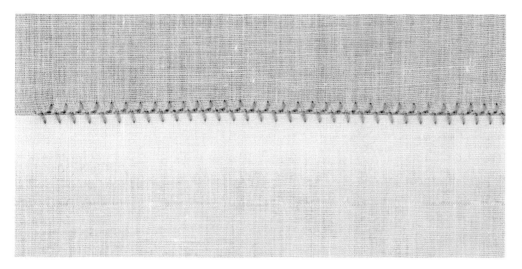

With a single needle and a decorative stitch, such as the feather stitch, you can stitch a double-fold hem and, if you are re-hemming, conceal the crease line of the original hem.

TIP Decorative stitching Is difficult to remove. If future lengthening may be needed, consider planning ahead by adding a growth tuck or two (these are folded tucks designed to let out later on for adding length). Another option is to stitch a hidden growth tuck on the underside of the hem, as was done on the baby dress shown in the photo on p. 150.

apart (4mm) also have larger needles (90 or 100). The larger needles may cause problems such as puckering on satin ribbon but may work fine on grosgrain ribbon ($^1/_4$ in.) or on some trims. Test first.

SINGLE-NEEDLE DECORATIVE STITCHING

As with twin-needle decorative stitching, when re-hemming it is important to choose the stitch carefully or it will be obvious that the decorative stitch is being used to cover a crease. Because the feather stitch on many machines looks so much

like a handsewn stitch, it is often a good choice for a double-fold hem, as can be seen on the hem of the baby dress in the photo on p. 150). It is beautiful when stitched right above the hem, with the stitches to one side catching the folded edge of the hem (see the photo above).

On single-fold hems, denser, satin-stitch-type decorative stitches can be stitched from the right side through both the garment and the hem (see the photo below). Slightly loosen upper tension. Stabilizing may be needed: Spray-starch (or use another spray-on or paint-

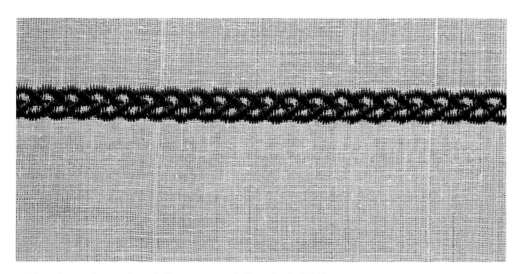

With a dense decorative stitch, you can stitch a single-fold hem.

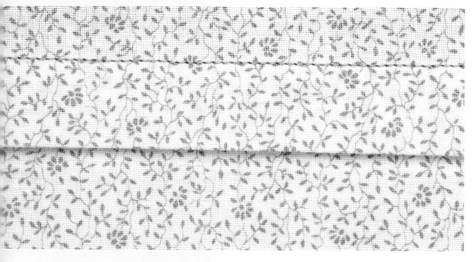

A folded tuck is a simple but attractive way to re-hem a garment while concealing both the crease line and the raw edge.

on stiffening product) and press, or on fabrics other than sheers, try a tearaway stabilizer. Always test first. Trim the excess fabric after stitching.

FOLDED TUCKS

Folded tucks are attractive and may even be used on velveteen and corduroy. When re-hemming, make the crease line of the original hem the folded edge of one tuck. You can conceal the raw edge of the hem in this tuck or in an additional tuck. (See the sidebar on pp. 134-135 for instructions on concealing a raw edge in a

TIP On many fabrics, the Parisian hemstitch or feather stitch may be added to embellish the tucks. With either stitch, first straight-stitch and press the tuck. For feather stitching, center the stitch over the straight stitching so that the feathers on one side are on the tuck and those on the other side are just above the tuck (see the organdy pinafore in the photo on p. 67). For Parisian hemstitch tucks, see pp. 102–103.

The contrasting turned-edge scalloped hem and collar border on this linen dress were appliquéd in place with the Parisian hemstitch for a handsewn pin-stitched look. The edging scallop stitch appliquéing a strip of yellow linen onto the grosgrain belt echoes the scallop shape.

(Girl's dress is an adaptation of "Margaret" by Children's Corner. Collar pattern is #4 from Collars, etc. Both available at heirloom shops. See Resources on p. 199.)

folded tuck.) Chapter 2 has tips for precision sewing, including stitching perfect folded tucks.

For a more delicate look on soft, lightweight fabrics, you can use the blind stitch with a satin-stitch foot to stitch one or more rows of small shell tucks. Shell tucks (see the drawings at right) are especially appropriate on garments for babies or little girls and for lingerie, such as slips or nightgowns. Fold the fabric as for a regular tuck, but stitch it with the blind stitch rather than a straight stitch. The tuck will be about $3/16$ in. deep. In order to create the scalloped effect, the stitch to the side must go over the folded edge.

ADDING A TRIM

With a single needle and a straight or zigzag-type stitch (including hemstitches, if the fabric is appropriate), you can add one or more rows of ribbon or trim, including those too wide for a twin needle. This works well when a hem needs to be let down more than halfway and the crease is above the top of the hem. You can either blind-hem the folded hem edge separately first or catch it in zigzag-type stitching on one side of the trim.

If you are using a zigzag-type stitch to attach the trim, you can stitch from the right side through both the garment and a single-fold hem. Trim the excess hem fabric after stitching. With a lace trim, you can cut away the fabric beneath the lace as well.

FAGOTING

Instead of letting down the original hem, you can simply add to it. Join a folded strip of fabric to the folded crease line with machine fagoting. The strip may be made from the excess fabric in the origi-

Shell tuck

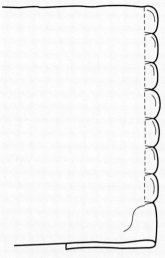

1. Fold fabric as for a regular tuck. Stitch with a satin-stitch foot and blind stitch. The zigzag over the fold creates the shell effect.

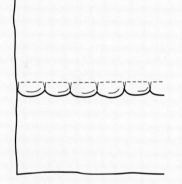

2. Open fabric, and press tuck in the direction desired. On a skirt, this would be down.

Other options for lengthening garments

Some garments (including many heirloom garments) may not have been blind-hemmed originally but may have had a ruffle or other decorative treatment at the lower edge. Options for lengthening these garments may be suitable for garments that were originally blind-hemmed as well. These include:

✗ Inserting a band above the ruffle or hem. The band may include one or more rows of entredeux, lace, embroidery, and so on, and be inserted with traditional heirloom techniques, or it may be a plain or embroidered strip of fabric inserted with fagoting.

✗ Unstitching growth tucks and pintucking the creases. Growth tucks may be let out to lengthen the garment, then twin-needle pintucks may be stitched over any visible crease lines. Additional rows of pintucks can be added for a pleasing effect.

✗ Adding a ruffle. A fabric or eyelet ruffle may be added to a garment that did not have one originally. For some garments, an alternative to lengthening the garment itself would be to wear a longer slip with a pretty eyelet ruffle under the garment; it can look as though it was always part of the design.

Drawing scallops

Draw the scallops on paper first. (I use 8½-in. by 11-in. graph paper.) Remember to make the scallop depth shallow.

Draw one line the hem depth from the bottom of the paper.

Starting at one side, draw the scallops on this line for as many scallops as will fit, using your own favorite method or one of the following options:

✗ Kitchen tools. Draw scallops using a plate, plastic lid, etc., with a curve that fits (or nearly fits) the desired scallop width and depth. For shallow scallops, use a small portion of a circle much wider than the desired scallop width.

✗ Scallop Radial Rule. The Scallop Radial Rule (order #121) and Mini Scallop Radial Rule (order #120), both from Katie Lane Quilts, are very handy because you do not have to go through your kitchen looking for the right-sized circle. The regular Rule has arcs in 1-in. increments for tracing 6-in.- to 10-in.-wide scallops. The Mini Rule (which I use the most) is for 2-in.- to 5-in.-wide scallops. For each width, there is a shallower and a deeper scallop. For turned-edge applications, I use the shallow version.

✗ The 6-Inch Design Ruler. Accurate scallops can also be drawn using a circle-making device, such as a compass or the 6-Inch Design Ruler by Collins (article #72). This ruler has a center hole (for pivoting) plus additional holes for drawing arcs up to 6 in. in diameter.

Note: Pivoting at the line representing the top of the hemline creates deep scallops that are difficult to fold under, so draw a line on the graph paper above the top hemline (most often 1 in. to 2 in. above) on which to pivot. Experiment with different pivot lines and radiuses until you get the desired scallops. I put cardboard under the graph paper, put a pin in the hole being used for pivoting, and use a different-colored pen or pencil for each scallop size to make them easier to distinguish.

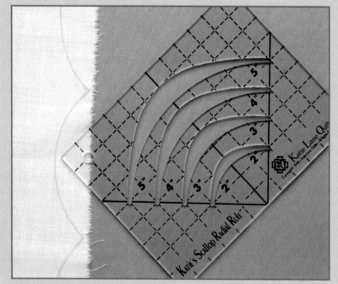

The Scallop Radial Rule can be used to draw arcs 6 in. to 10 in. wide. The Mini Rule is for 2-in.- to 5-in.-wide arcs. For each width, there is a shallower and a deeper scallop.

For the pillowcases with the contrasting hem (on p. 168), pivoting on a line 1¾ in. above the top hemline with a 2½-in. radius (using the center and 5-in. scallop holes on the Design Ruler) created the 3⅝-in.-wide and ¾-in.-deep scallops.

nal hem, if necessary. See pp. 134-135 for ways to finish the raw edges under the folded edges needed for fagoting.

Easy turned-edge scalloped hems

I have always loved the look of appliquéd turned-edge scalloped hems and borders, like those on the collar and hem of the dress on the facing page, but rarely did them because of the work involved in planning and drawing the scallops, as well as the difficulty in getting perfect turned edges. Now tools for drawing scallops and products that facilitate accurate and even turned edges, such as heat-resistant templates and water-soluble stabilizer and thread, have made shaped appliquéd hems surprisingly easy.

PLANNING SCALLOPED HEMS

There are patterns for baby, young girl's, and doll dresses with scalloped hems and for collars with contrasting scalloped borders available at most heirloom shops. (See Resources on p. 199.) But with the following tools and tips, you can adapt your own favorite pattern for a unique scalloped hem treatment.

When practical, start with fabric wider than the finished project requires, draw as many scallops as fit, and cut off the excess. If this is not possible, measure the finished width of the front of the project (excluding seam allowances), and divide it by a pleasing scallop width for that size project. This will give you the number of that size scallops that will fit across the front. (The back will usually be the same.) It will likely be a number with a fraction, so you will have to experiment with a slightly different scallop width, use scallops of different widths, or fudge by slightly overlapping or spreading as you draw the scallops.

It is much easier to have the dip of a scallop, not the point, centered on a seam. (This eliminates the problem of trying to have a perfect point at the bulk of a seam.) So on a project with seams, such as a skirt, seam the skirt front to the skirt back at one side seam, and start tracing with the center (dip) of a scallop there. If there is only one side seam, as on a pillowcase, press a crease halfway and start there.

On small, flat projects, such as the pillowcases on p. 168, plan to also have the dip of a scallop at the center front (and back). On larger projects or those on which the scallop hem is gathered, such as the dress hem on p. 160, the center scallop is not visually apparent so centering a scallop at the front is usually not necessary.

TURNING EDGES USING HEAT-RESISTANT TEMPLATE SHEETS

My favorite way to prepare turned-edge scalloped hems and borders is one I developed after seeing quilter Karen Kay Buckley use a heat-resistant template material called Templar for preparing turned-edge appliqués. (See chapter 3 for details on using Templar for appliqués.) I started experimenting with Templar for shaped appliquéd hems. It made beautifully smooth and accurate turned scalloped edges with less effort than any other method I have tried. You can use this technique to prepare your

TIP ✱ A pleasing scallop width (from point to point) will generally be narrower for smaller projects (for example, a toddler girl's dress or a small pillowcase) and wider for larger projects (for example, a larger size dress).

✱ Shallower scallops are easier to turn neatly and smoothly than deeper ones.

shaped hems whether you choose to stitch them by hand or by machine.

Templar, from Heirloom Stitches, comes in 8½-in. by 11-in. sheets. Other heat-resistant template products for cutting and pressing include: Perfect Shape No Melt Templates (9 in. by 12 in. each, from The Stem Emporium), No Melt Mylar Template Plastic Sheets (9 in. by 12 in. each, from Worldwide Template Products and available from Viking

dealers), and Heat Resistant Mylar (10 in. by 12 in. and 13 in. by 18 in., from Quilter's Rule).

To use heat-resistant template sheets for tracing, cutting, and pressing scalloped hems:

1. Lightly trace the scallops onto the dull side of Templar (or other heat-resistant template sheet with a dull side) using a sharp pencil, or onto

TIP Reduce scallop marking and cutting time in half by cutting scallops through two layers at once. Start by placing the center of a scallop (dip) at the center crease (or seam), and trace scallops to one end. Fold at crease, pin, and cut both layers at the same time.

Lay one long edge of a sheet of Templar over the top hemline drawn on the paper and trace the scallops onto the Templar.

For an even faster and more accurate option, tape the Templar in place, and use the Design Ruler (or compass) and the same pivot holes as before to draw the scallops directly onto the Templar.

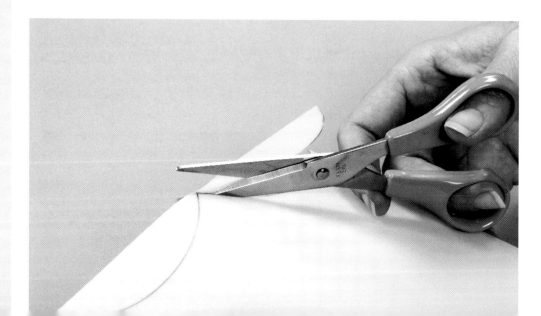

Cut out the scallops on the Templar.

the shiny side of Templar or any other shiny product using a template pencil.

2. Cut out carefully, cutting off as much of the pencil marking as possible. If more than a trace of regular-pencil marking remains, erase it. Remove template-pencil marking with a damp cloth. Smooth any rough edges with an emery board.

3. Align the scalloped Templar along the fabric edge, and trace the scallops onto the fabric. Start by aligning the middle of a scallop at the side seam or crease and continue around the hem (see the tip on the facing page).

4. Cut traced scallops from the fabric using scissors or a small rotary cutter. Clip only where necessary, usually only on very deep inside

curves. Test that the fabric marker will not be permanent when pressed, or remove marks after cutting but before pressing.

Cut scallops along the fabric edge following the traced line.

Larger scallops may be cut more quickly with a small rotary cutter.

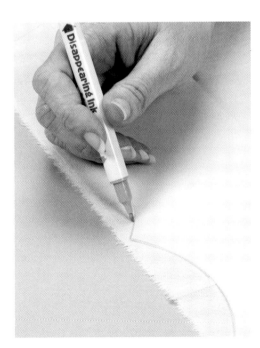

Use the scalloped Templar edge to trace the scallops onto the fabric edge. Align the middle of a scallop at the side seam or crease, trace as many scallops as fit on the Templar, then overlap one scallop to continue around the hem.

Align the scalloped Templar approximately ³⁄₁₆ in. below the scalloped fabric edge. Use a brush or Q-tip to lightly dampen the fabric above the Templar with starch, one scallop at a time.

For each scallop, press the inside curve first.

TIP To avoid warping the Templar:

- ✖ avoid a very hot iron setting;

- ✖ do not press down on the iron;

- ✖ as much as possible, use the sides of the iron and keep the iron on the fabric rather than on bare Templar.

Press each side of the scallop over the Templar using the side of the iron. Following the same steps on the next scallop will form a neatly folded overlapping point.

With sharper points, some fabric may extend beyond the point. Dampen the fabric with spray starch, fold it back, and press.

5. Protect your ironing-board cover with a piece of muslin or similar fabric. Align the cut Templar on the fabric about $^3/_{16}$ in. below the wrong side of the cut scalloped edge. Dampen (but do not saturate) the fabric above the Templar, one scallop at a time, with spray starch using a stencil brush or Q-tip. Fault-less Heavy and Spray 'n Starch brands both work well. I spray a small amount of starch into a small bowl or into the spray-can lid and work from that.

6. Use a dry iron (no steam), set at medium heat (wool/cotton, but test setting) to guide the seam allowance over the Templar. Leave the iron in place without pressure until the fabric is dry each time. Press the inside curve first. Then press each side of the scallop over the Templar using the side of the iron. When you press the next scallop the same way, you create neatly folded points. If any fabric extends over the point (as happens with sharper points), dampen it with spray starch, fold it back, and press. If you make a mistake, simply dampen that area and press it over the Templar again.

7. Seam the open side of the front and back together so that the middle of a scallop will align at the seam, cutting off any excess fabric.

8. Spray-starch and press. Use pins, glue stick, or a temporary spray adhesive (such as Sulky KK 2000) to hold hem in place for stitching.

SIMPLE FOLDED SCALLOPED HEM

The simplest scalloped hems are those where the raw lower edge of the hem is scalloped, the scalloped edge pressed under, and the hem folded to the wrong side and stitched. As can be seen on the pastel blue pillowcase on the facing page, only the shadow of the scalloped hem and the stitching securing it (usually decorative) are visible from the right side.

CONTRASTING SCALLOPED HEM WITH STRAIGHT LOWER EDGE

The white linen dress with the contrasting yellow scalloped skirt hem on p. 160 shows a more visible scallop treatment. For this hem, a scalloped border in a contrasting color is seamed to the lower edge of the project, then folded to the right side and stitched.

For a contrasting hem border:

1. Cut the project (for simplicity, I will call it a skirt) to the desired finished length plus a 1/4-in. seam allowance.

2. Cut the contrasting border the length of the desired hem depth plus a 1/4-in. seam allowance.

3. If there is a front and back border piece, as on the dress skirt, seam them (right sides together) at one side using a plain 1/4-in. seam.

4. Trace, cut, and press the scallops onto the border as explained on pp. 164-166.

5. Stitch the right side of the border to the wrong side of the skirt along the lower edge, matching the side seam, using a plain 1/4-in. seam.

6. Turn the border to the right side. Spray-starch and press. Use pins,

This pretty baby/boudoir pillowcase has a simple version of a scalloped hem. For it, the scalloped lower edge of the hem is folded to the wrong side and stitched. Only the shadow of the scallops and the decorative stitching, like the feather stitch here, show on the right side of the project. Additional embellishment could easily be added.

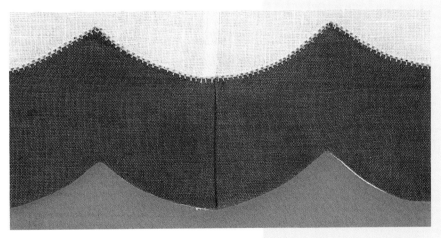

After pressing a contrasting border to the right side and securing it in place with pins or a temporary adhesive, French-seam the doubled layer (skirt and border). The finished seam is centered at the dip of a scallop. This hem is appliquéd with the Parisian hemstitch to resemble the hand pin stitch. The forward and back stitches are on background fabric, and the zigzag swings just wide enough to catch the hem.

glue stick, or a temporary spray adhesive (such as Sulky KK 2000) to hold the hem in place.

7. Estimate the midpoint (center of dip) of the last scallop on both of the unseamed outside edges. Mark

TIP For contrasting borders, prewash the background fabric and the border fabric separately, if colorfastness or shrinkage is a concern.

TIP To use a temporary spray adhesive, like Sulky KK 2000, to hold a hem in place for stitching: Lay the hem, one section at a time, wrong side up, over a press cloth or paper; spray lightly along the turned edge of the hem; and finger-press the hem in place. Do not press the hem with an iron at this point because the adhesive will not hold if heated. The adhesive will disappear within a few days.

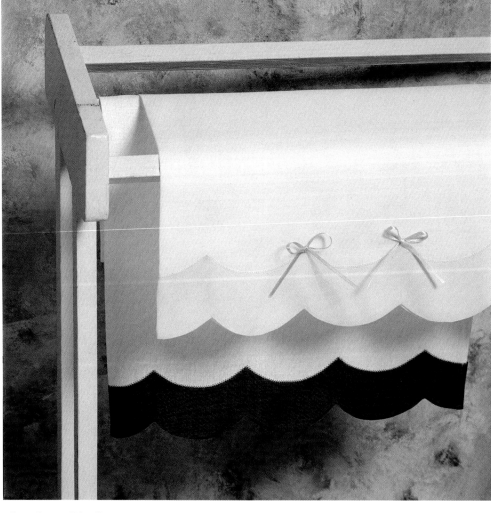

These beautiful pillowcases (one pima cotton, one linen) have contrasting hem borders scalloped along both the upper and lower hem edge. They may be folded over to use as elegant lingerie bags or personalized with additional hand or machine embellishment for a perfect gift (that you may decide to give yourself!).

a line just under $^1\!/_2$ in. toward the edge from this estimated last scallop midpoint on both edges. Cut along this line through both skirt and border layers, and continue for the entire length of the skirt.

8. Pin and French-seam skirt front to back including the doubled layer with the border. (Do not open the hem.) Pin wrong sides together, and adjust folded border, if necessary, so that it matches. Stitch just under a $^1\!/_4$-in. seam, press, and trim to $^1\!/_8$ in.

Fold right sides together, stitch just under a $^1\!/_4$-in. seam, and press.

9. Stitch the border in place with the handsewn-looking appliqué stitch of your choice.

CONTRASTING HEM SCALLOPED ON BOTH THE UPPER AND LOWER EDGES

The pillowcases above show a variation of a contrasting scalloped hem where the hem is scalloped along both the upper and lower border edge. This hem looks impressive and will take just a little more time, but it is not difficult.

For a contrasting hem scalloped along both the upper and lower border edge:

1. Follow steps 1 through 3 on p. 167 for a "Contrasting scalloped hem with straight lower edge."

2. Spray-starch and press the border fabric without stretching. Lightly crease at the center.

3. Draw the scallops on graph paper, using one of the methods discussed in the sidebar on p. 162, then trace onto Templar. Cut scallops carefully along this line.

4. Using scalloped Templar for the template, trace scallops along the top of the opened strip, aligning points just below the cut edge. Start by placing the center of a scallop (dip) at the creased center fold (or seam for a skirt), and continue tracing scallops to one end of the border strip.

5. Fold at center crease. Cut these upper scallops through both layers at once, using scissors or a rotary cutter.

6. Trace scallops along the lower edge, aligning the lower part of the curves about $1/4$ in. from the lower edge of the strip. Start at the center fold with the center of a scallop and continue tracing scallops for the entire width, taking care to align lower scallops with those at the top (see drawing at right). *Do not cut lower scallops.*

7. With the wrong side up (lower scallop markings should be visible), align the scalloped Templar about $3/16$ in. below the cut scalloped fabric edge. Lightly dampen the fabric above the Templar with starch using a stencil brush or Q-tip, and press it over the Templar, one scallop at a time, following the instructions on p. 166.

8. Spray-starch and press the lower edge of the pillowcase fabric. Stitch the right side of the border to the wrong side of the fabric, aligning center creases. Align the straight edges, and stitch along the traced lower scallop line. Use a straight stitch, length 1.5mm to 2mm, upper tension 4, a 70 Universal needle, and a basic zigzag or straight-stitch foot.

9. Trim to $1/8$ in. Clip to within a few threads at the inner points.

10. Turn the border to the right side. Press. Spray-starch, and press again. Use pins, glue stick, or a temporary spray adhesive (such as Sulky KK 2000) to hold the hem in place for stitching.

11. Fold in half, aligning the scallops. Estimate the midpoint of the last scallops at the outer edges. Mark a line just under $1/2$ in. toward the edge from the estimated midpoint of the last scallop. Cut along this line through both layers and continue for the length of the pillowcase.

12. Pin and French-seam the side of the pillowcase, including the doubled layer with the border. Pin the wrong sides together. Adjust the folded border, if necessary, so it matches. Stitch just under $1/4$-in. seam. Press. Trim to $1/8$ in. Fold

Drawing scallops for border

For contrasting hem scalloped along both the upper and lower border edge:

1. *Trace scallops along top of opened border strip, aligning points just below cut edge. Start with the center of a scallop (dip) at the creased center fold, and continue tracing scallops to one end of the strip (upper part of illustration).*

2. *Fold at center crease. Cut upper scallops through both layers at once, using scissors or rotary cutter.*

3. *Trace scallops along lower strip, aligning lower part of curves about $1/4$ in. from lower edge of strip. Start at center fold again, and trace scallops for entire width, aligning lower scallops with those at top (lower part of illustration). Do not cut lower scallops.*

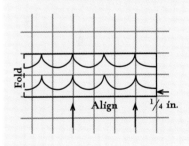

the right sides together. Stitch just under ¼-in. seam. Press.

13. Seam the end of the case with a French seam or other seam finish, such as a straight stitch, overcast, and trim. Press.

14. Stitch the border in place with the handsewn-looking appliqué stitch of your choice. Add any additional machine or hand embellishment you like.

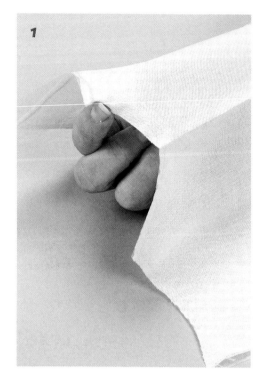

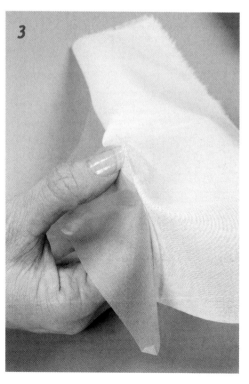

To form neat points when turning a faced scalloped hem right side out:

1. *Put your thumb inside the point between the hem and the facing (either side can be up). Fold the seam allowance on one side of the point to the back along the stitching, and pinch it between the thumb inside the point and that index finger.*

2. *Fold the seam allowance on the other side of the point to the back along the stitching line. Hold the overlapped fabric at the point in the pinch, too.*

3. *Continue to hold the pinched overlapped point as you fold the facing over until the point is turned. Having at least a little bit of fingernail on your thumb helps. If your thumb has no nail, slip one side of a pair of long tweezers into the point and pinch with that.*

TIP ✸ Water-soluble stabilizers may be easily pieced by overlapping a small amount either as you stitch or by covering the overlap with a press cloth and fusing with an iron.

✸ Covering with a press cloth or a piece of paper and pressing with a dry iron will also help stiffen a water-soluble product that is soft and difficult to manage.

✸ Experiment with different water-soluble stabilizer brands (some are more sensitive to humidity than others) or a heavier version (like Sulky's Super Solvy). Heavier and stiffer water solubles are easier to handle but will require longer soaking to completely dissolve.

SCALLOPED HEMS AND BORDERS PREPARED WITH WATER-SOLUBLE STABILIZER FACING

An alternative method for turning the edges of shaped hems is to stitch a water-soluble stabilizer to the right side of the shaped edge and then turn it to the inside of the hem like a facing. After the scallops are stitched in place, the water-soluble stabilizer can be dissolved by soaking it in water. If a shape is repeated many times, as it is on the scalloped skirt and pillowcase hems, I find the Templar method above the most efficient way to mark, cut, and prepare the hem. I use the water-soluble facing method more often for shapes that do not repeat over and over, like the shaped, contrasting border on the collar of the white and yellow dress on p. 160.

For a scalloped hem prepared with a water-soluble stabilizer facing:

1. Follow steps 1 and 2 on pp. 164-165 for tracing scallops onto Templar, except tagboard (such as a file folder) may be substituted for Templar as the template.

2. Trace scallops onto the lower edge of the project so that points are $1/4$ in. (or a little more) from the fabric edge.

3. Cut a strip of water-soluble stabilizer about the scallop depth plus 1 in.

4. Straight-stitch the water-soluble stabilizer to the right side of the hem following the traced scallop line. (Stitch length 1.5mm, with slightly loosened upper tension.)

   Hold the water-soluble taut with your hands as you stitch. On machines where the presser-foot pressure can be adjusted, decreasing the pressure slightly may make guiding easier.

5. Trim to about a $1/8$-in. to $3/16$-in. seam allowance. Clip only if scallops are deep.

6. Carefully turn the water-soluble stabilizer to the wrong side of the scallops, as you would a facing, gently forming the curves and points. The photos on the facing page show how to form neat points when turning the facing, eliminating the bulk created by pushing a point turner into points.

7. Press the scalloped hem from the fabric side. Then lightly spray-starch the lower part of the project one area at a time, position hem, and press. The water-soluble stabilizer will temporarily fuse the hem in place.

8. The water-soluble stabilizer may be removed after stitching by soaking in water.

SCALLOPED HEMS AND BORDERS PREPARED WITH WATER-SOLUBLE BASTING THREAD

Just as it was helpful to know several ways to turn edges for appliqués (chapter 3, the same is true for preparing shaped hems. You may simply prefer one method over another in certain situations, or if the products needed for one method are not on hand, it is great to have options.

Patti Jo Larson developed a really clever method to prepare shaped hems by expanding on the principle that turning edges is easier using a facing. She simply found a way to make part of the project the facing. Using water-soluble basting

Still another way to prepare shaped hems is to stitch the front and back project pieces right sides together along the traced scallops using water-soluble basting thread. After turning right side out and pressing (as at right), the scalloped edge is spritzed with water dissolving the thread. The pieces can then be separated and both have perfect turned edges (as at left).

thread, she stitches the front and back project pieces right sides together along the traced scallops. (Think of the back of the project as the facing.) After the "facing" is turned to the inside and pressed, the scalloped edge is spritzed with water, and the thread holding the "facing" to the fabric dissolves. The fabric and "facing" can then be separated, and both have perfect turned edges.

There are several advantages with this method. Since you prepare the front and back pieces at the same time, you only have to mark, stitch, and turn half as many scallops as you do with the water-soluble-facing method. And not having to soak and dissolve a water-soluble facing is a real time-saver.

For a shaped hem prepared with a water-soluble basting thread:

1. Follow steps 1 and 2 on pp. 164-165 for creating a Templar template, except tagboard (such as a file folder) may be substituted for Templar.

2. Trace scallops onto half of the project's lower edge or border so that points are ¹⁄₄ in. (or a little more) from the fabric edge. For example, for a contrasting skirt border, lightly trace scallops onto the wrong side of the back-border strip so that the scallop points are at least ¹⁄₄ in. from the edge. (The border front and back are not seamed ahead with this method.)

Other stitches that can closely resemble hand-appliqué stitches for scalloped hems are feather (ABOVE) and blind-hem (BELOW) variations. Align so that the straight stitches are on the background fabric, and the zigzag swings just wide enough to catch the hem.

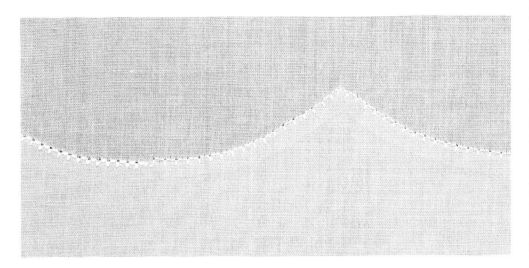

3. Thread the machine with water-soluble thread (such as YLI's Wash-A-Way) top and bobbin. With right sides together, straight-stitch the border back to the border front following the traced scallop line. (Stitch length 2mm, with slightly loosened upper tension.)

4. Trim to about a $1/8$-in. to $3/16$-in. seam allowance. Clip only if scallops are deep.

5. Carefully turn right side out, gently forming the curves and points.

6. Press the scalloped hem with a dry iron. Then lightly mist the scalloped edge with water to dissolve the thread. Press again. The front and back border strips with perfect turned-edge scallops can now be separated.

7. Seam front to back border on one side so that the seam is at a scallop dip. Continue by following steps 5 through 9 in "Contrasting scalloped hem with straight lower edge" on pp. 167-168.

For a pillowcase, or other project with just one seam, fold right sides together and crease at halfway point. Open and place the center of a scallop (dip) at the creased center fold, and continue tracing scallops to one end of the border strip (with points at least $1/4$ in. from the edge). Fold at the center crease. Stitch scallops through both layers at once using water-soluble thread. Turn and press as above, then open.

MACHINE STITCHING SCALLOPED HEMS TO RESEMBLE HAND-APPLIQUÉD HEMS

Most sewing machines have stitches that can be made to resemble hand stitches that were traditionally used to appliqué turned-edge shaped hems. (For details on how to create machine stitches that resemble hand-appliqué stitches, see chapter 3, pp. 59-61.) Additional hand or machine embellishment may also be added.

For stitching appliquéd scalloped hems:

✗ An open-toe (appliqué) foot is helpful so that the edge of the hem is visible.

✗ Start stitching on a straight or slightly curved area, such as the inside curve on a scallop, not on a point or at a seam.

✗ Try to anchor points securely with a stitch on or near the tip. This may take some experimentation with the stitch pattern. For example, with some stitches, one stitch pattern across the point gives better results than one pivot right at the point.

✗ To reduce puckering, slightly loosen (lower) upper tension, and try more spray starching and pressing and/or a lightweight tearaway underneath.

✗ A contrasting border will usually be stitched from the right side of the fabric. For simple turned-under shaped hems, it is easiest to stitch from the wrong side so that the hem shape is visible. If you do not like the way the stitching appears on the right side, then stitch right side up. If the fabric is not sheer enough for the hem shape to show through, lightly mark the stitching line along the top of the hem, or straight-stitch the hem in place from the wrong side and use that stitching line as a guide to decoratively stitch from the right side. If the straight stitch is short (usually about 2mm) and stitched with a fine needle and very fine thread, it should not be obvious after most decorative stitches are stitched over or beside it. Another option is to straight-stitch the hem in place using water-soluble basting thread (top and bottom), which can be dissolved afterward with water.

Questions

How much of the garment should be caught in each stitch to the side when blind hemming by machine?

The stitches should be almost invisible from the right side of the garment, which means that the stitch should barely catch the garment. However, there are other considerations that will affect how much the stitch should bite into the fabric, including the wearer, the occasions the garment will be worn, and the type of fabric. For example, on children's play clothes, durability is important; so it makes sense to catch a little more than a thread or two of the garment with each stitch. And on prints or loosely woven fabrics, the stitches can be a little wider without being visible than they can on a densely woven solid.

It is always a good idea to stitch a test sample, or at least start hemming at the back or in another inconspicuous place, to perfect the amount of bite into the garment as well as all other factors. If too much of the garment is being caught, adjust by decreasing the stitch width (or on adjustable blind-hem feet, by moving the guide to the left). Fine thread and slightly loosened tension are also important for the stitches to be almost invisible.

When shortening slacks that taper, how do you hem the narrower lower edge to the wider part of the pant leg above it without getting puckers?

First, avoid making a deep hem on any garment that angles. The more acute the angle, the shallower the hem should be. For slightly tapered slacks, try a $1^1/_4$-in. to $1^1/_2$-in. hem. (Of course, if there is a cuff, the hem must be deeper than the cuff.)

To avoid puckering, the narrower lower edge must be made as wide as the part of the pant leg to which it is being sewn. The easiest way I have found to do this is to open the lower edge of each inseam to about $1/_2$ in. from the new hemline, using a seam ripper. If more width is needed, open the seam a little more (to about $1/_4$ in. from the new hemline) and/or open the outside seam. After hemming, secure the seam just below the removed stitches with a few stitches by hand.

For a more professional finish, you can restitch these opened seams to angle out from the hemline to the lower edge. But for most casual slacks, I just leave the seam open; since it is at the seam allowance, it does not show.

Narrow Hemming

A simply beautiful finish to this elegant blouse, the Parisian hem-stitch narrow-hems and hemstitches the edges of the cap sleeves in one step. This easy-to-make blouse begins with a V-neck pattern and uses the corners of a handkerchief for the collar.

Narrow hems are called for in many applications. For example, the lower edge of blouses, nightgowns, sheer-fabric skirts, circular skirts, and many linings are best finished with a narrow hem, as are the edges of ruffles, fabric ties (for aprons or dresses), and tablecloths. Narrow casings, like those for the $1/8$-in. ribbon on each side of the neck-roll pillow covers on p. 135, can also be stitched with a narrow hemmer.

Yet the perfectly stitched narrow hem can be elusive. Pattern instructions for narrow hems usually read something like "Turn edge under $1/4$ in., press, stitch near fold, trim to $1/8$ in., then turn under, press, and stitch again." After many time-consuming efforts following this method, which resulted only in burned fingertips and uneven, unprofessional-looking hems, I decided to try the narrow hemmers available for my sewing machine.

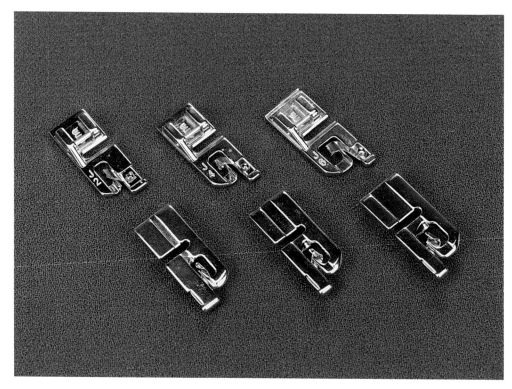

Typical narrow hemmers include (left to right) 2mm, 4mm, and 6mm hemmers. Each makes hems approximately the size of the channel cut out on its underside.

TIP ✖ The size hem that a hemmer will make can be estimated by the size of the curl on the foot and, more accurately, by the width of the channel cut out on the underside.

✖ Narrow hemming over seams requires a slightly wider hemmer than would otherwise be needed to hem a single layer of the same fabric. For curves, use the narrowest hemmer appropriate for the weight of the fabric.

Like many sewers, I was frustrated and disappointed with my first attempts at using these accessories—until I was asked to hem the sides of floor-to-ceiling fabric panels in every pastel color for one of my daughter Emily's dance performances. (This was before home sergers.) After narrow hemming more than 150 yards of broadcloth, I knew exactly how to use narrow hemmers! Since then I have taught more than 6,000 people how to narrow-hem successfully by sharing a few critical tips that are rarely included in instructions. A little practice definitely helps, but I promise you won't need to hem 150 yards to be able to use your hemmers for quick and neat narrow hems!

Fabric: Mostly light- to medium-weight wovens, although some knits such as tricot can be narrow-hemmed (usually with a zigzag-type stitch for a shell edge).

Thread: Appropriate for the fabric; most often Coats Dual Duty Plus Extra-Fine Cotton-Covered Polyester or fine machine-embroidery cotton threads (size 50/2 or 60/2).

Needle: Appropriate for fabric and thread being used, most often 70 or 80 Universal.

Foot: Narrow hemmer. Choose hemmer according to the fabric weight, the size hem desired, and the stitch to be used. Available hemmers vary by machine. Typical hemmers include:

✖ Rolled hemmer. For very lightweight fabrics only. It is used with a zigzag stitch to make a rounded rolled hem, as seen on some handkerchief edges. Some rolled hemmers can also be used with a straight stitch for a tiny flat hem.

✘ 2mm hemmer. For very lightweight fabrics (e.g., batiste). Makes hems approximately $1/16$ in. to $1/8$ in. wide.

✘ 3mm to 4mm hemmers. For light- to medium-weight fabrics (e.g., broadcloth). Makes hems approximately $1/8$ in. to $3/16$ in. wide.

✘ 5mm to 6mm hemmers. For light- to medium/heavyweight fabrics (e.g., poplin). Makes hems approximately $1/4$ in. wide.

✘ Shell hemmer. Designed to be used with a zigzag-type stitch on lightweight fabrics to create a wider, shell (scallop-like) hem. Depending on the needle-position capability of the machine, sometimes a shell hemmer will also work with a straight stitch.

Some hemmers are designed for straight stitching only; these hemmers have a hole rather than an oval opening for the needle. Some hemmers are designed for the hem to align with a zigzag stitch only; these may be called rolled or shell hemmers. And finally, some more versatile hemmers are designed to be used with either a straight or zigzag-type stitch. Hemmers in the latter two categories both have oval openings for the needle; they cannot usually be distinguished from each other visually.

Difficulties with narrow hemming are often the result of using the wrong foot. Contributing to this problem is the lack of uniform terminology in the sewing industry. The terms "narrow hemmer," "rolled hemmer," and sometimes "shell hemmer" are frequently used interchangeably. It is not uncommon for students in my classes who wanted to

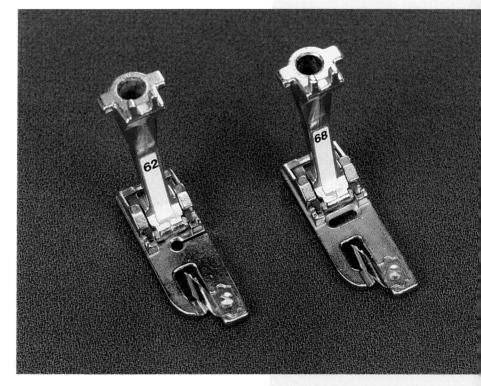

The hemmer at left is designed for straight stitches only (note the small round needle opening); the one at right is a shell hemmer, designed to align with zigzag stitches.

straight-stitch narrow hems to have unknowingly purchased a shell hemmer designed to be used with a zigzag stitch. With this type of hemmer a centered straight stitch is too far onto the hem to be secure, and on some machines, if you move the needle to the next position left, the needle totally misses the hem. When purchasing hemmers, consult a chart from the sewing-machine company or the machine manual to be sure you are getting the foot you need.

Stitch: Straight (other stitches for decorative edges will be covered later).

Length: 2mm to 2.5mm or appropriate for fabric.

Upper tension: Normal for fabric used.

Stabilizer: A small piece of lightweight tearaway stabilizer (2 in. to 3 in. square)

TIP A 2mm or 3mm hemmer comes with some machines. If you do not have a narrow hemmer, a 3mm or 4mm hemmer (usable with either straight or zigzag stitching, if available) is a good middle-range size to purchase.

is helpful when starting the narrow hem at a corner and to hem seams.

General procedure for narrow hemming

Most narrow hemming is done with a straight stitch, but the instructions that follow also apply to narrow hemming with other stitches. With a little know-how, you can easily narrow-hem even seemingly difficult areas, such as seams and corners.

GETTING STARTED

There are several methods for getting the hem started. This method is easy and works well even on difficult areas, such as starting the hem on a folded double layer of fabric for a shirt and facing.

1. Trim the ravels for a clean edge. (A rotary cutter and mat are great for this task.)

2. With the wrong side of the fabric facing up, form a tiny starting hem by folding the fabric edge over

After taking two to three stitches, stop with the needle down, and lift the presser foot.

twice where the narrow hem is to begin, as shown in the photo below. Pin with one pin. This hem must be approximately the same width as the channel on the underside of the narrow hemmer.

TIP If you are a novice, practice narrow crossgrain (i.e., selvage-to-selvage) hemming with a straight stitch on scraps of batiste using a 2mm hemmer or on broadcloth with a 3mm or 4mm hemmer. Start narrow hemming on a long side about ½ in. or more from a corner. (Later, you can tackle starting at a corner.) At this stage, just get comfortable with guiding the fabric into the hemmer. If you make a mistake, just start again in a new place. There is no need to rip out stitches on these practice pieces.

With the fabric wrong side up, form a tiny starting hem by folding the edge over twice and pinning. Make this hem about as wide as the channel on the underside of the foot.

180

3. Put the pinned narrow hem under the hemmer foot on the machine, and lower the presser foot.

4. Take two to three stitches near the inside folded-hem edge (just left of the pin) by turning the flywheel toward you by hand. Stop with the needle down, lift the presser foot (see the top photo on the facing page), and remove the pin.

5. Feed the fabric edge into the curl of the hemmer (see the photo below). You may have to give the fabric in front of the foot a slight tug.

6. Lower the presser foot, and slowly begin to stitch. It may be helpful to pull the thread tails gently toward the back for the first few stitches.

GUIDING THE FABRIC

Perfect narrow hemming requires slight guiding adjustments as you stitch. Using both hands to guide the fabric into the hemmer gives greater guiding control than using just one hand (see the photo above).

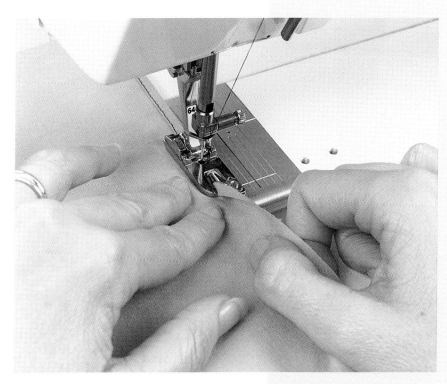

Two hands are needed for perfect guiding. The right hand guides the fabric edge directly in front of the foot. The index and middle fingers of the left hand gently push (or pull) the fabric at the left front of the foot, to keep the fabric edge at the upper left side of the ditch as it enters the foot.

With the right hand, slightly lift the fabric edge and guide it directly in front of the foot. Allow the fabric to slide freely through your hand. Watch to make sure that the fabric touches the inside of the curl on the right. It should never go under the right toe of the foot.

With the index and middle fingers of the left hand, gently push or pull the fabric at the left front of the foot to adjust how much fabric goes into the foot. Watch to make sure that the fabric edge is at the upper left side of the ditch as it enters the foot. If it is at the center of the foot, there will not be enough fabric for the hem. If it is over the ditch on the left, there will be too much fabric for the hem. The photos on p. 182 illustrate some common feeding mistakes to avoid.

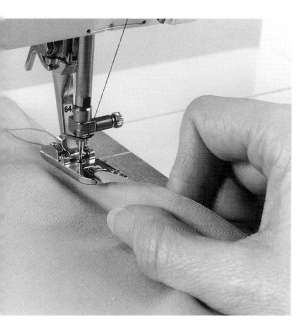

After removing the pin, feed the fabric edge into the hemmer curl.

Problem solving If the fabric edge is being folded over only once and the raw edge shows, start again and as you stitch, push a little more fabric into the hemmer with the fingers of your left hand. If this happens on a garment, remove the stitches back to the place where the hem is stitched correctly, and start again there. No pinning is necessary this time.

If the stitching is in the middle of the hem rather than near the inside folded edge—where it should be—or if extra fabric protrudes from inside the hem, use the fingers of your left hand to feed less fabric into the hemmer.

Common feeding mistakes to avoid

With narrow hemming, guiding is critical to success. These photos show four common feeding mistakes. Slight guiding adjustments will correct these problems.

Gap between the fabric and the inside of the curl on the right.

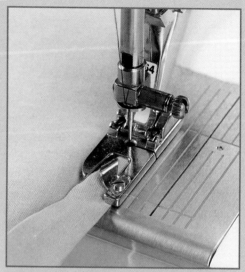

Fabric under the right toe of the foot.

Not enough fabric being fed for the hem.

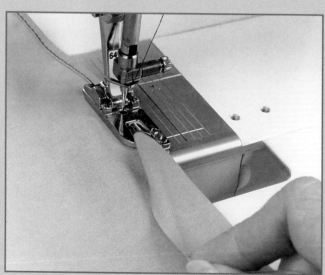

Too much fabric being fed.

If the hem is uneven, make sure you keep the fabric edge at the upper left side of the ditch as it enters the foot. Evenness will come with practice.

STARTING AT A CORNER

Some narrow-hemming applications—such as on folded facings or on rectangular scarves, napkins, place mats, and tablecloths—require starting at a corner. Putting stabilizer underneath ensures smooth feeding from the start.

1. Form the starting hem by folding the edge twice at the very beginning of the side to be hemmed. Put about $1/2$ in. of the corner of a small piece of tearaway stabilizer under this starting hem, and pin with one pin, as shown in the photo below.

2. Put the pinned narrow hem under the hemmer foot, lower the presser foot, and take two to three stitches on the pinned hem starting at the edge of the fabric. Stop with the needle down.

3. Lift the presser foot, remove the pin, feed the fabric edge into the curl of the hemmer, and lower the presser foot.

4. Gently pull the thread tails toward the back as you begin to stitch (see the photo on p. 34). The stabilizer enables the feed dogs to move the fabric easily past the edge without hang-ups or pushing the fabric down toward the bobbin.

5. Gently tear away the stabilizer when the stitching is complete.

NARROW HEMMING OVER SEAMS

Many applications require narrow hemming over seams. For example, when narrow hemming the lower edge of a blouse, it's necessary to hem over the side seams. By reducing as much bulk as possible, even serged or French seams can be narrow-hemmed. (French seams should be made very small if they will be hemmed over.)

1. Secure the seams at the end where the narrow hem will be. Instead of backstitching, which puckers lightweight fabric, an easy alternative is to use a very short stitch length (about 1mm) for the lower $1/2$ in. of the seam. Another option is to tie the thread tails together at the end of the seam.

2. To reduce bulk, trim the corners of the lower edge of the seam allowances (see the bottom photo on p. 184).

3. Press each seam open or in the desired direction.

4. To keep the seam allowance from shifting, either use fabric glue stick (see the bottom photo on p. 184) or zigzag baste (width 3mm, length 2mm) to hold the lower 1 in. in place as pressed.

TIP Narrow casings, like those for the $1/8$-in. ribbon on each side of the neck-roll pillow covers on p. 135 can be stitched with a 5mm or 6mm narrow hemmer.

To start narrow hemming at a fabric corner, pin the starting hem to the corner of a piece of tearaway stabilizer.

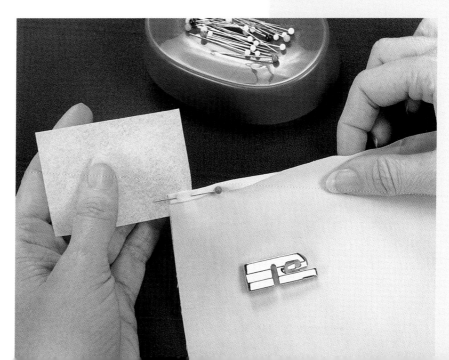

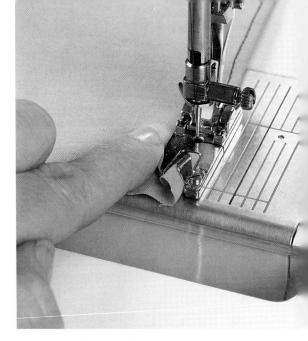

To keep the fabric in the curl when hemming seams and at the end of the hem, use your left index finger to press on the fabric next to the left side of the foot.

TIP Do not start stitching on a difficult area, like a seam, unless absolutely necessary. For example, to narrow-hem (or blind-hem) a skirt with side seams, start hemming at the back a few inches past a seam.

Before narrow hemming over seams, the corners of the lower edge of the seam allowances should be trimmed to reduce bulk; the lower 1 in. of the seam allowances should be held in place with glue stick (or zigzag basting).

5. Use a hemmer at least 3mm to 4mm wide if seams must be crossed. It is difficult to get seams through a 2mm hemmer.

6. Do not start the hem at a seam. As you approach the seam, stitch slowly and hold the fabric taut to help get over the thickness.

7. Remove any basting after stitching is complete.

Problem solving If the fabric works out of the curl of the foot as the seam goes through, use your left index finger to press on the fabric next to the left side of the foot, so the fabric cannot be pushed out.

If the seam gets hung up under the foot, lift the presser foot, put a small piece of tearaway stabilizer under the fabric behind the needle, lower the presser foot, and continue. The stabilizer is not caught in the stitching but helps move the fabric, by giving the feed dogs something they can grip.

ENDING A NARROW HEM

To avoid having a fabric tail protrude at the end of a narrow hem, trim about

¹/₄ in. of the corner before you hem it. (Special situations, such as ending on folded facings and continuous narrow hemming, are discussed on the next two pages.)

To keep the fabric in the curl all the way to the end, use your left index finger to press on the fabric next to the left side of the foot, as shown in the photo above.

NARROW HEMMING THE FACINGS

There are several ways to hem the facings you may encounter when narrow hemming, such as those at the lower edge of a blouse front. This method of narrow hemming the facing and garment together is easy and creates a neat hem with little bulk.

1. Trim the lower edge of facings to eliminate bulk. Trim ¹/₄ in. at the facing edge, angling to nothing near the fold, as shown in the photo at left on the facing page.

2. Use glue stick to hold the lower 1 in. of the facing in place to prevent shifting.

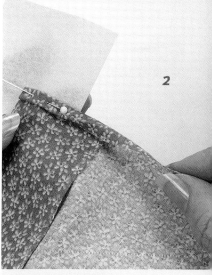

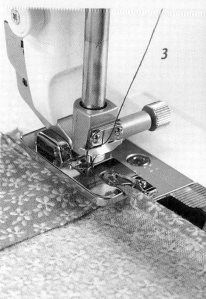

To narrow-hem a garment and facing together (e.g., at a blouse's bottom edge):
1. Trim the lower edge of the facings at an angle to eliminate bulk.
2. Fold both layers of fabric (garment and facing) together twice to form the starting hem, and pin to a piece of tearaway stabilizer.
3. Stitch the entire doubled layer before feeding any fabric into the curl of the hemmer.

3. Fold both the garment fabric and the facing together twice to form the starting hem at the fold, and pin to the corner of a piece of tearaway stabilizer, as instructed in "Starting at a corner" on p. 183 and shown in the top right photo. Prepare the hem on the other facing the same way, except pin without stabilizer.

4. Use at least a 3mm to 4mm narrow hemmer. Start as instructed for a corner, except stitch the entire doubled layer before feeding any fabric into the curl of the hemmer (see the bottom right photo).

5. Continue stitching the narrow hem as usual, until you reach the facing at the other end. At that point, stop with the needle down, raise the presser foot, and ease the fabric out of the curl of the foot.

6. Pull the fabric in front of and behind the foot taut, to form a matching hem under the foot. (Coax the edge under with your finger, a straight pin, or an awl, if necessary.)

7. Lower the presser foot, and stitch the remaining hem. (Remove the pin when you get to it.) For neatness, knot the thread tails at the end of the stitching, bury about 1/2 in. of the tails, and trim off the rest.

NARROW HEMMING CURVES

Gradual curves, such as you would have on round or oval tablecloths and flared skirts, are not difficult to narrow-hem. If the curve is tight, reshape it to be more gradual whenever possible. For example, sharp curves on shirttails can usually be rounded (or squared, once you are comfortable handling corners). Use as narrow a hemmer as possible for the weight of the fabric.

Keeping the right amount of fabric fed into the hemmer takes a little more effort on curves. Stitch at a slow speed, and keep the edge of the fabric at the upper left side of the ditch as it enters the foot.

CONTINUOUS NARROW HEMMING

With some applications—such as on flared skirts, round tablecloths, and some blouses—the beginning and end of the narrow hem meet. To join the end of narrow-hem stitching to the place it was started:

1. Stop, with the needle down, just before the front of the foot reaches the spot where the narrow hem began.

2. Lift the presser foot, and slide the fabric out of the curl of the foot.

3. Form a matching folded hem on the fabric beneath the foot by pulling the hem slightly taut from in front of and behind the foot. (You may have to use your fingers, a straight pin, or an awl to help form the hem.)

4. Lower the foot, and stitch over the folded hem. (The fabric is under the foot, not in the curl for this inch or so of stitching.)

5. Continue until you overlap the beginning of the hem by a few stitches.

HEMMING ADJOINING SIDES OF A CORNER

This easy method of narrow hemming adjoining sides, adapted from an Elna educational leaflet, makes an attractive mitered corner with little bulk.

1. Fold about $1/4$ in. to $3/8$ in. of the corner to the wrong side, and straight-stitch across the fold. (Stitch and save test samples to know corner size to fold for each of your hemmers.)

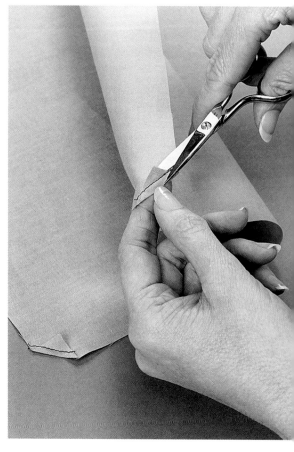

To narrow-hem adjoining sides, first fold the corner to the wrong side and straight-stitch across the fold. Trim the excess fabric up to the stitching.

For applications where the beginning and end of a narrow hem must meet, stop with the needle down just before the front of the foot reaches the beginning of the stitching. Lift the presser foot, and slide the fabric out of the foot. Form a matching hem beneath the foot, lower the foot, and stitch over the folded hem until you overlap the beginning.

2. Trim the excess fabric up to the stitching, as shown in the photo at right on the facing page.

3. Form the starting hem at the beginning of one side, and pin it to the corner of a small piece of tearaway stabilizer, as usual.

4. Continue as instructed in "Starting at a corner" on p. 183, hemming the entire side.

5. Form and pin the starting hem for the adjoining side to stabilizer. Hem this side (see the photo below).

6. After the stitching is complete, gently remove the stabilizer.

7. For a neat appearance, tie and bury the thread tails.

Narrow hemming with specialty stitches

You can use stitches other than straight stitches for narrow hemming to create beautifully finished edges on nightgowns, slips, ruffles (including smocked ruffles), and tablecloths. On some machines, you can use utility and decorative stitches with certain narrow hemmers, and the stitches will align properly. On other machines, two steps are required, in which case the narrow hem is first basted with a straight stitch, then the decorative stitch is sewn over the hem. As you can see on the ruffled edges of the pillow and the pinafore-style bib in the photos on p. 66, either method gives you the option of creating a decorative finish rather than a plain one.

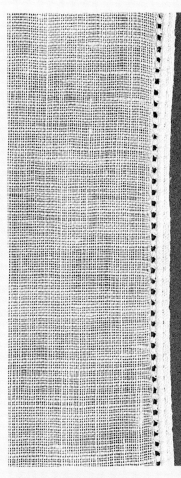

Narrow hemming combined with the Parisian hemstitch produces a finished decorative edge similar to those on hand-hemstitched handkerchiefs.

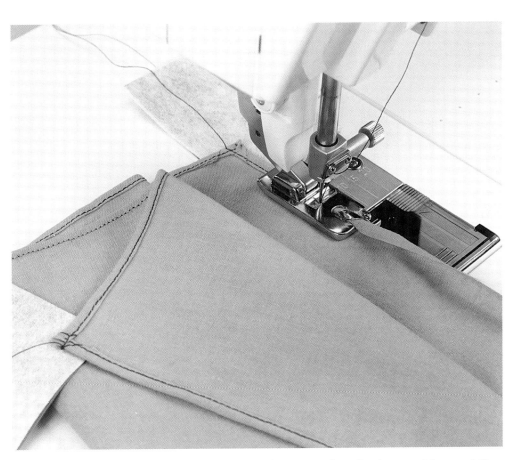

After stitching the entire first side, form and pin the starting hem for the next side to stabilizer and continue.

When a decorative stitch aligns properly on the hem, you can narrow-hem and create the decorative edge at the same time (one-step method).

ONE-STEP METHOD

If the stitch you wish to use aligns as needed on the hem, you can stitch the narrow hem and create the decorative edge at the same time (see the photo above). If the stitch does not at first align properly, try the following remedies:

✗ Check that the stitch is being made in the appropriate direction, and if necessary, mirror the stitch. If the stitch cannot be mirrored on your machine, look for another similar stitch that is stitched the right direction and try it.

✗ Try a different stitch width.

✗ Try a different hemmer.

✗ If it is possible on your machine to change the needle position with the stitch you are using, try that.

✗ On some programmable machines, you can program the stitch into memory with the correct alignment.

TWO-STEP METHOD

If the stitch you wish to use cannot be made to align properly, use the two-step method:

1. Baste the narrow hem, using a narrow (usually 3mm or less) hemmer with a long (about 4mm) straight stitch. Upper tension should be loosened.

2. Stitch the utility or decorative stitch over the basted narrow hem to create the desired decorative edge (see the top photo on the facing page). If necessary for proper stitch alignment, the fabric may be turned so the narrow hem is to the left. Use a satin-stitch foot, and adjust upper tension as needed.

3. Remove the basting stitches.

Finished decorative edges

Shell, picot, scalloped, or hemstitched edges make lovely finishes for delicate garments and table linens. For all the following decorative edges:

Foot: For the one-step method, use a 2mm to 4mm narrow hemmer with a wide needle-hole opening to allow for zigzag stitching. For some machines, these may be called rolled or shell hemmers.

For the two-step method, use a 2mm or 3mm straight stitch or straight/zigzag stitch narrow hemmer first. Then use a satin-stitch foot for the decorative stitching.

SHELL EDGE

A shell edge is a pretty and practical way to finish edges on baby garments and lingerie. Since it creates a very soft folded edge, it is especially useful for finishing

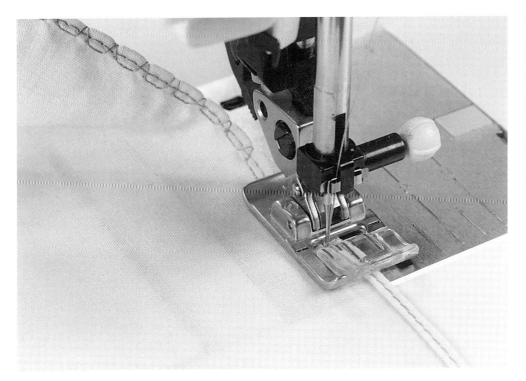

If necessary you can baste the narrow hem first, then add the decorative stitch (two-step method). Remove the basting stitches afterward.

TIP In addition to shell edges, the blind stitch can be used to create decorative shell tucks (see p. 161). Shell tucks are appropriate for the same types of baby, little-girl, and lingerie items as recommended for the shell edging and would be very attractive on a garment on which the neck, armhole, and lower edges were finished with the shell edging.

neck and armhole edges on slips and gowns, where lace or other finishings may be too rough for these sensitive skin areas.

Fabric: Soft, lightweight woven fabric such as batiste. Tricot may also be used.

Thread: Fine cotton (size 50/2 or 60/2) or extra-fine cotton-wrapped polyester.

Needle: Appropriate for fabric and thread, most often 70 Universal.

Stitch: Blind stitch (also called blind-hem stitch) or a variation of it. This stitch creates an edging that more closely resembles a handsewn shell edge than a simple zigzag stitch does. Mirror imaging may be necessary for the zigzag part of the stitch to go to the right, as illustrated.

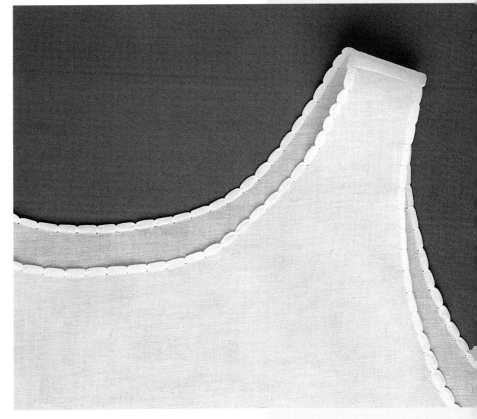

A shell edge creates a soft folded edge that is good for lingerie and baby garments.

Blind stitch

Variation of blind stitch

Stretch blind stitch

Edging scallop

Width: Varies with hemmer. Start with 3.5mm to 4.5mm, then adjust.

Length: Varies with machine. Start with about 1.5mm, then adjust. Each shell or scallop should be no longer than ³⁄₈ in.

Upper tension: Slightly tightened (adjusted to a higher number), so that there is enough pull to form the shell shape.

1. Start the narrow hem as usual, except stitch until there is a zigzag stitch to hold the starting hem before you feed the fabric into the curl of the hemmer.

2. For proper alignment, the straight stitches in the stitch pattern should go into the single layer of fabric just to the left of the hem. The zigzag must go "into the air" just to the right of the hem. If the alignment is wrong, try the suggestions listed for the one-step method on p. 188. If none helps, use the two-step method instead (see p. 188), and baste the narrow hem with a long straight stitch first. Then stitch over it with a blind stitch to create the shell effect. Remove the basting.

Problem solving If the shell effect is not being formed, tighten upper tension. If there is puckering, loosen (decrease) upper tension.

For curves, use the narrowest hemmer that will give the desired results. If the curve is very sharp and cannot be reshaped, consider using a different edge finish.

PICOT OR SCALLOPED EDGES

The stretch blind stitch and the edging scallop—the same stitches used for the decorative edges described in chap-ter 3—can be combined with narrow hemming for a more finished edge.

Fabric: Medium-weight wovens (broadcloth, most cotton or polyester/cotton prints) with the stretch blind stitch for the picot decorative edge; lightweight wovens (batiste) for the edging scallop.

Thread: Fine machine-embroidery thread—size 50/2 or 60/2 cotton or size 40 rayon.

Needle: 80 Universal on broadcloth, 70 Universal on batiste.

Stitch: Stretch blind stitch; edging scallop. Engage mirror imaging, if necessary, to make the stitches in the direction shown.

A simple zigzag can also be used with some hemmers for a finished decorative edge; the narrow hem will roll rather than stay flat. A relatively close zigzag (width 2.5mm to 3mm, length 1mm) with a 2mm or rolled hemmer makes an especially attractive decorative edge for ruffles.

Width: Start at about 4mm, then adjust.

Length: Start at about 0.5mm, then adjust.

Upper tension: Slightly loosened for picot; slightly tightened for scallop. Test.

Problem solving The right side of the stitch must clear the folded-hem edge on the right. If the alignment is wrong, try the remedies suggested for the one-step method (see p. 188). If none of these helps, use the two-step method (see p. 188). Baste the narrow hem with a long straight stitch. Then stitch over it with either the stretch blind stitch or the edging scallop. Remove the basting.

HEMSTITCHED HANDKERCHIEF EDGE

If your machine has the Parisian hem-stitch (also called pin stitch or point de

Paris) or the picot stitch, you can combine either stitch with narrow hemming for a beautiful hemstitched edge, as shown in the photo at right on p. 187 and on the armhole edges of the blouse in the photo on p. 176.

Fabric: Appropriate for hemstitching; mostly linen and cotton.

Thread: Very fine machine-embroidery cotton (80/2, 70/2, or 60/2).

Needle: Most often 120 Universal. Experiment with others.

Stitch: Parisian hemstitch (pin stitch, point de Paris) or picot stitch. Engage mirror imaging, if necessary, to form the stitch in the direction shown.

Width: Varies. Start at about 2mm, then adjust.

Length: Varies. Start at about 2.5mm, then adjust.

Upper tension: Normal to slightly tightened to create enlarged holes.

Problem solving Because the picot stitch has a simpler stitch pattern, it may be easier to use with narrow hemmers than the Parisian hemstitch, especially on more difficult fabrics.

For this edge, the forward and reverse stitches must be on the single layer of fabric to the left of the narrow hem, and the zigzag part of the stitch should go to the right to catch the hem. If you are unable to get this alignment with either of these stitches, use the two-step method (see p. 188). Use a regular needle (70 or 80 Universal) to baste the narrow hem with a long straight stitch. Then switch to the larger needle to hemstitch over it.

Questions

When narrow hemming with a decorative stitch to create a picot, scalloped, or hemstitched edge, which side of the fabric do you use as the right side?

With solid-color fabrics without seams (for example, tablecloths, or ruffles before they are attached), you can use whichever side you like best as the right side.

On projects with seams, you probably want the narrow hem to turn to the wrong side. Stitch a test sample on the fabric. If the underside of the stitch (on the right side of the fabric) doesn't look just as nice as the top side (often it does), adjusting upper tension should help. An alternative is to use the two-step method (see p. 188). Narrow-hem to the wrong side as usual, except use a long straight stitch, then turn the fabric over and stitch the decorative stitch from the right side. As always, test your setup on a scrap first.

Picot or scalloped edges can be created by stitching over a folded edge and trimming from the back [see pp. 46–47] or by combining the stitches with narrow hemming for a more finished edge. When would you choose one method over the other?

On projects where durability is important, the narrow-hemmed decorative edge is probably a better choice. Depending on the fabric, however, a narrow-hemmed edge may be too bulky and stiff for some projects—like gathered ruffles, for example. Of course, personal preference is a consideration also. One method may be easier to do or may look better on a certain fabric or location on a garment than the other method.

Parisian hemstitch

Picot stitch

Appendix A

What to Look for in a Sewing Machine

The goal of this book is to help you use the sewing machine you have to its fullest potential. But because I am constantly asked for machine recommendations, I have included in this appendix a discussion of the features that I look for in a sewing machine for fine machine sewing. The information can be helpful for understanding features you have on your current machine, as well as for when you are in the market for a new machine.

Not everyone wants or needs the same capabilities on a sewing machine. Like many home sewers, I do general garment construction, mending and hemming, and home decorating. If handling these applications was all I wanted from a machine, many basic machines would serve my needs. Even for most machine heirloom-sewing techniques, such as attaching laces and entredeux, a good straight and zigzag machine (one that has good-quality tension and feeding for handling the lightweight fabrics) is all that is required. However, once I became fascinated with machine versions of related fine machine-sewing techniques like hemstitching, fagoting, and shadow work, my machine wants became more sophisticated. As shown throughout this book, many of these techniques are possible on mechanical machines; but the capabilities and features that have developed with the computerized sewing machines have opened up creative possibilities we never would have dreamed possible just a few years ago.

Stitches

Accommodating the display and selection of large numbers of stitches has become a major challenge for machine companies. In addition to checking the availability of certain stitches on a particular machine, it is important to consider the user friendliness of the stitch display and selection process. Along with good basic utility stitches (straight, zigzag, blind hem, multiple zigzag for mending and sewing elastic, double overlock for some seaming, and consistent good-quality buttonholes), I look for the following:

Of the hemstitches, I look principally for the Parisian hemstitch to resemble pin stitching by hand and the Venetian stitch to resemble entredeux. Other stitches that are not used as much as the Parisian and Venetian, but are nice to have for decorative rows, include the four-sided, triple honeycomb or Rhodes, and Turkish stitches. The last two stitches resemble the honeycomb and the double-overlock stitches, but each step of the stitch pattern is repeated, which is necessary for hemstitching.

For related techniques, I look for the feather or briar stitch for decorative embroidery and fagoting, the tracery scallop for twin-needle shadow-work scallops, and the edging scallop, which creates scallops over a folded edge without necessitating trimming around each scallop. I also look for other scallops that make pretty decorative stitches, even though trimming is necessary when they are used for edging.

Finally I look for any other decorative stitches (such as flowers, leaves, bows,

and so forth) that would be appropriate for creating the look of hand embroidery or purchased Swiss embroideries.

General features

Most upper-end machines have a majority of the following features, but take note whether the ones you care about most are easy to identify (have readily identifiable symbols) and are convenient for you to select and use.

Good-quality, well-marked tension mechanisms While the newer "automatic, self-adjusting" tension systems are great, the upper-tension setting nonetheless should be adjusted to obtain the best results for certain fabrics or techniques. The upper-tension dial or function should be well marked, so that you can easily note the adjusted setting for future reference, before returning to the normal setting.

Good-quality feeding mechanism Both good feeding and tension are crucial for any sewing but especially for sewing on lightweight fabrics and for techniques like fagoting. The feeding mechanism must hold the fabric firmly and move it evenly.

The following features are helpful but not absolutely necessary:

Ability to stop with needle up/down as desired Engaging "needle down" allows you to adjust fabric as you go without shifting the fabric under the foot. It is also helpful when pivoting the fabric to turn a corner, especially with decorative stitches. Since I use this feature often, I like to be able to engage it with a button right over the needle bar or with the foot pedal.

Ability to stop automatically at the end of the stitch pattern
This function is also very helpful for turning corners with hemstitches and other decorative stitches—for example, when stitching around a square collar.

Speed reducer
An even, slow to medium sewing speed gives the best results for decorative stitching. Stitching at all-out speed or at a very uneven speed (pumping) can affect tension, stitch length, and the general quality of the decorative stitch.

For decorative sewing, including twin-needle stitching, I usually engage the speed reducer, which allows me to stitch up to a medium speed but gives me much more control for a smooth sewing rhythm.

Stitch width and length features
The indicators should be easy to read, visible at all times, and well marked (ideally with meaningful numbers, i.e., millimeters). Settings should be easy to change (not requiring multiple steps) and changeable in small increments; automatic settings are often too wide and too long, so the ability to override them and make adjustments in small increments is desirable.

A wide stitch width (6mm or wider), though not often needed, is useful for fagoting and for a prettier shape for scallops (especially twin-needle scallops) as well as for other decorative stitches.

Balancing or fine adjustment/tuning mechanism
The mechanism to balance stitch alignment should be easy to use, and the adjustments should be indicated with numbers or with a position that is easy to record accurately for future reference (see the sidebar on p. 85).

Ability to change needle positions with as many stitches as possible
Being able to change needle positions ensures that the desired stitch can be aligned as necessary for the desired foot. For example, it is possible to combine decorative stitches, such as the edging scallop or Parisian hemstitch, with narrow hemming, but changing needle positions is often necessary for proper alignment.

Ability to use twin needles
Twin needles are needed for twin-needle pintucks and twin-needle shadow work.

Mirror imaging with as many stitches as possible
The ability to mirror the stitch (ideally, horizontally as well as vertically) often comes in handy. For example, mirroring enables you to stitch the project in the most convenient position—with the bulk of the garment to the left and out of the way—for hemming or for sewing both sides of a trim or lace with decorative stitches, such as the Parisian hemstitch. Mirroring is also useful for combining decorative patterns (for example, leaf and flower patterns) in the most attractive way.

Convenient reverse button
An instant reverse button in a convenient location, such as right over the needle bar, is very handy. You don't want to have to take your eyes off your work to find the button.

Embroidery and programming capabilities
It is now possible to create your own embroidery design combinations, including ones that can look very much like expensive Swiss embroideries. If this type of work interests you, check whether the embroidery designs are appropriate for the uses you intend and check the size of the designs—many machines now allow designs to be elongated while maintaining the same density. (This feature makes a broader size range possible with the desired density for satin stitches such as scallops.) Also consider the ease or difficulty of programming and editing.

Special features

Table For a freearm machine, a large, removable sewing surface allows for more control when guiding.

Thread cutter/holder It should be in a convenient location to cut threads after stitching and hold them for the beginning of the next stitching.

Needle threader It should be easy to use and preferably built in.

Securing or tie-off option This is very useful for securing the beginning and end of embroidery motifs.

Light Brightness and location are both important.

Low-bobbin warning It should be readily visible.

Portability Nothing beats classes for "hands-on" learning of all the wonderful things you can do on your machine. But classes mean you will regularly have to transport your machine (for more on this subject, see p. 199). Check how easy the machine is to pack up and how heavy it is to carry.

Updateability Since the marriage of computer technology and home sewing machines, machines are changing much more rapidly than in the past. Some machine companies make additional stitches available, usually in the form of software. If you are interested in decorative stitching, this is an advantage, since you do not have to purchase a new machine to get more stitches. However, it is important to realize that a machine company will not keep making accessories for previous models indefinitely.

There are also machines that allow the home sewer, with increasing technological refinement, to create stitch designs. Even though most home sewers do not regularly use this function, it is nice to know you can add stitches yourself.

Good instruction manual Since most machines are imported, the manuals are often awkwardly translated from a foreign language. Check the clarity of the instructions and of the photos or illustrations. A good index in the back of the book and a table of contents in front make looking up specific information easier. It is very helpful to have all the presser feet and stitches named and illustrated with suggested uses. (Many machine companies have additional instructional materials available—a workbook, leaflets, magazines, and so on.)

Brand-specific features

There are a few other advantageous features that are unique to certain machines (at least for now). They include: a knee lift, built-in dual feed, the ability to return to the last settings you used with a stitch, bobbin-tension bypass for easily sewing right side down with heavier threads on the bobbin, and large embroidery motif capabilities. Any of these that is important to you will certainly affect your machine choice. No one machine has absolutely everything!

Presser feet and accessories I probably would not reject a machine that I loved just because of deficiencies in the presser feet. Although they are not usually ideal, feet from different machines are sometimes interchangeable. (Test before relying on being able to interchange feet, however.) Refer to pp. 12-16 for more detail.

Identification Feet and accessories should have identification on them so that you can easily tell what you have and can track down its intended purpose in the manual or from a dealer if necessary.

Instructions If good instructions on using an accessory are not in the machine manual, they should be included with the purchase of the accessory.

Availability of special feet The standard zigzag, satin-stitch (embroidery), buttonhole, zipper, and blind-hem feet should come with the machine. (Ideally they should easily snap on and off a shank on the needle bar and be stored in a compartment conveniently located on the machine.) Find out whether the additional presser feet you want most are available for the machine.

Price Additional feet should be reasonably priced; if they are too costly, you may be reluctant to purchase them.

Ease of use Test-sew with the presser feet you expect to use the most. Certain special feet available for some machines, particularly narrow hemmers and pintuck feet, yield good results very easily, while using those for other machines seems like a battle.

Choosing a dealer

When you are in the market for a new machine, make a list of the features you want most. There likely will be several machines that will fit your needs. When you have decided which ones to consider, make an appointment before going to test them to be sure the dealer will be available.

Take pieces of the fabrics you use most. (Many dealers will have only starched, stiff "demo" cloth available.) Ask to stitch the techniques you are most interested in (including buttonholes) yourself. Remember, for the best results, the thread and needles should be changed to those appropriate for each fabric and technique.

The helpfulness of the dealer is definitely a consideration. A dealer's knowledge about the particular kind(s) of sewing you do, while not absolutely necessary, is an asset because it will mean more reliable tips, recommendations for the best feet and accessories, and help with troubleshooting when you have stitching problems.

Classes provided by the dealer are very important. Inquire about which ones are included with machine purchase. Also check on the warranty and how the dealer handles service.

Price is usually a big concern, of course. Ask the dealer to let you know when the model you like goes on sale. Also, you may want to consider a used machine. Often perfectly good used machines are available because their owners just wanted to upgrade.

All this will take time. Do not let yourself be pressured into a hurried decision. A sewing machine is a major purchase, and you will be happier if you have taken the time to find the best machine-and-dealer combination for you.

Upgrading

I would recommend upgrading when your present machine no longer meets your sewing needs. If all you want to do is basic sewing and you have a machine that does a good job of it, then buying a new, top-of-the-line machine does not make sense. But if you wish you could finish edges with a pretty decorative scallop (that you don't have to trim around) or attach lace with the Parisian hemstitch, for example, then it is worth taking the time to investigate machines that satisfy your wish list. The other time to consider upgrading is whenever your current machine needs repairs that cost more than you want to spend.

Appendix B

Machine Settings for Decorative Techniques

This chart provides stitch numbers along with suggested starting points for stitch width and length (in parentheses) for the machines with which I am most familiar—the ones brought to my classes the most. There are many other machines capable of these techniques, including models on which stitches are not numbered and therefore could not be listed. If your machine is not on this chart, use the stitch illustrations (page numbers indicated) and the guidelines for settings at the beginning of each technique in the appropriate chapter to determine how to set your machine.

Machine	Edging, Appliqué		Twin Needle	Hemstitches		Fagoting
	Picot (p. 46)	Scalloped (p. 48)	Shadow Work** (p. 71)	Parisian (p. 83)	Venetian (p. 83)	(p. 137)
BABY LOCK						
BL8800	—	—	9**	19 (W2, L2)	—	27 (W5.5, L2)
Encore	—	—	5 (W3.5, L1)	49 (W2, L2)	50 (W3, L3)	27 (W5.5, L2)
Ellageo	—	8-24 (auto)	7-48**	11-20 (W2, L2)	—	11-28 (W5.5, L2)
BERNINA						
930	5* (W4, L0.5)	—	20 (W3, L1)	—	—	6 red (W4, L2)
1090,1090QE, 1090S	same as 930	—	19** (W4, L0.75)	21 (W2, L2)	Only on QE-14 (W3, L2.5)	13*** (auto)
1130, 1230, 1260, 1260QPE	5* (W4, L0.3)	23 (W4, L0.3)	24 (W2.5, L0.75)	26 (W2, L2); QPE****	18 (W3.5, L1.3, long stitch button); QPE****	11 (13 on 1130)*** (auto)
1530	A2/5* (W4, L0.3)	H1/7* (W4, L0.3)	H1/8** (W3, L1)	H1/4 (W2, L2)	H1/5 (W3, L2.5)	A1/9 *** (auto)
1630	same as 1530	G1/7* (W4, L0.3)	G1/8** (W3, L1)	G1/4 (W2, L2)	G1/5 (W3, L2.5)	same as 1530
150, 150QE	CPS-N0018* (W4.5, L0.3)	CPS-D0122* (W4.75, L0.5)	CPS-D0123 (W2.75, L1)	19, QE 18 or 25 (W2, L2)	22 or D0120 (auto)	21 (W5.5, L2)
145	—	47* (auto)	40 (W3, L1.5)	21 or 22 (W2, L2.5)	—	24 (auto)
160, 163	same as 150	38* (W auto, L0.6)	4 (W3, L1) or same as 150	23 (W2, L2)	22 (auto)	21 (W5.5, L2)
200, 185, 180, 170, 165	18* (W4.5, L0.3)	CPS-427* on 200, 427* (W4.75, L0.5)	719** (W5 center needle, L1)	720 (W1.5, L2.5), or 330 (W2, L2.5)	701 (W3, L2.75)	334 (W5-6, L3.5)
BROTHER						
PC-3000, PS-3000	—	—	63 (W3.5, L1)	49 (W2, L2)	50 (W3, L3)	27 (W5.5, L2)
Ult-2001, 2002	—	†	2-17 (W3.5, L1)	3-04 (W2, L2)	3-08 (W3, L3)	2-11 (W5.5, L2)

* Mirror image or put fold to the left.
** Width will vary with twin needles and presser foot. Test carefully. Twin-needle width limit may be needed to center the stitch.
*** Engage continuous reverse and balance approximately +26.
**** 1260QPE—Hemstitches are the second and third "Quilting" stitches following the script alphabet. Settings—same as 1530.
† The edging scallop stitch may be programmed into models with "My Custom Stitch." The coordinates may be obtained at Brother's website (www.brother.com).

(continued on p. 196)

Machine Settings for Decorative Techniques (continued from p. 195)

(continued from p. 195)

Machine	Edging, Appliqué		Twin Needle	Hemstitches		Fagoting
	Picot (p. 46)	Scalloped (p. 48)	Shadow Work** (p. 71)	Parisian (p. 83)	Venetian (p. 83)	(p. 137)
ELNA						
Carina & most disc models	Built-in 2 (W4, L0.5)	Built-in 3 (W4, L0.5)	Disc 4 (W3.5, L1)	Disc 126 (W4)	Disc 140 (W4)	Disc 104 (W4)
7000	5 (W4.4, L0.5)	15 (W5, L0.6)	14 (W3.1, L1.2)	746 (W1.8, L2.5)	747 (W3.7)	742 or 721 (auto)
8000	6 (W4.4, L0.5)	14 (W5, L0.5)	81 (same as 7000)	68 (W1.8, L2.5)	69 (W3.7)	71 or 62 (auto)
9000, Diva	same as 8000	86 (same as 8000)	90 (W3.7, L1.2)	120 (W1.8, L2.5)	121 (W3.7)	127 or 891 cas. 2 (W5, L1.8)
9006	21 (W5.5, L0.45)	38 (W5, L0.35)	27 (W4, L1)	24 (W2, L2.5)	70 (program 31 times, size 1-2)	25 (W5, L2)
6003, 6003Q	4 (W4.5, L0.5)	23 (W4.5, L0.3)	3 (W3.5, L1)	13 (W2, L2)	31 (W4, L2.5)	15 (W6, L2)
6004	22 (W4.5, L0.5)	43 (W5, L0.3)	34 (W3, L1)	31 (W2, L2)	66 (W4, L1.5)	32 (W6, L2)
CE20	150* (W3.5, L0.45)	52 (W5, L0.3, elongate x 1)	148 (W3.5, L1)	149 (W2.5, L2)	39 (W4, L2)	28 (W6, L1.5)
6005 Heirloom	4 (W4.5, L0.4)	—	27 (W4.5, L2)	45 (W2, L2)	47 (W3.5, L2.5)	50 (W5.5, L1.5)
Xquisit	1/14 (W auto, L0.4)	4/05 (W reduced, L0.4)	6/01 (W reduced, L auto)	2/09 (auto)	2/10 (auto)	3/08 or 3/09 (auto)
KENMORE 385						
-19601	31 (W3.5, L0.3)	—	22 (W3, L1)	30 (W2.5, L2)	—	25 (W5.5, L2.5)
-19030	7 (W4.5, L0.5)	—	19 (W3, L1)	12 (W2, L2)	21 (W4, L2)	16 (W5.5, L2.5)
-19153	31 (W4.5, L0.5)	—	22 (W3, L1)	30 (W2, L2)	—	25 (W5.5, L2.5)
NEW HOME (JANOME)						
6000	26 (W4, L0.5)	—	22 (W3, L2)	I27 (W & L2.5)	I181 (W4, L3)***	19 (auto)
7000	15 (W4, L0.4)	29 (W5, L0.35)	same as 6000	16 (W & L2.5)	53 (W3, L auto)***	17 (W5, L2)
7500	43 (W5.5, L0.4)	60 (same as 7000)	47 (W4, L1)	44 (W & L2.5)	84 (W3)***	45 (same as 7000)
8000	21 (W5.5, L0.45)	38 (same as 7000)	27 (same as 7500)	24 (W2, L2.5)	70 (program 31 times, size 1-2)***	25 (same as 7000)
9000	150* (W4, L0.3)	52 (same as 7000)	148 (same as 7500)	26 (same as 8000)	81 (50%) or 39 (W4, L2)***	28 (same as 7000)
4000	22 (W4.5, L0.5)	43 (W5, L0.3)	34 (W3, L1)	31 (W2, L2)	66 (W4, L2)***	32 (W6, L2)
5700	26 (W5, L0.4)	54 (W5, L0.3)	29 (W3, L1)	23 (W2, L2)	40 (W4, L2)***	same as 4000
4800	28 (W4.5, L0.5)	56 (W5, L0.3)	33 (W3, L1)	26 (W2, L2)	42 (W4, L2)***	31 (W6, L2)
10000	89 (W4.5, L0.5)	53 (W5, L0.3)	92 (W3.5, L1)	85 (W2, L2)	100 (W4.5, L2)***	94 (W6, L1.5)

* Mirror image or put fold to the left.

** Width will vary with twin needles and presser foot. Test carefully. Twin-needle width limit may be needed to center the stitch.

*** Substituting a similar stitch. A good option: adjoining rows of Parisian to resemble Venetian (see p. 99).

| Machine | Edging, Appliqué | | Twin Needle | Hemstitches | | Fagoting |
	Picot (p. 46)	Scalloped (p. 48)	Shadow Work** (p. 71)	Parisian (p. 83)	Venetian (p. 83)	(p. 137)
PFAFF						
1471	18 (W4.5, L0.5)	—	38 (W4, L14)	78 (W3, L2.5)	programmable***	29 (W6, L2.5)
1473	17 (W4.5, L0.5)	54 (W4.5, L0.4, balance 6)	same as 1471	165 (W2, L3)	169 (W3.5, L2.5)	same as 1471
1475	same as 1473	same as 1473	same as 1471	same as 1473	same as 1473	same as 1471
7510, 7560	5 (W4.5, L0.5)	—	81** (W7, L4)	57 (W2, L2)	58 (W3.5, L3)	17 (auto)
7530	5 (same as 7510)	51 (W5, L8)	program an arch	97 (W2, L2.5)	100 (W3.5, L3)	17 (auto)
7550, 7570	5 (same as 7510)	61 (W4.5, L8)	141 (W4, L9) or program an arch	112 (W2, L2.5)	115 (W4, L2.5)	17 (W6, L2.5)
2140	31 (W4.5, L0.5)	78 (W4.5, L8)	81** (W7, L11)	139 (W2, L2.5)	142 (W4, L2.5)	11 (W6, L2.5)
SINGER						
DSXII †	10 (W4, L1)	—	74 (W2, L2)	75 (W0.5, L3)	77 (W2.5, L3)	70 (W4, L auto)
XL-1000, 150	—	—	Straight-Stitch Menu**	Dec-Stitch Menu (W reduced)	Dec-Stitch Menu (W regular)	Dec-Stitch Menu (auto)
XL-5000	—	—	Rose 2, row 2, #2 (reduced)	Rose 1, row 2, #1 (reduced)	Rose 2, row 2, #3 (reduced)	Rose 1, row 1, #3 (regular)
VIKING (HUSQVARNA)						
6000 series	Cam A orange (W4, L0.3)	Cam G green (W4, L0.3)	Cam D red or H green (W3, L0.3)	Cam C yellow	—	Cam D yellow (W4)
990	Built-in 10 (W4, L0.3)	—	2-8 (W3, L1)	2-3 (W2, L2.5)	—	2-19 (W6, L2.5)
500	10 (W4.5, L0.3)	—	32 (W3.5, L1.5)	12 (same as 990)	13 (auto)	34 (W5.5, L2)
530, 535 Lily	8 (W4.5, L0.2)	—	4 (W4, L0.8)	17 (W2, L2.5)	18 (auto)	11 (W6, L2)
540, 545 Lily	9 (same as 530)	—	36 (W3.5, L2)	12 (same as 530)	13 (auto)	34 (same as 530)
550, 555 Lily	1-18 (same as 530)	5-23* (W4.5, L0.5, elongate 1)	1-26 (same as 540)	6-5 (same as 530)	6-6 (auto)	1-24 (same as 530)
600, 605 Rose	15 (same as 530)	—	32 (W4, L1.5)	19 (same as 530)	20 (auto)	34 (same as 530)
1100, #1, & 1+	A29 (W4.5, L0.2)	D29* (same as 550)	A32 (W3.5, L2)	D6 (W2, L2.5)	D7 (auto)	A35 (W6, L2)
Designer II, Quilt Designer	$A_1$24 (W4.5, L0.2)	$E_1$25* (same as 550)	$E_1$6 (W3.5, L2)	$D_1$6 (W2, L2.5)	$D_1$7 (auto)	$E_1$8 or $D_1$15 (W6, L2)
Designer I	A24 (W4.5, L0.2)	H24* (same as 550)	E6 (W3.5, L2)	D6 (W2, L2.5), v1.31-D46 (auto)	D7 (auto)	D15 (W6, L2)

* Mirror image or put fold to the left.

** Width will vary with twin needles and presser foot. Test carefully. Twin-needle width limit may be needed to center the stitch.

*** Venetian hemstitch program for Pfaff 1471 (Courtesy of Louise Gerigh at Pfaff.)
    width   18 02 18 34 18 18 18 18
    length 00 14 28 14 00 28 00 28

† Width and length numbers refer to settings marks on the machine, with "1" for the leftmost mark.

Appendix C

Caring for Your Sewing Machine

It is well worth the little time and effort it takes to care properly for your sewing machine, both for maintaining the stitching quality and for avoiding the inconvenience and cost of repairs.

Cleaning and oiling

Before starting a sewing project and any time you are having stitching problems, clean your sewing machine. Follow the instructions in your machine manual.

Occasionally (about every three to six months, depending on your sewing habits), do a more thorough cleaning. Clean out any lint, dust, threads, broken needles, sequins, and any other foreign objects. (Children put some amazing things into sewing machines!) Most routine machine cleaning can be done adequately with a brush. But occasionally I use "canned air" to remove lint that cannot be reached with a brush. (Blowing into machines with your mouth is not recommended.) Be sure to aim the nozzle so that lint is forced out of the machine, not farther into it. There are also mini-vacuums and vacuum attachments available.

Use a soft cloth to wipe any visible lint or dust from the outside of the machine. The needle bar in particular collects a lot of greasy fuzz and should be wiped. Remove any sticky residue on spool spindles with rubbing alcohol. If rubbing alcohol will not remove the sticky residue that tape and labels may leave on presser feet, spool spindles, or the machine bed, try Goo Gone or Goof Off, both available at hardware stores. As always, test on an inconspicuous area. Stains on the outside of the machine can usually be cleaned safely with Formula 409 or similar product, but check with your dealer or test first.

"Floss" the tension discs to remove the buildup of residue from some threads, especially poor-quality threads. Raise the presser bar to the up position, and set the upper tension to "0". Fold a piece of soft (but not fuzzy) cotton fabric in half, and put some rubbing alcohol along the fold. Slide the fold up and down through the tension discs, as if flossing. (If there is a separating plate, floss each side.) Remember to return your tension-setting dial to the normal setting afterward.

If oiling is recommended for your machine (check the manual), oil it after cleaning. Use only the sewing-machine oil recommended for your machine. After oiling, run the machine unthreaded to work the oil in, then "sew" (without thread) a fabric scrap to absorb any excess oil.

Almost all oilers leak unless kept upright. I keep mine in a cup or compartment with other sewing notions near my machine, rather than in the accessory tray.

Maintenance and repair

Some machine companies suggest a schedule for routine dealer maintenance and others don't. Check your machine manual and ask your dealer for recommendations, but use common sense, too. There are many variables that affect how often your machine will need professional care, the main factor being how careful you are about keeping your machine clean and oiled (if your machine requires oil). If you keep your machine covered when not in use and clean it often, it will need maintenance far less often than the machine that is not so well cared for. Generally computer machines are more sensitive to lint than older mechanical models and should be serviced more often. Other factors affecting the maintenance schedule include how often you sew, the kind of sewing you do, your climate, and, of course, stitching quality.

Whenever you take your machine for service, include a few scraps of the types of fabrics you stitch the most so that the machine can be adjusted and tested on those fabrics.

When you are having stitching problems, first run through the troubleshooting routine on p. 6, and check the problem-solving section of your machine manual. When it is necessary to take the machine in for repair, leave it set up as it was when the problem occurred (i.e., same thread, needle, and so on). Also take a sample of the stitched fabric that shows the problem. This will help the dealer find out what's wrong.

Power surges and magnets

Surge protectors give some protection but cannot prevent damage to a sewing machine from lightning or a severe power surge. If your area is prone to power surges or lightning, it makes good sense to disconnect your machine from the power between uses or at least during storms. You may disconnect the power cord at the outlet or at the machine. If you disconnect it at the machine and the other end of the cord is still plugged into the outlet, do not leave the cord touching the machine.

Representatives from Bernina, Elna, New Home, Pfaff, and Viking all say that the magnets in magnetic pincushions are not strong enough to cause problems with their machines. Technical representatives from Brother would prefer not to have magnets near any of their computerized sewing machines or memory cards.

Transporting your machine

To travel with your machine, position it so that it cannot topple. To prevent theft, do not leave it unattended if it is visible. Avoid leaving a machine in a trunk or closed car on very hot days. Cold temperatures should not damage your machine but may cause it to run sluggishly until the lubrication warms up. You can avoid this problem by letting the machine warm to room temperature before you start sewing.

For long-distance transporting, the best protection is to pack a machine in the fitted Styrofoam pieces and box in which it originally came. It is rare for a machine packed this way to be damaged. (When you purchase a machine, save its packing materials and box.) If you need a box and no longer have yours, a dealer may have extras and be willing to lend or give you one.

To ship a machine, pack it in its original box and insure it. If you are shipping it ahead for a seminar, take the tracking number with you.

For air travel—to a sewing seminar, for example—many sewing educators recommend putting the machine, packed in its original box, into a large soft-sided piece of luggage. Fill in any space around the box with fabric, clothes, and so on. The luggage conceals that fact that you have a valuable item (which helps prevent theft) and provides a handle. When you check the bag, tell the agent that there is a sewing machine inside (for security and so that they can put a fragile sticker on it.)

Airlines may not cover sewing machines under their regular liability. Check with your homeowner's insurance company to see if it will cover any damage or theft that the airline will not. Additional coverage may be purchased from the airline when you check the bag. The airlines and machine companies with whom I spoke did not recommend hand-carrying a sewing machine onboard unless the machine is very small and light. If you do, remember to remove needles, pins, seam rippers, screwdrivers, etc. beforehand.

All the machine companies I surveyed (Bernina, Elna, New Home, Pfaff, and Viking) said that airport security devices will not harm their machines.

If you are concerned about traveling with your machine, see if a machine dealer in the seminar area has machines for rent. At the seminar, transporting your machine to the classroom in one of the luggage-type bags with wide wheels is safer than strapping it onto separate luggage wheels. Use elevators rather than escalators when pulling or carrying a machine.

Resources

Sources of Supply

Buttons 'n' Bows
14086 Memorial Dr.
Houston, TX 77079
(800) 769-3251

Clotilde, Inc.*
B3000
Louisiana, MO 63353
(800) 772-2891
www.clotilde.com

Fabric Boutique
1701 Old Minden Rd., #11
Bossier City, LA 71111
(318) 742-0047

Farmhouse Fabrics
270 Church Rd.
Beech Island, SC 29842
(888) 827-1801
www.farmhousefabrics.com

Heirloom Stitches
P. O. Box 1774
Fairfield Glade, TN 38558
(800) 261-4218

Londa's Sewing Etc.
404 S. Duncan Rd.
Champaign, IL 61821
(217) 352-2378
www.londas-sewing.com

Margaret Pierce, Inc.*
P. O. Box 4542
Greensboro, NC 27404
(336) 292-6430

Nancy's Notions*
333 Beichl Ave.
P. O. Box 683
Beaver Dam, WI 53916-0683
(800) 833-0690
www.nancysnotions.com

Nostalgic Needle Works
5763 Airport Blvd.
Mobile, AL 36608
(877) 739-7444
www.nostalgicneedle.com

Peanut Butter-n-Jelly Kids
3607 Old Shell Rd.
Mobile, AL 36608
(334) 342-8017

Pintucks & Pinafores
4300 Paces Ferry Rd.
Atlanta, GA 30339
(888) 342-6478
www.pintucksandpinafores.com

Indicates mail order only

Publications

Creative Needle (for smocking, heirloom-sewing, and related needle-art enthusiasts)
1 Apollo Rd.
Lookout Mountain, GA 30750
(800) 443-3127
www.creativeneedlemag.com

Sew Beautiful (for smocking, heirloom-sewing, and related needle-art enthusiasts)
149 Old Big Cove Rd.
Brownsboro, AL 35741
(800) 547-4176
www.marthapullen.com

Threads (for sewing and other fiber-art enthusiasts)
63 S. Main St.
P. O. Box 5506
Newtown, CT 06470-5506
(800) 888-8286
www.threadsmagazine.com

Index

Index note: page references in bold indicate drawings; page references in italics indicate photographs.

Index